The Practice of
Multimodal Therapy

The Practice of Multimodal Therapy

Systematic, Comprehensive, and Effective Psychotherapy

ARNOLD A. LAZARUS, Ph.D.

McGRAW-HILL BOOK COMPANY

New York • St. Louis • San Francisco • London • Paris • Tokyo • Toronto

Thomas H. Quinn, Michael Hennelly, and Karen Seriguchi were the editors of this book. Christopher Simon was the designer, and Paul Malchow supervised the production. This book was set in Caledonia by Com Com, Inc..

Printed and bound by R. R. Donnelley and Sons, Inc.

LIBRARY OF CONGRESS CATALOGING IN PUBLICATION DATA

Lazarus, Arnold A
   The practice of multimodal therapy.
   Bibliography: p.
   Includes index.
   1. Psychotherapy.   I. Title. (DNLM: 1. Psychotherapy.
WM 420 L413p)
RC480.L39   616.89'14   80-29561
ISBN 0-07-036813-9

1 2 3 4 5 6 7 8 9 RRD RRD 8 0 7 6 5 4 3 2 1

I dedicate this book to:
Ettye and Elias, Doreen and Isaac,
Leonard and Mary

Contents

Preface

This book is addressed to practitioners who are genuinely interested in achieving a higher level of efficiency and effectiveness with the people who consult them. While the intelligent layperson may extract sufficient do-it-yourself procedures to derive personal benefit, it is written primarily for professionals. My intended reference groups are psychologists, psychiatrists, social workers, counselors, psychiatric nurses and any other "health service providers" to whom people turn for emotional help. Since I spend the bulk of my professional time training graduate students enrolled in a Doctor of Psychology (Psy.D.) program, I have held this audience most strongly in mind. The more experienced and sophisticated clinician may elect to skim through or skip over certain chapters, but I trust that there are sufficient provocative and stimulating ideas scattered throughout to provide value even to seasoned veterans.

The last thing we need is another psychotherapeutic system to be added to the hundreds already in existence. Multimodal therapy is not a *system,* it is an *approach* that provides humanistic integration, systematization and a comprehensive "blueprint" for assessment and therapy. It deliberately avoids the pitfalls of *theoretical* eclecticism while underscoring the virtues of *technical* eclecticism. The upshot is an armamentarium of more than thirty-six specific procedures (see Appendix 2 for a glossary of the most frequently used techniques). The major objective is the achievement of rapid and durable results. The emphasis throughout is essentially pragmatic and empirical.

A number of people cared enough to offer me critical suggestions and constructive ideas. Since 1972, close collaboration with Allen Fay, M.D., a brilliant and creative psychiatrist and an A to Z friend has added immeasurably to my clinical acumen and treatment repertoire. His detailed and incisive review of the manuscript was in and of itself a profound learning experience. The openness and willingness to share ideas, methods and techniques that characterizes my colleagues and associates at the various Multimodal Therapy Institutes is another source of inspiration. I inflicted weekly readings of the manuscript on the Kingston, New Jersey and on the New York City members who listened attentively and responded honestly and insightfully. I also want to thank the personnel of the Multimodal Therapy Institute in Virginia Beach for their generous assistance in helping to improve the Life History Questionnaire (Appendix 1). I thank Dr. Larry Minter for troubling to send me a detailed and most informative letter after reading the initial draft. I want to thank my clients for willingly allowing me to borrow tape recordings of specific sessions that contained segments which I thought worth including in this book. (Following Albert Ellis, I encourage many of my clients to tape record each session and to study the recordings as a homework assignment between meetings. Whenever necessary, case material has been modified to maintain confidentiality and to protect the actual identity of the clients in question.) I thank Edith Cohen, Alyce Koblan and Linda Provenzano for so graciously carrying out the tedious task of transcribing the tapes. Finally, I want to thank my wife Daphne, my daughter Linda and my son Cliff for providing the type of nuclear family base that encourages me to write books.

* * *

In addition to authors whom I will cite in this book, a number of other clinicians have published papers on multimodal applications. In the multimodal treatment of agoraphobia, Kwee and de Waal (1975) and Popler (1977) have published papers in Dutch and English respectively. Kwee (1978) discusses multimodal methods in neurotic depression, and in a broad-ranging article (Kwee, 1979) he outlines the evolution of multimodal thought and presents the pros and cons of this approach to symptoms and problems of daily living. Richard (1976) addressed the field of behavioral medicine from a multimodal perspective. Bair and Leventhal (1979) have written about the multimodal management of essential hypertension. Yokley and McCarthy (1980) have described the use of paraprofessional resources in multimodal therapy. I am optimistic that enterprising clinicians and reseachers will find many problems and settings in which the BASIC I.D. schema will facilitate understanding and result in constructive and durable change.

We are too restricted by the parochial teachings of our own past to have learned to use effectively all dimensions of treatment. It is my hope that professionals dedicated to bringing about helpful changes in their patients' behavior will seek and welcome similar changes in their own behavior. We will achieve the goal of multi-dimensional treatment more quickly to the extent that we approach our patients with open minds and a relentless committment to study and confront the complexities of human behavior.

Seymour L. Halleck, THE TREATMENT OF EMOTIONAL DISORDERS

Psychologists who will be extant in the year 2000 will have to be . . . enormously more broadly *trained than the subspecialized people turned out today.*

Gardner Murphy, PSYCHOLOGY IN THE YEAR 2000

Either therapists can successfully influence behavior or they cannot, and they have little choice of what to claim. If they wish to say they cannot do so, or may not do so in just those areas where human concern is greatest, and are therefore not at all responsible for the behavior of their clients, one must ask what right they have to be in business.

Perry London, THE MODES AND MORALS OF PSYCHOTHERAPY

Introduction

"I feel very depressed. I'm nearly 42 years old, and what have I got to show for it? My wife says I treat her like my mother and has threatened to leave. My children treat me like dirt. I'm frustrated at work—in fact I hate my boss. At times it all seems too much and I have even thought of doing away with myself. My doctor thinks I'm a hypochondriac and never takes anything I tell him seriously, but recently I've been getting these awful headaches and for all I know it may be something serious."

Clinicians will hear the foregoing litany of complaints, or variations thereof, dozens of times a month. The way in which this information is received, analyzed, assessed, processed, dissected, interpreted, investigated, responded to, and ultimately managed or dealt with varies enormously from therapist to therapist. Those wedded to diagnostic classification will want to determine whether this man is manifesting an affective disorder, an anxiety disorder, or is perhaps suffering the consequences of his "dependent personality" or some other DSM III category. Others, to rule out organic pathology, may call for elaborate medical and neurological investigations. Some would see this as a problem in family dynamics calling for the treatment of the entire family. Many other views would undoubtedly be proffered—an assertiveness problem, a lack of rational self-talk, poor integration between child-adult-parent ego states, or any number of ideas drawn from the more than 250 different therapies in use today (Herink, 1980). In other words, clients are apt to be assessed and treated according to the therapist's particular orientation, which may not be appropriate for that given individual.

Most therapists would agree that it would be desirable for this 42-year-old man to "find himself," to effect a happier marriage and

1

family life, to derive gratification from his work, fulfillment from life, and freedom from his aches and pains. How is this best achieved? Is there a "correct" way to attain happiness in place of misery, serenity instead of turmoil? Should he be hospitalized, tranquilized, desensitized, hypnotized, psychoanalyzed, or psychosynthesized? Would experts from different schools ever reach a consensus?

Last year, I sent the following letter to three well-known therapists who are also writers, researchers, and theoreticians—Drs. Albert Ellis, James Framo, and Hans Strupp.

Dear Colleague:

Will you please take a few minutes out of your busy schedule to assist me with the following survey?

Problem: You are asked to visit a 19-year-old lad in the hospital. He has made a serious suicidal attempt but is now medically on the way to recovery. While it may not be your customary practice to visit clients in hospitals, in this case a special appeal (by a referring physician, or a close family friend, or some other persuasive person) has led you to meet with the young man in order to evaluate the situation and come up with treatment recommendations.

Request: In the space below, will you please jot down your main hypotheses about what you might expect to find out. For example, a "behavior therapist" might jot down the following possibilities: *Probably lacks assertive social skills that resulted in learned helplessness and a loss of positive reinforcement. May also be hypersensitive to criticism and rejection. After excluding organic factors (e.g., drug abuse) will probably benefit from desensitization techniques and assertiveness training.* What sorts of antecedent and/or maintaining processes would *you* look for?

Here are their respective replies:

Dr. Albert Ellis: Probably is self-downing, self-pitying, and depressed; and has made himself these ways by largely believing (1) "I MUST do well and be approved by significant others; isn't it awful if I am not; and what a rotten person am I for not doing as well as I MUST! and (2) Conditions under which I live MUST be easier and more enjoyable; isn't it horrible when they aren't; and what a horrible world this is for not being as good as it MUST!" May well benefit from rational-emotive therapy, including some skill training in social relations and in getting more of what he wants in life as he changes his MUSTurbatory philosophy.*

Dr. James Framo: (1) In all suicide attempts, in my judgment, there is a family connection—a communication to an intimate. (2) Therefore, I would arrange a family diagnostic session to determine what's going on. (A fuller explanation is presented in my article "Family theory and therapy," *American Psychologist,* 1979, *34,* 988–992.)

Dr. Hans Strupp: I would expect to find some recent experience that proved to be a devastating blow to the patient's self-esteem (rejection, loss, etc.). His history will probably reveal that his self-esteem has always been rather shaky due to grossly disappointing and traumatic experiences in early childhood (hostile, rejecting, exploitative parents). Equally important, there would have to be enormous rage directed against some significant person in the patient's present life that ties in with comparable rage at a parent figure. Being unable to direct his rage outward, he has turned it against himself. Profound desperation and hopelessness are of course a part of the picture, as is great ambivalence toward a love object. There is probably other evidence of poor ego controls and acting-out tendencies of a destructive sort. From a therapeutic standpoint, I would attempt to deal with these issues from a psychodynamic perspective.

After receiving these replies I posed the same situation to several other colleagues and obtained even more divergent answers. Let us discuss this hypothetical case from a multimodal perspective.

It may prove equally effective to treat this young man by rational-emotive therapy, or family therapy, or psychoanalysis. All he may require is the *attention* of a professional or virtually any nonjudgmental outsider. His suicide attempt may have been a miscalculated

---

*Note, however, that what I have just said is *statistically probable* and not a *certain* or *absolute* answer. This means that the great majority (but hardly *all*) of the suicidal young males I have seen for the past twenty-five years have had the kind of MUSTurbatory thinking I have just mentioned and that this kind of cognizing has significantly contributed to their depression and suicidal attempts. My records actually show that when I used RET with some 300 seriously suicidal clients during this period of time not a single one actually killed himself or herself during treatment and only two, to my knowledge, subsequently did so—one a few months and one a full year after treatment had ended. Since therapy with these clients consisted of inducing them to surrender their MUSTurbatory cognitions not only with the kind of rational restructuring for which RET is famous (that is, active disputing of clients' irrational beliefs), but also with the use of a number of other cognitive, emotive, and behavioral techniques designed to modify their absolutistic thinking, their successful treatment provides some backing for the rational-emotive hypothesis that irrational ideation is probably a principal (though not the only) cause of severe depression and of suicidal urges.

endeavor to give a message to his loved ones: "Show me that you care by sending me to a therapist." On the other hand, if his family is highly dysfunctional, and he receives rational-emotive therapy or psychoanalysis without the active involvement of the entire network, his chances for recovery will probably be limited. If he is incipiently schizophrenic (probably in need of antipsychotic medication) and made the suicide attempt in response to command hallucinations, rational-emotive therapy, family therapy, and psychoanalytic therapy may all prove useless.

Perhaps this particular young man will respond best to a combination of an existential encounter group plus individual assertiveness training. Or perhaps a priest or some spiritual revival meetings may do more for him than any formal methods of psychotherapy. Could the best "therapy" for him be a year on a kibbutz in Israel or six months on a farm in Vermont? Or should he rather undergo Erhard Seminars Training (est) and Transcendental Meditation (TM)?

The multimodal therapist asks: *Who or what is best for this particular individual?* The approach is personalistic and individualistic. Multimodal therapists are on the lookout for individual exceptions to general rules and principles. By assessing seven parameters of "personality," multimodal therapists search for apposite interventions for each person.

Multimodal therapy is perhaps best described as *systematic eclecticism.* In the clinical area, rigid adherents to particular schools have receded into a minority. Practitioners who employ a diverse range of methods and theories have replaced them. Does this constitute progress? Yes and no. The limitations of orthodoxy have become apparent, and it is encouraging that more and more therapists are inclined to place the practical exigencies of their patients' problems before the theoretical constraints of their own ideologies. But in so doing, to quote the recondite Eysenck (1970), many have embraced "a mish-mash of theories, a hugger-mugger of procedures, a gallimaufry of therapies, and a charivaria of activities having no proper rationale, and incapable of being tested or evaluated." The typical eclectic therapist chooses his or her methods, theories, and techniques largely on the basis of subjective appeal. "I use whatever makes sense to me and whatever I feel comfortable with," is a frequent refrain. As I have pointed out over the years (Lazarus, 1971, 1976 a,b) this type of theoretical or unsystematic eclecticism can only breed confusion worse confounded.

A therapist who wishes to be effective with a wide range of problems and different personalities has to be flexible, versatile, and *technically* eclectic. Technical eclecticism implies using many techniques drawn from different sources without also adhering to the theories or disciplines that spawned them. One need not agree with gestalt principles to use gestalt techniques; one may employ free association to arrive at affect-laden material without subscribing to a single psychoanalytic tenet. Technical eclectics try to answer the basic pragmatic question: What works for whom and under which particular circumstances?

In scientific research, eclecticism cannot be condoned—it can result only in a plethora of contradictory notions. In laboratories it is necessary to test one or two variables at a time to separate the passive, inert, and incidental ingredients from the active and specific. It is essential to withhold, isolate, or withdraw potentially active factors not only to determine what actually works but also to find out *why* it works. Such procedures in clinical practice—withholding potentially helpful interventions—are unprofessional and inhumane. Whereas a rigorous scientist cannot afford to be eclectic, an effective therapist will not withhold seemingly helpful techniques, regardless of their point of origin.

Does the foregoing imply that a practicing therapist cannot contribute to scientific knowledge or clinical advancement? Indeed, he or she can, but mainly retrospectively. Over years of technically eclectic practice, the clinician who remains a systematic and perceptive observer can detect various trends and "helpful clusters." These findings need to be expressed in terms that can be tested, and they must be consonant with current scientific findings. The evolution of multimodal therapy has followed both of these precepts.

The Multimodal Evolution: A Personal Note

As a child, I would see my father, uncles, and older cousins carefully reviewing the merchandise in their small retail businesses. "What specific items have been selling well? Why have they been good sellers and what can we do to ensure that they continue selling well? What items have not been sold? Why have they failed to move, and what can we do to encourage a better turnover?" Systematic plans to encourage the movement of fast-selling products were coupled with proposals for the disbursement of sluggish merchandise.

This "stock-taking mentality" rubbed off. Even as a trainee therapist I kept careful inventories. "Who seems to be deriving benefit from my ministrations? Who seems to be making no headway? How can I enhance the gains of the former and diminish the losses of the latter?" I have continued to keep careful stock over the years. In many ways, the contents of this book represent the culmination of more than two decades of such stock-taking. The following sorts of questions are addressed: What methods seem most effective with which individuals suffering from what problems? With whom are they most effective, and with whom are they least helpful? What specifically can be done to achieve more successes and fewer failures? Why do certain procedures prove so helpful to some and so unhelpful to others? What specific factors seem to enhance treatment outcomes? How can we best ensure long-term, positive follow-ups?

As an undergraduate, I sought counsel when my interest in pursuing a career in psychotherapy grew. My basic dilemma was whether to pursue my goals via the medical-psychiatry route. I was told that, unless I became especially interested in biological treatments, a medical training would not make me a more competent psychotherapist. In retrospect, my background in academic and clinical psychology has made me lean toward educational models rather than disease analogies, but most of my clinical skills have come from the research literature plus *personal observation* rather than from academic schooling. I made a point of observing competent therapists behind one-way mirrors and have thus been afforded the privilege of sitting in on sessions conducted by experts. In several instances, I was permitted to serve as a co-therapist. I also observed (in the stock-taking tradition) the impact of my personality on the people I was treating. An initial Freudian and Rogerian nondirective orientation gradually gave way to a more active and strongly humanistic training and retraining (psychoeducational) approach to therapy.

As a graduate student, I became aware that performance-based methods are usually better than purely verbal and cognitive approaches at effecting change. Initially, I was strongly influenced by Joseph Wolpe and his coterie of "conditioning therapists." Whereas my academic professors and clinical supervisors viewed behavior as the outward manifestation of more fundamental psychic processes, I soon saw that behavior per se is often clinically significant. It became obvious that people could acquire insight or alter significant beliefs, and still engage in persistently self-destructive behavior. Conversely, a change in behavior often led to a dynamic redistribution of internal activity—after behaving differently, people were inclined to feel and think differently. Yet the psychiatric establishment continued to regard behavior as "the tip of the iceberg," as symbolic of unconscious complexes, as symptomatic of an underlying disease. To offset this unfortunate tradition, and to legitimize behavioral intervention as an essential part of effective clinical practice, I introduced the terms "behavior therapy" and "behavior therapist" into the scientific and professional literature (Lazarus, 1958).

Initially, I went too far into the behavioral mode. While I was never a radical behaviorist, I nevertheless embraced animal analogs, extrapolated from infrahuman to human levels of functioning, and my speech was heavily laced with jargon from the literature on classical and operant conditioning. I ignored some important process variables and overemphasized *techniques.* The variety of new techniques I introduced into the behavioral literature included methods of group desensitization (Lazarus, 1961), "emotive imagery," (Lazarus & Abramovitz, 1962), desensitization procedures for preorgasmic women (Lazarus, 1963), "time projection" and other methods for overcoming depression (Lazarus, 1968b), assertiveness-training groups (Lazarus, 1968a), and several other variants of standard behavioral procedures (cf. Wolpe & Lazarus, 1966).

As early as 1965, I wrote a paper on the need to treat alcoholism from a multidimensional perspective (Lazarus, 1965a). By 1966 I had become suspicious of what I subsequently termed "narrow-band behavior therapy" and published "Broad spectrum behavior therapy and the treatment of agoraphobia" (Lazarus, 1966). This article not only challenged narrow stimulus-response formulations, but also elaborated on the notion that dyadic transactions, or interpersonal systems, were an integral part of the genesis and maintenance of agoraphobia. Subsequently, after conducting preliminary follow-up inquiries, I seriously questioned the durability of narrow-band behavior therapy. I advocated a "broad-spectrum" approach in my book *Behavior Therapy and Beyond* (Lazarus, 1971), one of the first texts on what has come to be called "cognitive behavior therapy."

The reason for employing techniques that were considered outside the boundaries of traditional behavior therapy was that more systematic follow-ups revealed a disappointingly high relapse rate for people who were exposed to behavioral methods alone. Referral to the case notes of those individuals who had maintained their therapeutic improvements revealed that they had achieved "a different outlook and philosophy of life and increased self-esteem in addition to an increased range of interpersonal and behavioral skills, presumably as a result of therapy" (ibid., p. 18). The synergy of behavioral and cognitive methods has become more and more apparent.

The Importance of Follow-ups

Since its inception, behavior therapy literature has seldom cited follow-ups of more than one or two years' duration. Long-term, systematic follow-up studies have been conspicuously absent. It is difficult to interview people even three to five years after they have terminated therapy. Apart from the obvious fact that many people move and are difficult to locate, some contend that follow-up inquiries are a violation of their privacy. Yet the development of durable treatments depends almost entirely on adequate follow-up data. I used to rely almost exclusively on follow-up *questionnaires*, but I have found that they tend to yield false positives. Telephone interviews with former clients are slightly more reliable, but, whenever possible, I prefer face-to-face meetings, and I also try to interview (with the clients' permission) spouses and other family members. Clients' family members, employers, friends, and associates are far less reluctant to disclose negative findings.

My therapeutic procedures have been more heavily influenced by the results of my follow-up inquiries over the past ten years than by any other single factor. When do behavior therapy techniques suffice? What sorts of people with what types of problems seem to require more than behavior therapy? When stepping outside the bounds of behavior therapy, which effective "nonbehavioral" methods are best incorporated into what types of specific treatment programs for which particular problems, under what sets of circumstances, and with which individuals? (cf. Paul, 1967). The answers to some of these questions emerged from several follow-up inquiries that commenced in the early 1970s. In brief, behavior therapy seemed adequate for people with situational crises, specific adjustment problems, circumscribed phobias, various sexual inadequacies, discrete habit disorders, the less pervasive anxiety and tension difficulties, and some psychobiological disorders. Those who needed support over a difficult period, or reassurance about difficult life decisions, and those who lacked assertive and other social skills also seemed to derive enduring benefit from such behavioral interventions as relaxation, desensitization, social skills training, the correction of misconceptions, and behavior-rehearsal.

Follow-ups revealed that, while behavior therapy often enabled some seriously disturbed individuals to make impressive headway, these gains were usually not maintained. (N=19, of whom 13 had relapsed within three years.) Thus, severe obsessive-compulsive individuals would benefit from flooding, response-prevention, and participant modeling procedures, only to relapse within a few months or, at best, a year or two later. (Monthly booster sessions proved helpful in some instances, but "motivation" became a problem, as most people saw no reason to continue therapy while functioning so much better.) Those individuals who had been highly anxious with intermittent panic attacks also tended to relapse after receiving behavior therapy. Unimpressive follow-up findings emerged in cases with self-destructive tendencies and among those who displayed guilt, rage, depression, and withdrawal, sometimes coupled with suicidal gestures. The entire range of addictions fared poorly after a three-year follow-up (i.e., addiction to drugs, alcohol, or food).

Note that I avoid diagnostic labels and nosological categories. A wealth of literature attests to the poor reliability and dubious validity of psychiatric labels. I use them only when filling out insurance forms for my clients, or when other establishmentarian demands dictate the need for these formal diagnostic entities (e.g., when testifying in a court of law). In my own vernacular, everything from situational crises to mild, moderate, or severe psychological disturbances are reflected by the degree of involvement across a person's BASIC I.D. (i.e., excesses and deficits in *b*ehavior, *a*ffect, *s*ensation, *i*magery, *c*ognition, and *i*nterpersonal relationships, as well as in biological and *d*rug-related issues).

In essence, follow-ups revealed that behavior therapy was significantly less effective with cases involving extended interpersonal (systems) problems; when cognitive restructuring called for more than the correction of misconceptions or the straightforward alteration of negative self-talk; when intrusive images conjured up a gloomy and troubled future; and when affective reactions were characterized by extremes (e.g., pervasive anxiety with intermittent panic attacks, or chronic anaesthesia or deadness of feeling). To reiterate, behavior therapy techniques frequently ameliorated these complex problems, but more than two-thirds of these cases relapsed within two years.

The search for additional, systematic interventions that will yield enduringly positive results remains the mainstay of my professional endeavors. Since its beginnings (Lazarus, 1973b) the multimodal approach has provided a comprehensive, but not cumbersome orientation that appears to offer impressive outcomes and encouraging follow-ups. A three-year follow-up of twenty "complex cases" who had completed a course of multimodal therapy (e.g., people suffering from obsessive-compulsive rituals, extreme agoraphobia, pervasive anxiety and panic, depression, alcohol addiction, or enmeshed family and marital problems) showed that fourteen maintained their gains or had made additional progress without further therapy; two felt the need for medication from time to time, for which they had consulted their family physicians (one person had suffered from extreme panic attacks; the other was prone to bouts of recurring depression), one man considered himself "pretty good," although his wife revealed that he was still "too compulsive"; and three other cases (an anorectic woman and two alcohol abusers) had failed to maintain their initial gains. A 70% successful follow-up with a sample of complex and difficult cases, some of whom were seemingly intractable, is most encouraging. We expect someday to be able to report ten-year follow-ups of people who undergo multimodal therapy, but at the three-year interval, we have found very few relapses with straightforward "neurotic disorders."

With difficult or complex cases, the mean duration of a "complete" course of multimodal therapy is approximately 50 hours (i.e., about a year of therapy at weekly intervals). Initially, acutely disturbed people or those with special problems may require more frequent sessions, but once a week is often the best interval for "homework assignments" to have their full impact. The present orientation also lends itself extremely well to crisis-intervention and short-term therapy. Fewer than 25% of the clients I see in my private practice seem to require, or are willing to undergo, as much as 50 hours of therapy. At one extreme, I have one client who has received almost four years of multimodal therapy, the first year of which consisted almost entirely of support and trust-building. While I have not used multimodal therapy with people in mental institutions, in day treatment centers, or with mentally retarded individuals, others have reported gratifying results using multimodal methods in these settings (e.g., Brunell, 1978; Brunell & Young, 1981; Pearl & Guarnaccia, 1976; Roberts, Jackson & Phelps, 1980).

As I hope to show in this book, the multimodal orientation transcends the usual multifactorial or multidimensional approaches to assessment and therapy. It offers a systematic framework that ensures comprehensiveness without sacrificing detail. It provides a compass, a cognitive map, and continuous cross-checks that promote diagnostic accuracy and therapeutic efficiency. It also provides specific vehicles for "treating the whole person" while "talking the client's language." Above all, it provides specified procedures for assessing and remedying intraindividual *and* interpersonal (systems) problems.

Parity as a Way of Life

An outlook that personifies my dealings with all people, be they friends, relatives, colleagues, students, or clients, is the principle of parity, that is, a belief that we are essentially equal to one another. This egalitarian outlook pervades the entire interpersonal modality. "There are no superior human beings—not royalty, heads of state, religious leaders, heads of large corporations, famous actors, athletes, doctors, lawyers, or teachers" (Lazarus & Fay, 1975).

Therapists who believe that some people are superior to others, and especially those who regard themselves as superior to their clients, will obviously give very different messages about matters of inferiority and superiority than those of us who view all human beings as different, indeed unique, but equal.

In therapy, the client undergoes profound changes when one manages to convey that while some people possess superior skills and abilities in many areas, this does not make them superior human beings. As Ellis (1962, 1975, 1977c) has emphasized for many years, we are all fallible human beings with limitations as well as assets. To go through life respecting others for their exceptional capacities, but never deifying them, enables one to derive vicarious enjoyment and learning from others' achievements instead of envy and self-denigration. As long as one subscribes to a vertical model of human superiority in which some people, as people, are elevated above others, acquisitiveness, power, and aggression will dominate one's interpersonal dealings. Never looking up to anyone on a proverbial pedestal (or down on anyone from a pedestal) promotes a sense of *being* based on love, intimacy, and productive activity (cf. Fromm, 1976).

Clearly, when most clients enter therapy, they have been brainwashed by our hierarchically minded society into believing that some people are better than others, and that they, themselves, are inferior to most. Many will elevate the therapist to godlike eminence (and all too many therapists will perpetuate this and, much worse, actually believe it). Initially, it may prove useful to capitalize on this "halo effect" to galvanize certain clients into productive action, but, as therapy proceeds, I prefer to disabuse clients of these distorted perceptions, much as one enlightens subjects after an experiment that may have relied on subterfuge.

The ability to grasp and fully assimilate the philosophy of parity into one's modus vivendi is not easy. For one thing, prestige merchants and status-seekers are ubiquitous, and it is easy to fall into their traps. For another, everyone in our Western civilization has been socialized in terms of a vertical scale of accomplishment tied into the inferiority-superiority dichotomy. Thus, I have encountered more resistance in promulgating the parity philosophy than in any other venture to date. The most common reaction is disbelief in my sincerity. "You don't really believe that there are no superior people." I would urge the reader to think most seriously about what impact the thorough and sincere adoption of parity as a way of life will have on his or her life in general and in the professional sphere in particular.

Chapter 1

Multimodal Therapy:
Basic Rationale and Method

The aim of multimodal therapy is to reduce psychological suffering and to promote personal growth as rapidly and as durably as possible. We avoid psychiatric labels where possible and strongly emphasize the need for therapeutic pluralism. In stressing that few, if any, problems have a single cause or a unitary "cure," we recognize that human disquietude is multileveled and multilayered. But, instead of making these observations in global or undifferentiated terms, practitioners of multimodal therapy dissect human personality into discrete but interactive modalities or dimensions. By assessing each individual through each of these specific modalities, and then examining the salient interactions among them, one is better able to achieve a thorough and holistic understanding of the person and his or her social environment.

The Seven Modalities

We are beings who move, feel, sense, imagine, think, and relate to one another. At base we are biochemical/neurophysiological entities. Our personalities are the products of our ongoing *b*ehaviors, *a*ffective processes, *s*ensations, *i*mages, *c*ognitions, *i*nterpersonal relationships, and *b*iological functions. The first letters of each of these modalities form the acronym BASIC IB. If we call the biological modality "D," for "Drugs," we have the more compelling acronym BASIC ID. (It is most important to remember that "D" stands for much more than drugs, medication, or pharmacological intervention, but also includes nutrition, hygiene, exercise, and the panoply of medical diagnoses and interventions that affect personality). The

13

BASIC I.D. (as in "identity") is an alternative and preferred acronym that represents "human personality."

Multimodal therapy involves the comprehensive assessment and treatment of the "BASIC I.D." By working in this manner, we do *not* fit clients to the "treatment"; we demonstrate instead precisely how to fit the therapy to the requirements of the client. The fundamental assumption is that BASIC I.D. comprises the entire range of human personality; that there is no problem, no feeling, no accomplishment, no dream or fantasy that cannot be subsumed by BASIC I.D.[1]

Multimodal therapy attends to specific problems or difficulties within a given modality as well as the interaction between this modality and each of the six others. Let's assume that a person is evoking powerful affective reactions to a cognitive appraisal (e.g., a real or imagined threat to his or her psychological integrity). This, in turn, triggers repercussions in behavior, sensation, and imagery, as well as interpersonally and biologically. In other words, the involvement or activation of one modality will, to a greater or lesser extent, influence every other modality. A multimodal elaboration of the statement, "When Mr. Smith has a headache, he worries because he is a hypochondriac," would proceed as follows: When Mr. Smith has a headache, he becomes quiet and withdrawn (behavior), starts feeling anxious (affect), experiences the pain as "an internal hammer with hot spikes driven into the skull" (sensation), and pictures himself dying of a brain tumor (imagery) while convincing himself that the doctors have probably missed something seriously wrong (cognition). During these episodes, he talks monosyllabically while his wife fusses over him (interpersonal) and resorts to aspirins and other pain killers (biological). Multimodal elaboration of any problem not only spells out who or what may be maintaining the ongoing difficulties, but also enables one to pinpoint logical therapeutic approaches by examining the interactive aspects of the identified problems.

On those relatively rare occasions when affective reactions are due solely to a biological disorder (e.g., a space-occupying lesion, an endo-

---

[1]Sociocultural, political, and certain environmental factors fall outside the BASIC I.D. These external factors influence "personality," but while there is obvious reciprocity between subjective and objective events, sociological variables are not part of "temperament and personality." Of course, it is imperative to know the cultural heritage of any person before endeavoring to assess or modify his or her BASIC I.D. As Nathan and Harris (1980) strongly emphasize, "psychopathology and society are inextricably bound together."

crinological imbalance, a neurological deficit), the entire BASIC I.D. is still implicated. A brain tumor that causes heightened irritability and aggressive outbursts will have an impact on the sufferer's behavioral repertoire, other affective reactions, sensations, images, and cognitions, as well as many of his or her interpersonal dealings. (It is worth mentioning at this point that when a multimodal assessment reveals lacunae or inconsistencies across the BASIC I, the D modality calls for a particularly thorough investigation. Thus, organic factors are not likely to be overlooked when one conducts a multimodal assessment. This point will be amplified in the chapters on diagnosis and assessment.)

As Plutchik (1980) has shown, emotions or affective responses are triggered by some stimulus that is evaluated cognitively by the individual. From a multimodal perspective, the sequence of events that results in emotional disturbance may proceed as follows:

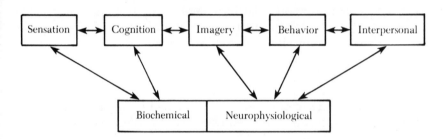

First, through one or more of the senses, a person hears something, touches or is touched by something, sees, smells, or tastes something that is cognitively appraised (i.e., perceived as a danger or a loss), closely followed by images (a succession of fleeting yet vivid pictures of gloom and doom) that result in overt behavior (e.g., flight or fight) and that usually have other interpersonal repercussions (e.g., avoidance or control). The biological modality influences each link in the chain by introducing various chemicals into the system (e.g., adrenalin). There is close-knit interaction among the various modalities; hence, the arrows go in both directions.

The affective chain does not invariably follow a Sensory-Cognitive-Imagery-Behavioral-Interpersonal sequence. The "firing order" may commence with any modality. Thus, a person may launch an anxiety attack simply by dwelling on frightening thoughts and images that lead to unpleasant sensations (e.g., heart palpitations and dizziness). Impulsive people are likely to trigger an affective reaction by saying or doing something that has immediate interpersonal ramifications. A person blurts out a stupid remark at a party. A hush descends upon the group, and he understands their air of disapproval. He blushes and begins to perspire, and imagines the comments that people will make behind his back. He gets up and walks out of the room. Here the firing order was Behavior-Interpersonal-Cognition-Sensation-Imagery-Behavior. Without our succumbing to trait theories, it may be mentioned that many people appear to have reasonably well-defined and predictable "modality firing orders" that tend to remain constant across different situations. As we shall see, this has important implications for the selection of appropriate therapeutic techniques.

To know the principal ingredients of a person's BASIC I.D.—his or her salient behaviors, affective reactions, sensory responses, images, cognitions, interpersonal dealings, and biological propensities—is to know a great deal about that individual as well as his or her social network. To appreciate further the interactions of the various modalities—how certain behaviors influence and are influenced by affects, sensations, images, cognitions, and significant relationships—is to achieve a level of prediction and control that leaves very little to chance.

The BASIC I.D. represents the fundamental vectors of human personality just as A B C D E F G represent the notes in music. There are no H I J K L M N O P. Combinations of A B C D E F G (with some sharps or flats) will yield everything from "chopsticks" to Mozart. Or take the primary colors—red, yellow, and blue. When mixed in various ways, they produce the secondary colors—green, orange, purple, and so on. Thus, our hypothesis is that every condition that human flesh and the psyche is heir to can be accounted for by BASIC I.D. Love, hope, faith, ambition, greed, optimism, joy, sexual drive, assertiveness, disappointment, anticipation, anger, disgust, fear, grief, ecstasy, surprise, failure, awe, contempt, acceptance, boredom, or whatever other action, feeling, sensation, mental picture, idea, personal bond, or physical factor a person may experience resides in the BASIC I.D. "Faith" or "spiritual" components, for example, arise out of a strong cognitive-affective bond. It must be emphasized again that every modality is present, to a greater or lesser extent, in every other. This is a truly "dynamic" theory of personality. To "know" or to "understand" another person is to have full access to his or her

BASIC I.D. Self-knowledge implies an awareness of the content of one's own BASIC I.D. as well as insight into the interactive effects therein.

The Essence of Multimodal Assessment

A detailed and comprehensive assessment is often a sine qua non for effective therapeutic intervention. The cliche "diagnosis must usually precede treatment" points to the obvious fact that when the real problems have been identified, effective remedies (if they exist) can be administered. To accommodate the ephemeral nature of human psychology and the complexity of human thought, feeling, and action, some extremely intricate diagnostic procedures have been devised. These are useless to the practicing clinician. Some are so intricate that they almost demand access to digital and analog computers! Is there a detailed and comprehensive assessment schema that is (1) easy to remember and (2) easy to administer? Furthermore, could such a schema (3) clearly point the way to more effective treatment interventions? I believe that multimodal assessment procedures readily satisfy these three criteria.

By way of illustration, let us assume that we are given one hour to evaluate an individual. Clearly, many different questions can be posed within that time frame. Some theorists may gear their questions to childhood memories, toilet training, and the like. Others may elect to apply objective test items, or administer the Rorschach, or devise in vivo excursions. A multimodal assessment would focus on the following issues:

1. What behaviors are getting in the way of your happiness? What would you like to start doing? What would you like to stop doing? What would you like to do more of (increase)? What would you like to do less of (decrease)? What do you regard as some of your main strengths or assets?

2. What makes you laugh? What makes you cry? What makes you sad, mad, glad, scared? How do you *behave* when you feel a certain way (e.g., sad, mad, glad, or scared)? Are you troubled by anxiety, anger, depression, guilt, or any other "negative emotion"?

3. What do you especially like to see, hear, taste, touch and smell? What do you dislike seeing, hearing, tasting, touching, and smelling? Do you suffer from frequent or persistent unpleasant sensations (such

as aches, pains, dizziness, or tremors)? What are some sensual and sexual turn-ons and turn-offs for you? What bearing do your sensations have on your *feelings* and *behaviors?*

4. What do you picture yourself doing in the immediate future? How would you describe your "self-image"? What is your "body-image"? What do you like and dislike about the way you perceive yourself to be? How do these images influence your behaviors, moods, and sensations?

5. What are some of your most cherished beliefs and values? What are your main should's, ought's, and must's? What are your major intellectual interests and pursuits? How do your thoughts affect your emotions?

6. Who are the most important people in your life? What do others expect from you? What do you expect from others? What are the significant people in your life doing to you? What are you doing to them?

7. Do you have any concerns about the state of your health? What are your habits pertaining to diet, exercise, and physical fitness? Do you take any medication or drugs?

These questions, of course, more or less follow the BASIC I.D. After an hour of such questioning, highly central and significant information will be obtained. Obviously, in clinical practice, our assessment phase is not limited to one hour and it is possible to dwell in much greater depth and detail on each modality and the interactions among them. (See the Life History Questionnaire in Appendix 1 for more detailed items and for a wide range of questions covering the BASIC I.D.)

When conducting a multimodal inquiry, the astute clinician can readily detect lies, distortions, and other inconsistencies. A BASIC I.D. survey enables the therapist to determine the client's specific strengths and weaknesses across the interactive dimensions of "personality," and it clearly reveals the degree of self-knowledge in each specific area.

How and where does a person acquire his or her behavioral outputs, affective responses, sensory delights and displeasures, images, cognitions, and interpersonal skills and deficits? These elements are predominantly *learned*—developed and cultivated through past experience and maintained largely by ongoing rewards. Strengths and weaknesses, assets and liabilities throughout the BASIC I are all products of learning, conditioning, modeling, and similar social and psychological processes. Those who dwell on disease analogies and medical models to account for the BASIC I are sadly in error. But to overlook the D modality and thus to ignore these medical and disease implications is equally hazardous.

A Classic Case

At the beginning of 1974 a colleague asked me to see a second cousin of his, whom he described as "a desperate case." The client was 32 years old, living with his mother, and had been suffering from multiple fears, generalized anxiety and panic attacks, psychosomatic problems, obsessions and compulsions, and hypochondriasis. "He's a basket case, an emotional cripple," my colleague informed me.

The client's mother accompanied him and explained that he was "very nervous," adding that he had always been "delicate." He was agoraphobic and would not leave the house unaccompanied by his mother. He felt overwhelming panic when he tried to do so. He had specific phobias of illness and death, and his compulsive washing and cleaning rituals were tied to germ phobias. While he had "sort of been afraid all my life," he traced the beginning of his major fears to age 17, when he had completed high school and was about to leave for college.

A detailed life history revealed that he was an only child whose mother had been overprotective and whose father was often drunk and abusive. Early in life he felt alienated from his father. As he grew older, he played the role of his mother's protector, often interceding when his father became nasty to her. His mother would then say to him, "I don't know what I'd do without you." At age 17 he was in a quandary. He wished to go to college, but how could he abandon his mother? The eruption of his panic attacks and pervasive feelings of anxiety led his mother to collude with him. He was "too sick to leave home." That seemed to set the stage for a paradoxical relationship in which he functioned as his mother's protector at the same time he developed an infantile dependency on her.

Three years later his father died of a coronary thrombosis. His mother's widowed sister moved into the home, and the client now assumed the role of a "double protector." He was the "man of the house" who looked after his aunt and mother, even though he never left the house without his mother. He began complaining of numerous physical ailments and, together with his mother, made the rounds of various specialists. He had gastrointestinal work-ups, neurological and endocrinological examinations, as well as many routine tests such as chest x-rays and electrocardiograms. These medical tests and examinations revealed no organic pathology, and a year later (when he was 21) his internist referred him to a psychoanalyst.

The father had left the family a life insurance policy of $100,000 plus an Army pension and a few other financial assets that enabled the client to see his analyst several times a week. Six years and some $50,000 later he felt that psychoanalysis was not helping him. His fears, phobias, compulsions, somatic concerns, and family situation remained unaltered. He still had no friends, no independence, no mobility. He stayed at home, watched television, read, played cards with his aunt, went grocery shopping with his mother, and spent many hours preoccupied with bathroom rituals.

His aunt's sister-in-law had a son who majored in psychology and recommended a local "behavior therapist." According to the client, they embarked on a course of in vivo desensitization, thought-stopping, and progressive relaxation. After two months he was able to go to and from the supermarket without his mother, but when he had a panic attack he retreated back into the home and terminated his behavior therapy. Over the next few years his situation deteriorated. Frequent nightmares of dying added to his burdens. His compulsions increased in number, as did his psychosomatic complaints. He became prone to outbursts of temper at his mother. By the time he was referred to me, he had received—in addition to psychoanalysis and his brief bout with behavior therapy—drug therapy, electroconvulsive therapy, primal therapy, transactional analysis, transcendental meditation, and existential therapy. He still suffered from agoraphobia and numerous other phobias, bathroom rituals, and other obsessive-compulsive problems.

An indictment of the field?

Before discussing the specifics of the multimodal approach that was employed with this client, let us first ask ourselves, What is happening here? Is this some "resistant patient" who doesn't want to get better and who will fight desperately to maintain his status quo? Is he a "therapist killer" who will continue making the rounds of various therapists and therapies to "defeat" them and add more and more systems to his collection of "trophies"? Is he a "therapist shopper" whose modus vivendi now requires him to "be in therapy"?

Significantly, in his search for help, the client avoided the lunatic fringe. He consulted only reputable physicians, psychiatrists, a most highly respected psychoanalyst, and licensed clinical psychologists. Even the value of meditation training has been subsequently documented by a Harvard physician (Benson, 1975) and a Princeton psychologist (Carrington, 1977). Why then did he experience no relief from his suffering? How can his first therapist justify the $50,000 he took while prescribing more and more of the same over a period of six years, without any evidence of results? (This therapist refused to send me a written report, but on the telephone, explained that the client's main problems stemmed from pre-Oedipal conflicts. The remainder of the conversation was laced with similar jargon and trait theories that hindered meaningful communication.) Because Janov (1972) claims that primal therapy is "the *only* cure," which "renders all other psychologic theories obsolete and invalid" (p. 19) we are entitled to ask why our client was not cured by primal therapy. Similarly, did he just happen to see a poorly trained transactional analyst, a half-baked existentialist, an unqualified behavior therapist, and so forth? How far do we beg the question before concluding that something is seriously wrong with our field?

Some theorists and therapists stress commonalities between divergent therapeutic approaches. They seek similarities and point out where different systems and methods overlap. But to ignore differences is to overlook significant factors that may account for a critical variance. Multimodal therapy obviously has much in common with many psychotherapeutic approaches. Is there anything unique about it? Do multimodal therapists do anything that differs from what other psychotherapists do? Let us return to the "classic case."

Proceeding multimodally: How and where to intervene

The initial interview consisted mainly of rapport-building. While obtaining information about the client's problems and some antecedents, I attempted also to inspire hope. The client's morale was not high. He was discouraged sufficiently to be considered "depressed," and he was hesitant about embarking on yet another futile venture. I pointed out that some people would maintain that he had a vested interest in resisting change and asked him if he anticipated opposing me or whether he could picture himself cooperating with me. (This question was intended to smoke out oppositional tendencies and to promote some degree of compliance.) I also suggested that we should agree to have four sessions to determine whether he would work with or against me. After the initial interview he was given a Life History Questionnaire. At the end of the second session I drew up the following Modality Profile:

Behavior:	Avoidance
	Playing sick role
	Absence of mobility or involvement
	Bathroom rituals
Affect:	Fear
	Panic
	Anxiety
	Impetuous anger
	Discouraged/depressed
Sensation:	Dizziness, palpitations
	Tremors
	Aches/pains
	etc.
Imagery:	Poor self-image
	Feuding parents
	Teasing from sadistic teacher
Cognition:	"Other people see me as odd and peculiar."
	"No woman would ever want to get close to me."
	Contamination notions
	Musts and shoulds
Interpersonal:	Timid, inept, hermit-like
Drugs/Biology:	Regularly takes Valium 10 mg t.i.d.
	Eats junk foods
	Flabby, unfit, overweight

This cursory profile took 10 to 15 minutes. One advantage of writing down specific problems across the BASIC I.D. is that it provides a "blueprint" for the client and therapist in establishing treatment goals and in evaluating progress. There is a second but equally important advantage: It serves to educate the client by expanding his/her knowledge about the treatment process. This enables the client to assist the therapist in choosing wisely from a broad array of therapeutic strategies.

What would be a logical point of intervention with this client?

After perusing the Modality Profile and rereading his Life History Questionnaire, I decided to start with his Imagery and Biological modalities. I shared my rationale with the client by pointing out that he was obviously physically unfit. He was overweight, sat around the house, and took little exercise. I stressed the mind-body connection and pointed out that an immediate objective was to have him attain a high level of physical fitness. Much emphasis was placed on the notion that someone who is in top physical shape, in A-1 condition, was far less likely to play host to anxiety, or suffer from low self-confidence or psychosomatic afflictions. We discussed the role of good nutrition, and I underscored how his current eating habits could have contributed to his emotional problems.

Before he embarked on a physical-training regimen, I insisted that he undergo a thorough medical check-up, including blood tests and a stress electrocardiogram. "I want to be sure there are no defects," I told him, "because I'm going to push you like a coach or a trainer getting an athlete or a fighter ready for a big event." This communication was intended to serve several purposes. He had led me to believe that he very much wanted someone to "take charge," and I was willing to do so initially to mobilize adaptive behaviors. The image of an athlete being trained to win the "big event" had metaphorical overtones that fitted his needs and perceptions. He did not appear to want me to play a supportive or avuncular role, but he resonated to the image of the hard-driving Army sergeant who acts tough with his men, but who, deep down, has a soft spot for them.[2] This information was gained by asking him to describe the way he related to his previous therapists and to outline what he would consider ideal therapist-client interactions.

The medical examinations revealed slightly elevated cholesterol and triglycerides, which reinforced the need for a change in his dietary and exercise habits. His blood pressure was also slightly high. He became a member of his local YMCA and, while his mother knitted in the lobby, started walking and then jogging around the track, and gradually added swimming and bodybuilding to his training program. A major cognitive relabeling was deliberately emphasized. Instead of viewing heart palpitations with alarm and terror, his new association was to be in terms of cardiac output, collateral circulation, and cardiovascular activity.

---

[2]His father had been "an Army man" but was a *bad sergeant*—irresponsible and abusive without the redeeming virtue of basic compassion.

Within a month he started looking trimmer and his jogging time and distance had increased. Although he still complained of endless aches, pains, and imaginary afflictions, I consistently ignored these to avoid reinforcing his hypochondriacal tendencies. Concurrently with his physical training and nutritional changes (basically, he was to curtail his intake of fats and oil, refined products, and those with sugar or salt, while whole-grain breads and cereals, fresh fruits, and vegetables took the place of his junk foods), he also started a systematic program of *exercises in coping imagery.* (See Appendix 2.)

One of my fundamental assumptions is that, before people are capable of doing certain things in reality, they first need to rehearse them in imagery. A corollary to this notion is that if people cannot picture themselves performing an act, they will probably not be able to do it. Thus, if someone who wishes to quit smoking says, "I can't picture myself *not* being a smoker," that person will probably be unable to give up the habit until he or she is able to capture that image. The client had no picture of himself as a functioning individual—moving about, dealing with people, having gainful employment, developing friendships, dining in a restaurant, making love to a woman, being at a party, and, of course, leaving his mother to her own devices.

We constructed a hierarchy of situations, starting with some simple desensitization images (walking half a block from his home and gradually increasing the distance until he would visualize himself driving to the supermarket without his mother, driving to the YMCA alone, and so forth), and then added imaginary social situations (picnics, cocktail parties, formal dinners, etc.). We employed role-playing to enact various interpersonal encounters. I had recommended group therapy as an adjunct to his individual therapy, but he remained opposed to the idea and I decided not to insist, as I was driving him fairly hard in other areas.

One of his major anxieties revolved around the theme of being alone in a strange city and becoming ill. We discussed the fact that he could go to the nearest hospital emergency room and be attended to by the physician on duty. I wanted him to gain the cognition that the world is full of benevolent others, better trained and more capable than his mother of ministering to him. Accordingly, I presented the following image: "Imagine that you are all alone in Chicago. You become ill and are admitted to a hospital. . . . Now imagine the scene in the hospital. . . . The doctors are standing around your bed, talking to each other, helping you, curing you. . . ." At this point the client started hyperventilating, sobbing, retching, heaving, and panicking. It transpired that this image had elicited a "forgotten memory" that evoked a full-blown abreaction. When he finally calmed down, he recounted vivid memories of an event that took place when he was 7 years of age. He was in a hospital after a tonsillectomy and was coming out of the anesthetic, when he could barely make out some people hovering around his bed. His mother was talking to someone about his frail and sickly make-up. "I hope he lives to see 21!" she declared. I asked him why his mother labelled him "frail and sickly," and he replied that perhaps it was because he was prone to infections and high fevers as a child, which is why the doctor had recommended a tonsillectomy. But his mother's alleged postoperative commentary about the delicate state of his health—"I hope he lives to see 21!"—seemed to have left an indelible impression.

As we explored the repercussions of his mother's appraisals at subsequent sessions, it seemed evident that his somatic and psychosomatic tendencies stemmed from her attitudes. His mother's pronouncement at the time he was coming out of the anesthesia seemed to play a central etiological role. He was (1) in a semiconscious, perhaps highly suggestible, postoperative (traumatic) condition, when (2) an authority (mother) proclaimed him to be frail and sickly, which, in turn (3) centered on self-deficiency as a focal guiding concept.

Regardless of the accuracy of this brief analysis, the client was obviously upset by these real or imagined events, and something had to be done to alleviate his distress. In multimodal therapy, we try to cover the entire BASIC I.D. whenever feasible. The following "antidotes" were prescribed:

Behavior:	Use "Self-inoculation." Several times a day, close your eyes, relax, and repeat to yourself, "I am not frail and sickly." "I never was frail and sickly."
Affect:	Try to get in touch with anger or indignation in place of anxiety.
Sensation:	Use "directed muscular activity"—pounding a foam rubber pillow—as an exercise to assist with anger-arousal.
Imagery:	Picture yourself going back in a "time machine" so that you, at age 32, appear "out of the future" to reassure

yourself, at age 7 in that hospital bed. That little boy (you in the past) senses something special about that 32-year-old man (you at present) reassuring the child that he is not frail and sickly.

Cognition: Understand that your mother was projecting her own hypochondriacal and anxious feelings. There is and was "no objective reality" to her remarks.

Interpersonal: Discuss your recollection of this event with your mother. Be confrontative, but do not attack or blame. (Behavior-rehearsal may be necessary before implementing this assignment.)

Biology/Drugs: Keep working at improving physical fitness, and phasing out the Valium.

As these recommendations were discussed and applied, other feelings and associations emerged. For example, he raised his ongoing fears about death, and he discussed his ambivalence, particularly his antagonistic feelings, toward his mother. (Incidentally, his preoccupation with death seemed to abate after a most fatuous intervention. The client was born in 1942. I asked him where he had been in 1941. He answered, "I wasn't born until 1942." I then said, "Oh, so you weren't alive in 1941. . . . In other words, if you were not alive in 1941 or 1931 or 1921, it means that you were dead during those years. Tell me, was 1941 or 1906 or 1873 a particularly bad year for you? Do you remember suffering and being dreadfully unhappy in 1920? So when you die, it will be back to 1941 or 1901 or 1899 for you. What's the big deal?")

He would become discouraged by setbacks from time to time. I found that he responded poorly to reassuring or direct morale-building behaviors, but tended to snap out of his depressions when I used "paradoxical statements." For instance, I would say: "Well, as everybody knows, you are frail and sickly, weak, defective, about to fall apart, living on borrowed time, inferior, contaminated, deficient. . . ." He would laugh, utter some expletive, and therapy would proceed in a positive direction.

One of the coping images that called for repeated rehearsal was the scene in which he pictured his mother begging him not to leave home, not to desert her. On three or four occasions, we had family therapy sessions in which the client was seen with his mother and his aunt, but these meetings proved unproductive as far as I could tell. After therapy had been going on for about a year, and the client managed to start coming to his sessions without his mother, her attitude toward me and the therapy became extremely antagonistic. She refused to have any further family meetings and tried to persuade her son to terminate therapy.

The therapy lasted for just under two years, and during the hundred or so hours, we employed many techniques while covering the BASIC I.D. We used self-monitoring, imaginal and in vivo densensitization, thought-stopping, a variety of imagery techniques, stress inoculation, cognitive disputation, role-playing, and gestalt and psychodrama procedures (e.g., the empty chair technique, as well as the imagery procedure of going back in time to complete "unfinished business"),[3] and we spent several sessions talking about such values as "long-range hedonism," and the various effects of living by categorical imperatives (what Karen Horney in 1950 called "the tyranny of the should"). His bathroom rituals decreased through the use of response-prevention and contingency contracts. (Instead of his spending four hours in the bathroom performing his rituals, we agreed that he would reduce the time by half or forfeit watching his favorite television shows for an entire week. Thereafter, they were systematically whittled down from two hours to less than 45 minutes.)

By the nineteenth or twentieth month after starting multimodal therapy, most of the negative items on the client's Modality Profile had been erased. By that time he was willing and able to travel alone, and his numerous fears, compulsions, and anxieties were well under control. However, he was still living with his mother and her sister; he had not looked for gainful employment; and he had not gone out on a date. Getting him to move out of his mother's home, to find a job, and to start socializing with women proved especially difficult. I used just about everything in my clinical repertoire—imagery, assertiveness training, interpretation, contingency contracts, rational disputation, and many other tactics, including "coercive persuasion." In the latter, I painted an ugly verbal picture of him as a bewildered, nervous, and incompetent recluse who would lapse into his pervasively neurotic ways if he refused to risk taking the three essential steps of leaving home, gaining employment, and dating women. I

[3]Appendix 2 provides a description of the techniques mentioned throughout the text.

might add that his mother did not make the task easy. She played on his sense of obligation and managed to ignite his residual doubts and fears on several occasions. It seems that I was more persuasive and had greater credibility than his mother, for I prevailed. He moved into an apartment, obtained a job with a company that was willing to give him managerial training, started dating one of the secretaries, and finally lost his virginity at age 34.

A feature of his therapy that proved extremely helpful was the identification of the modality firing order that led to most of his anxiety attacks. He began to realize that his fears usually followed an S-I-C-B-C sequence. First, he would become aware of some minor *sensation* (a slightly rapid heartbeat, some facial tension), which would produce frightening *images* (fleeting scenes of operating rooms and intravenous drips), whereupon his *cognitions* would signal "danger!" and add a "what if" to the equation (generally "what if I become catastrophically ill?"), whereupon he would retreat *behaviorally* and intensify the vicious circle by dwelling on further *cognitions* ("something must be dreadfully wrong with me"). Having identified the order of events, we were able to prescribe effective measures. As soon as he experienced a negative sensation he was to use the differential relaxation plus breathing techniques he had been shown. He was then to switch to various success and coping images, while subvocally chanting, "Keep cool, keep calm, and cut the crap!"

In therapy, "talking the client's language" often adds up to tracking his or her modality firing order (identifying sequential proclivities) and intervening in the relevant modalities. An A-B-S-C sequence calls for a different treatment from a B-C-S-A or a C-S-A-B sequence, and so forth. We call this process *tracking* (see Chapter 5 and Appendix 2).

Follow-up Information

One year later (I had seen him a couple of times during that year for some "booster sessions" after he had suffered needless discouragement following some minor episodes of anxiety), he had changed jobs (he was earning a good salary plus commission from selling life insurance), had moved to a better apartment, was enjoying "plenty of sex," had become an excellent squash player, and was taking up horseback riding. On the negative side, he remained somewhat phobic—he avoided crowded places and insisted on having the aisle seat in a theatre. In my estimation, he was still overconcerned about his health and, while he looked remarkably trim and fit, seemed to be overdoing the health foods and the jogging.

At a four-year follow-up, his progress had been maintained. He was now into water-skiing and had made two trips to Acapulco. He was thinking about "settling down and getting married" but was still "playing the field." He had won an award as "the insurance salesman of the year" and, during the follow-up interview, had the audacity to attempt to sell me life insurance! He was in training for a 26-mile marathon and was "trying out vegetarianism." While he still reported some discomfort in crowded places, he claimed to be less claustrophobic. Interestingly, his mother's view of the treatment outcome was that her son had been corrupted. He overheard her telling someone that he used to be "such a good boy," but by the time that "awful psychologist" got through with him, he started running around with women and picked up other loose morals. "But we get along just fine," he told me, "because she has learned to keep away from certain subjects."

Discussion

I doubt whether anyone can deny that certain constructive objectives were achieved. Some might argue, however, that these benefits may have come about with or without multimodal therapy. Others may even claim that the positive gains occurred in spite of the therapy. When I first presented this case at a professional meeting, a psychoanalyst claimed that the therapy was "superficial" and predicted that the client's basic inability to form mature attachments would find him seriously depressed within three to five years. I found this comment extremely myopic, especially since the client had undergone six years of psychoanalytic therapy with no discernible improvement.

But how can I claim that my therapy was the active ingredient that produced the observed improvements? Perhaps the client needed six years of psychoanalysis, plus behavior therapy, plus drug therapy, electroconvulsive therapy, primal therapy, transactional analysis, transcendental meditation, and existentialism—all of which merely primed him to respond to whatever brand of therapy happened to be number nine. Would he have done as well if he had not received any previous treatment? Would it have taken only two years to overcome most of his anxieties if he could have received multimodal therapy in 1964?

There is no way, of course, to answer these questions. From a strictly scientific point of view, I can offer no definite proof that multimodal interventions were responsible for the gains that accrued. If I filled this book with case after case after case of clients who failed to benefit from other therapies but who achieved their treatment goals via multimodal interventions, the reader might finally agree that it stretches one's credulity beyond the breaking point to ascribe most of our positive outcomes to fortuitous effects. Do I think that his previous therapy made him more accessible to multimodal therapy? On the contrary, more "unlearning" was required to correct impressions that he had acquired from previous therapists. I say this because similar cases who received no previous treatment have tended to respond more rapidly to multimodal methods.

In terms of overall statistics, during the past seven or eight years, more than 75% of the people who have consulted me have achieved their major treatment goals. Three-year follow-ups have revealed a relapse rate of less than 5%. While the multimodal approach can claim no special or consistent effects with floridly regressed individuals, sociopathic personalities, repeated substance abusers, and highly resistant or "unmotivated" individuals, some of these recalcitrant cases have benefitted from our ministrations when the match and artistry between client and therapist enabled thorough coverage of the BASIC I.D. How to reach those people whose excesses and deficits across the BASIC I.D. are rigid, encrusted, and pervasive rests heavily on the therapist's sensitivity, wisdom, and talent. That is why this book will address both the art and science of effective therapy.

Clinically, my colleagues who practice multimodal therapy report gratifying treatment outcomes, very often with people who had not derived benefit from other methods. Statistics at the Multimodal Therapy Institute in Kingston, New Jersey, where qualified multimodal therapists and trainees have treated in excess of 700 cases over the past five years, reveal a consistent 75% to 80% success rate, usually with cases that had not benefitted much from previous treatment.

The clinical successes achieved by my associates and myself are the main justification for this book, which will spell out in detail exactly how we go about the enterprise of effective psychotherapy. I will not emphasize *why* I think our methods are effective; rather I will stress *what* interventions seem to help specific individuals under given circumstances. Theoretical excursions into the domains of the ultimate causation of psychological problems, and definitive explanations of therapeutic success and failure, remain largely speculative and unproductive. The history of science reveals that many false paths were enthusiastically followed by thinkers who preferred theories to observations. The current state of psychological knowledge does not permit the development of an accurate theory of human functioning. Even in medicine, "what" questions have clearly proved extremely useful. Physicians know what to do for some illnesses without knowing their etiology or the mechanisms of action of the effective remedy. The exact mode of action of innumerable medications is unknown despite the fact that millions may have benefitted from them. Multimodal therapy outlines what and what not to do, when and when not to do it, and how to double-check the impact of one's interventions.

Before describing more precise and detailed clinical assessment procedures, it may clarify matters to examine the general terms and constructs that multimodal therapists employ in their conceptual frameworks.

Chapter 2

Basic Concepts for the Practice of Multimodal Therapy

The clinician's view of causality will largely determine his or her selection of therapeutic techniques. Those who believe that unconscious conflicts underlie most behavior problems will be inclined to direct their clients' attention away from overt responses. Instead, they will focus on the fundamental intrapsychic derangement. If demoniacal possession is postulated, exorcism will be the treatment of choice. The view that emotional disorders stem largely from maladaptive conditioning will call for deconditioning techniques. The notion that faulty thinking is at the base of most psychological disorders points to cognitive disputation as the mainstay of therapy. Organically oriented practitioners will favor medical or chemical interventions. The present chapter addresses the theories that form the substratum of multimodal intervention.

What specific constructs, principles, theories, terms, and concepts are needed to account for the vagaries of human conduct? Do we have to postulate the existence of the unconscious, the soul, psychic energy, Oedipal desires, organ inferiority, archetypes, defense mechanisms, drive reduction, actualizing tendencies, extinction, ego states, or various innate urges or instincts? If psychotherapists heeded Occam's razor (which holds that explanatory principles should not be needlessly multiplied), and if they respected the principle of parsimony (the view that between two equally tenable hypotheses, the simpler is to be preferred), the entire profession would enjoy a completely different ambience. At present, different schools of therapy use the same terms in different ways and spawn neologisms that foster in-group cohesion at the expense of general communication.

In my opinion, it is unnecessary, pretentious, and unproductive to invent a new vocabulary to explain supposed breakthroughs in psy-

33

chotherapeutic theory or technique. I am extremely suspicious of the "psychobabble" that has arisen (Rosen, 1977) and note with alarm how many of my colleagues eagerly memorize the latest neurophysiological gibberish and parrot various catchphrases. Jargon appears to be used for three main reasons. First, it covers up the speaker's ignorance and presents a front of erudition to the uninitiated. Second, it provides a vehicle for group identification. And third, it lends an air of mystification that has an allure for all too many. It retards the advance of knowledge to employ complex, abstruse, or obscure terms. Psychotherapists could communicate their ideas with an admirable degree of precision if they used everyday language instead of esoteric jargon. It could be argued that certain technical terms are useful for rapid and shorthand communication, but couldn't we keep these to the bare minimum?

Having stated the foregoing sentiments, I now return to the question, What terms, concepts, theories, constructs, and principles are necessary for the implementation of multimodal therapy? In a broad sense, we are products of the interplay among our genetic endowment, our physical environment, and our social learning history. To state that *learning* plays a central role in the development and resolution of our emotional problems is to communicate very little. What exactly is meant by "learning?" Do the same "laws of learning" apply to the acquisition of movements, habits, responses, expectancies, and values? Exactly how, when, where, and why are certain behaviors, outlooks, insights, fantasies, and interpersonal patterns acquired? While there are gaps in the theories and metatheories of the "learning theorists" and while some of their basic tenets and conclusions contain logical inconsistencies, virtually everyone agrees that *association* plays a key role in all learning processes. For a connection to be made between events, they need to occur simultaneously or in close succession. For present purposes we may ignore the spate of studies that address the precise role of contiguity, reinforcement, latencies, and so forth, and note only that two stimuli that occur frequently in close temporal proximity are likely to become associated. An association may be said to exist when responses evoked by one stimulus are predictably and reliably similar to those provoked by another stimulus. (V. M. Bekhterev originally termed this process the "association reflex." The term "conditioned reflex" was then introduced and subsequently changed to the "conditioned response.") In this regard, *classical and operant conditioning* are two central concepts.

Again, when using these concepts, we need not become embroiled in the controversies that surround them. There is persuasive evidence, for instance, that in humans, most conditioning does not occur automatically, but is cognitively mediated (Bandura, 1974; Brewer, 1974; Mahoney, 1974). Nevertheless, for our purposes I am simply saying that when someone tells me that she never drinks orange juice because as a child her mother tried to disguise the bitter taste of certain medicines by adding orange juice to the mixtures, I explain the aversion by "classical conditioning." When a child complains of frequent headaches for which physicians can detect no organic reason, and I learn that his mother fusses over him and cuddles him when he feels indisposed, I think in terms of "operant conditioning." In therapy, one endeavors to overcome "classically conditioned" problems by the deliberate introduction of new associations (as in desensitization techniques that help the client insert coping images and feelings of serenity in place of anxiety). Difficulties engendered by "operant conditioning" call for a reorganization of consequential behaviors.

Allied concepts that are closely linked with classical and operant conditioning, such as "stimulus generalization," "response generalization," "discrimination," "higher order conditioning," "extinction," "spontaneous recovery," "positive reinforcement," "negative reinforcement," "punishment or aversive stimuli," "stimulus control," "intermittent reinforcement," "self-reinforcement," and various elaborate "schedules of reinforcement," have been invoked to account for a wide range of human experiences and encounters. (Comprehensive accounts of the application of these principles in the modification of abnormal behavior are presented by Redd, Porterfield & Andersen, 1979; by Rimm & Masters, 1979; and by Wilson & O'Leary, 1980.) If we rely solely on the phenomena of classical and operant conditioning to account for human thoughts, feelings, and behaviors, how far can we get? Surprisingly far, but not far enough. As Bandura (1969) emphasized, if we had to rely solely on conditioning for all our learned responses, errors made during the acquisition phase of various skills would prove hazardous. It would probably prove fatal to rely on trial and error or successive approximation methods when learning to swim or to drive a car. In mastering these tasks and many complex occupational and social requirements, success often depends on imitation, observational learning, and identification, which Bandura (1969, 1977) subsumes under *modeling and vicarious processes*. Human survival is greatly facilitated by our ability to acquire new responses by watching someone else performing an activity and then doing it ourselves. We may learn what and what not to do by observing negative consequences befalling others, and some of us even avoid dangerous stimuli by heeding symbolic cues (e.g., "Warning: The Surgeon General Has Determined That Cigarette Smoking Is Dangerous To Your Health").

Cognitions and Levels of Awareness

Do we need to add any other modes to classical (respondent) conditioning, operant (instrumental) conditioning, and modeling and vicarious processes? Clinicians who try to limit themselves to this triad will soon realize when dealing with clients that people are capable of overriding the best-laid plans of contiguity, reinforcements, and example by their own thinking. Thus *private events* (thoughts, feelings, images, and sensations) must be added to the pool of basic concepts.

People do not respond to some *real* environment but rather to their *perceived* environment (cf. Beck, 1976; Ellis, 1962; Ellis & Grieger, 1977; Mahoney, 1974; Mischel, 1973). The cognitive domain addresses the idiosyncratic use of language, semantics, problem-solving competencies, encoding and selective attention, expectancies, and goals and performance standards, as well as the specific impact of beliefs, values, and attitudes on overt behavior.[1] As Bandura's (1978) principle of "reciprocal determinism" underscores, people do not react automatically to external stimuli. Their *thoughts* about those stimuli will determine which stimuli are noticed, how they are noticed, how much they are valued, and how long they are remembered.

As we enter the realm of private events, without succumbing, it is hoped, to the pitfalls of mentalism or dualism, it soon becomes evident that different people display different degrees and levels of awareness. People are capable of disowning, displacing, and denying numerous thoughts, wishes, feelings, and impulses. Furthermore, it has been demonstrated time and again that during altered states of consciousness one may have access to memories and skills that are

---

[1]The main cognitive errors include: overgeneralization, dichotomous reasoning, perfectionism, categorical imperatives, "cannot" versus "will not," "catastrophizing," non sequitors, misplaced attributions, insisting on fairness, jumping to conclusions, seeking the right answer, and excessive approval-seeking.

not amenable to conscious recall. A compelling example was provided by Wachtel (1977) in recounting the experience of a friend and colleague who, when recovering from anesthesia, began to speak Hungarian. She had been born in Hungary but had emigrated to America at an early age. In her completely wakened state, she knew no Hungarian. As Wachtel put it: "Upon fully recovering from the anesthesia she proceeded to communicate in excellent English again, and to this day remains, in everyday life, blissfully ignorant of how one would ask the time of day in Budapest." Most important, however, is the observation, made by innumerable clinicians, that memories not readily accessible to conscious recall are nevertheless capable of influencing behavior.

If we were to add *nonconscious processes* and *defensive reactions* to our assemblage of basic concepts, would we be falling into the quagmire of Freudian fiction? Are these concepts not the same as "the unconscious" and "defense mechanisms"? Emphatically not! The psychoanalytic notions of "the unconscious," with its topographical boundaries, separate divisions, putative complexes, and intrapsychic functions, are tied into an elaborate mosaic of untestable inferences replete with untenable state, stage, and trait theories of personality development. Whereas psychodynamic theory views "defense mechanisms" as perceptual, attitudinal, or attentional shifts that aid the ego in neutralizing overbearing id impulses, our use of the term "defensive reactions" is a simple and direct acknowledgment of the empirical fact that people are capable of truncating their own awareness, of beguiling themselves, of mislabeling their affective responses, and of losing touch with themselves (and others) in a variety of ways. Thus, they will frequently overintellectualize and rationalize. While attempting to reduce dissonance, they may deny the obvious or falsely attribute some of their own feelings to others (projection). They can readily displace their aggressions onto other people, animals, or things (e.g., yelling at one's children, kicking the cat, or punching the door instead of attacking one's spouse).

How does a concept like "nonconscious processes" differ from "the unconscious"? When we refer to "the unconscious" we are talking about an entity. Of course, even the most ardent psychoanalysts do not infer an autonomous homunculus, but the mere notion that there is such an entity as "the unconscious" leads to reification. The term "nonconscious processes" merely acknowledges (1) that people have different degrees of self-awareness and (2) that despite a lack of awareness or conscious comprehension, unrecognized (subliminal) stimuli can nevertheless influence one's conscious thoughts, feelings, and behaviors. Shevrin and Dickman (1980) have surveyed several diverse fields of empirical research and have provided experimental evidence that suggests that "nonconscious psychological processes" are a conceptual necessity. They demonstrate that both conscious experience and nonconscious psychological processes are necessary for a full understanding of the way in which human beings know, learn, or behave.

In objective vernacular, defensive reactions are "avoidance responses." What do they avoid? Pain, discomfort, and negative emotions like anxiety, depression, guilt, and shame. If we diligently avoid the surplus meanings that psychodynamic theory attaches to the mechanisms of defense and adhere to empirical observations, we circumvent the traps that ensnare those who accept the veracity of psychoanalytic principles. Thus, we do not regard "sublimation" as "the translation and modification of impulses/wishes into pursuits which are consciously acceptable to the ego and superego" (Reid, 1980, p. 84). Rather, we regard sublimation as a distraction, as a channeling of effort and concentration in one direction rather than in another. When a young man inquired how to handle his sexual needs during the final stages of his wife's pregnancy, he was advised to masturbate and/or sublimate. In this context, "sublimation" referred to the fact that if he exercised, jogged, and became involved in several absorbing activities, his sexual urges were likely to be less compelling.

A multimodal therapist might make the following observations about a client: "He tends to displace many of his mother's attributes onto his wife. To her dismay, he then behaves like a petulant child. Many of his problems revolve around his images of childhood protection versus adult responsibility. In other words, he is in a state of conflict about relinquishing his childlike, attention-seeking, and self-indulgent patterns of behavior." On hearing the foregoing, a transactional analyst might claim that we were alluding to various *ego states,* as well as *games, transactions,* and *scripts* that reflected the *archaeopsyche* or Child ego state (Berne, 1961) appealing to the *Nurturing Parent.* A Freudian psychoanalyst might be more succinct and refer mainly to the *unconscious conflict* that gave rise to the client's attitude toward his wife. At a purely descriptive level, both the transactional analyst and the psychoanalyst are correct. In many of his transactions with his wife, the client does play childish games, and he appears to be following a script (or what Adler called the *life-plan*) that asks for considerable parental stroking and nurturing from his wife. And the essence of his ongoing conflict (many elements of which lie outside his realm of awareness) amounts to the activation of the incompatible response tendencies of the boy versus the man. Thus, it has often been said that the main differences between separate schools of psychological thought are merely a matter of semantics. This notion is false and misleading.

If we look more closely at the theories, metatheories, and assumptions that underlie transactional, psychoanalytic, and Adlerian representations of personality and human functioning, contradictory notions and divergent points of reference are readily discerned. Transactional analysts, unlike psychoanalysts, do not rely upon a theory of deep unconscious processes. The Adlerian concept of a life-plan or lifestyle is not the same as the TA view of a script. Adlerians regard the life-plan as largely unconscious. Adler (1963) had written: "The life plan remains in the unconscious, so that the patient may believe that an implacable fate and not a long-prepared and long-meditated plan for which he alone is responsible, is at work." Berne (1972) stressed "(1) that the life-plan is usually not unconscious; (2) that the person is by no means solely responsible for it." Indeed, a step-by-step analysis of the manner in which the life-plan is attained would be construed quite differently according to Adlerian precepts and transactional ideologies. Those who believe that the main dissimilarities between various schools of psychological thought are merely terminological, have failed to appreciate certain basic and significant differences. It is easy to borrow freely from the theories of Adler, Berne, Freud, Jung, and many others as long as one glosses over essential differences in their respective ideologies. The net result is an agglomerate of incompatible and contradictory notions. I remain strongly opposed to ideas of achieving a rapprochement between psychoanalysis and behavior therapy. I think that Birk (1970), Feather and Rhoads (1972), Marmor (1971), Wachtel (1977), Woody (1971), and many others are all mistaken to seek "integration" and to advocate "psychobehavioral" or "psychodynamic behavior therapy." Behavioral and psychodynamic views of human development, meaning, and function rest on different epistemological foundations (cf. Messer & Winokur, 1980).

It seems almost reactionary, if not undemocratic, to resist "integration." It sounds so sensible to advise dynamic psychotherapists to pay heed to behavioral learning, and to encourage behavior therapists "not to ignore the manner in which unconscious processes and conflicts shape such learning" (Marmor & Woods, 1980). Perhaps the confusion stems from an erroneous assumption that phenotypical similarities must reflect genotypical commonalities. Vodka and water appear to be identical until you taste them. Many superficial similarities exist in psychoanalysis and behavior therapy, but upon closer inspection, basic paradigmatic differences emerge (Messer & Winokur, 1980). Psychodynamic behaviorism makes about as much sense as democratic fascism! Isn't multimodal therapy a conglomeration of psychoanalysis, behavior therapy, and many other systems? Definitely not. While using effective techniques from many available sources, multimodal practitioners do not subscribe to any of their underlying theories.

Let me clarify this by referring once more to the client who was conflicted about relinquishing his childlike attitudes and behaviors. When we use the term "conflict" we appear to be in concert with psychoanalysts, since "basically, psychoanalysis is a psychology of conflict" (Arlow, 1979). This phenotypic similarity even extends to the fact that both psychoanalysis and multimodal therapy would consider the resolution of the conflict essential for a successful treatment outcome. Both would even agree that there was opposition between conscious and unconscious (nonconscious) impulses. After this point, however, we part company. Psychoanalytic theory considers unconscious impulses to emanate from predetermined dynamic systems and forces within the psyche, and to interact in specified ways with id, ego, and superego functions and other topographical divisions. Thus, psychoanalytic theory assumes that the client's current conflicts have their roots in early infancy, and the likelihood of an unresolved Oedipal conflict might be posited as the basis of many of his present-day marital and sexual interactions. When I refer to "nonconscious processes," I mean simply that people are not necessarily aware of certain connections between past and present events, and that these connections can influence ongoing behaviors, perceptions, and emotions. No additional psychic mechanisms or dynamic forces are implied. We are not closet analysts!

Need we add more terms to our glossary of basic concepts? To recapitulate, we have *classical and operant conditioning, modeling and vicarious processes, private events, nonconscious processes,* and *defensive reactions.* These psychological constructs can explain most of our behaviors, affective responses, sensory reactions, mental images, and cognitive processes. However, as we enter the interpersonal modality and examine various dyadic and more complex interactions, communication breaks down (literally and figuratively) unless we add other explanatory concepts. In this regard, family theorists and therapists have supplied the necessary vincula.

Family Systems

Family therapists contend that "symptoms" or "problems" should not be viewed as individual attributes but as devices for maintaining the integrity of the family system, while simultaneously being maintained by the system. Individual therapy, or even couples therapy according to some family therapists, misses the whole by focusing on one or two parts. Each unit is said to be influenced by, and, in turn, influences the state of all the other units. From a multimodal perspective, it is a serious mistake to shift *all* attention away from disturbed *individuals* to dysfunctional *systems*. To argue that, since individuals form an integral part of a family system, only the larger unit (the family) should be the focus of therapeutic attention, is like saying that, since the family is part of a neighborhood, which is part of a community, which is part of a society, we should devote our attention solely to the ecosystem. Multimodal therapists maintain that more rapid, elegant, and longer-lasting gains are achieved when the therapist swings the focus of attention back and forth from the individual and his or her parts to the individual in his or her social setting. It should not be a question of *whether* to treat the individual or the family but *when* to concentrate on one or both. Although Haley (1976) states that "to interview an individual is one way to intervene in a family" (p. 11), he usually insists that the entire family be present. "The therapist should ask that everyone living in the household come in for the first interview" (p. 15). Multimodal therapists prefer to start with the "presenting client" and his or her "presenting complaints" and then to determine whether the identified client is the person most in need of therapy, and whether the presenting complaints are the "real" problems. Fay (1980) stresses that the person who arrives at the therapist's office is not necessarily "the patient." *"The patient is the person who wants a change* and who seeks professional assistance" (p. 34, italics in original). When family members are concerned about an individual, they are the patients, because they are distressed about their relative's well-being and/or perturbed about their own welfare. In our experience, to insist that everyone be present initially tends to scare away those "nonpatients" who first wish to establish a constructive alliance with the therapist before involving the truly problematic system.

Having stated my major objections to family therapy per se, let me now acknowledge a special debt to family systems theorists, especially to structuralists (e.g., Minuchin, 1974) and to those who employ strategic interventions (e.g., Haley, 1976; Watzlawick, Weakland & Fisch, 1974). They have underscored the fact that people not only "communicate," they also "metacommunicate" (i.e., communicate about their communications). Thus, when relating to and communicating with each other, people can step back, as it were, and examine the content and process of their own relationships and patterns of communication. (The ability to metacommunicate characterizes all "quality" relationships between friends, relatives, and lovers). Since language is so clearly tied to thought and action (e.g., Korzybski, 1933; Hayakawa, 1964; Postman, 1976), we need to talk *about* a language, which calls for a metalanguage, if not a meta-metalanguage (Watzlawick, Weakland & Fisch, 1974).

Here is a straightforward clinical example of the use of metacommunication. Mrs. Smith, aged 49, had been tense and anxious since the death of her mother one and a half years before. Although "a good wife and mother" in her own right, she had always depended on her mother for advice and guidance. She was "sad and depressed" for several months after her mother's demise, but she had recovered from these feelings only to become fearful and tense. For the first time in her life she experienced panic attacks and feared that she might lose her mind. "Am I a schizophrenic?" she asked. I reassured her that there was nothing psychotic about her thoughts, actions, or feelings. We proceeded to work on her anxieties and tensions and embarked on a course of social skills training and "independence training," while also discussing her ongoing relationships and the evolution of her own dependence. She remained overly concerned about the state of her "sanity and mental health" and I continued to offer reassurance. I also took the position that perhaps she secretly desired to go insane, but that intervention proved unproductive. When, by the fifth or sixth session she again asked, "Are you sure I'm not a schizophrenic?" I decided to take a different tack. "Actually, you are much worse than schizophrenic," I said. "In fact, you are a perfect candidate for the State Home for the Very Nervous, Bewildered, and Confused." She giggled and said, "I'm serious." I answered, "So am I." She burst into laughter and changed the subject.

The metacommunication behind my exaggerated irony was that if she were really psychotic or incipiently psychotic, I could not afford to make fun of her concerns. The use of hyperbole in this context offered even more reassurance than the oft-repeated, "I assure you, Mrs. Smith, that you have no need to worry about being or becoming psychotic." There is a wealth of literature on the uses of *paradox* in therapy (Fay, 1978; Frankl, 1960, 1978; Haley, 1973; Rabkin, 1977; Watzlawick, Weakland & Fisch, 1974), all of which uses draw their impetus from the process of metacommunication.

In summary, human personality is shaped and maintained by our associations (classical and operant conditioning) and by our patterns of imitation (modeling and vicarious processes). We are often unaware of motivating factors and tend to avoid unpleasant stimuli through a variety of devices (nonconscious processes and defensive reactions) while trying to integrate our thoughts, feelings, images, and sensations (private events). Finally, much of the foregoing is superseded by our use of language and our capacity to respond to communications within and about communications (metacommunications). Basically, our emotional problems can be reduced to the fact that we act on false or insufficient information. Of course, we are essentially biochemical/neurophysiological beings. The reader who is interested in the psychobiological foundations of psychotherapy and behavior change is urged to read Schwartz (1978).

Let us now discuss the specific application of these concepts to the clinical arena. The initial interview is regarded as extremely important for setting the tone and content of the relationship and ascertaining client-therapist expectancies. The next chapter will therefore discuss significant do's and don'ts during the first session.

Chapter 3

The Initial Interview

During the initial interview, multimodal therapists behave similarly to most practitioners who are interested in establishing rapport, in assessing and evaluating presenting complaints, and in determining the best course of treatment. Nevertheless, multimodal clinicians are apt to follow some important points of departure. In this chapter both the commonalities and differences between multimodal and other methods should emerge.

When one is about to meet a client for the first time, a myriad of questions comes to mind. What will this person be like? What problems will be presented? What will be withheld? What sorts of expectations will the client have about therapy in general? Will there be many hidden agendas? How much rigidity, defensiveness, resistance, or hostility will be evident? Will this be someone with whom a constructive therapeutic relationship can be established?

At the end of an initial interview, I feel that it is reasonable to expect any competent clinician to be able to answer most of the following questions:

1. Were there any signs of "psychosis" (e.g., thought disorders, delusions, incongruity of affect, grossly bizarre or inappropriate behaviors)?
2. What were the presenting complaints and their main precipitating events?
3. Was there evidence of self-recrimination, depression, or homicidal or suicidal tendencies?
4. What was the client's appearance with respect to physical characteristics, grooming, manner of speaking, and attitude (e.g., friendly, hostile, sullen, acquiescent)? Was there any disturbed motor activity (e.g., tics, mannerisms, rigid posture, fidgeting)?

5. What seemed to be some significant antecedent factors in this person's life?

6. Who or what appeared to be maintaining the client's maladaptive behaviors?

7. Was it fairly evident what the client wished to derive from therapy?

8. Were there any clear indications or contraindications for the adoption of particular therapeutic styles? (For example, did a basically directive or nondirective initial stance seem preferable? At what pace should the therapy best proceed?)

9. Can a mutually satisfying relationship be put into effect, or should the client be referred elsewhere?

10. What are some of the client's strengths and positive attributes?

11. Why is the client seeking therapy at this time—why not last week, last month, or last year?

12. Did the client emerge with legitimate grounds for hope?

In expecting clinicians to be able to answer these questions after an initial interview, we are obviously not thinking of those severely regressed, nonverbal, or seriously deranged individuals who may require sedation, instruction, strong reassurance, or those who simply crave the opportunity to experience the quiet presence of another human being. The implications contained in the twelve points are evident. The initial interview not only identifies significant trends, problems, and functional connections, but also provides a framework for assessing the broader structure and cadence of the interactions to follow.

The first four points are the most objective—presenting complaints, presence or absence of psychotic symptoms, aggressive or self-destructive tendencies, and overall appearance and mannerisms. They call for perceptiveness and observational skills. The next item (significant antecedent factors) implies that the clinician will search for continuities, contexts, and background issues. In this regard, knowledge of the premorbid state is often essential. It is also of primary importance to pinpoint precipitating events and their bearing on current influences. This leads to the next item (who or what seems to be maintaining the problems?). By ascertaining precise ways in which significant others react to the client's difficulties, one establishes to what extent systems or interpersonal factors may take precedence over individual or intrapersonal events. (This point will be amplified in several places. See Chapters 4, 5, and 8.)

Point number 7 (determining what the client wishes to derive from therapy) alludes to the fact that clients' hidden agendas and ulterior motives will send naive or gullible therapists off on tangents. (Clinical vignettes presented later will describe several ways of "staying on target.") Next, it is important to assess the client's demands as to the quality of personal interaction. The active, talkative, directive therapist will not be well received by the client who desires a particularly good and attentive listener. Some clients thrive on a battery of do-it-yourself homework assignments; others feel overwhelmed and require a much slower pace of interaction. The therapist should ask, "Can I dispense what this person seems to require?" If not, a judicious referral is strongly indicated.

Point number 10—the client's strengths and positive attributes—provides an important base on which to build additional adaptive skills. Cognizance of the things that people have going for them enables the therapist to assist clients in realistic goal-setting and facilitates the selection of appropriate techniques. To cite an obvious example, the extremely timid individual usually requires a course of desensitization before undertaking assertive excursions in vivo.

Point number 11—why the client has come for help at this particular time—puts one in touch with immediate antecedents and precipitants.

The final point—the arousal of hope—is considered by some to be at the core of therapeutic change (Frank, Hoehn-Saric, Imber, Liberman & Stone, 1978). Frank et al., contend that people do not seek psychotherapy primarily for the relief of specific symptoms; they seek help because they are demoralized. A person without hope is a person without a future. But false hope only intensifies the pain eventually. To be able to inspire legitimate hope is an essential aspect of the artistry of effective psychotherapy. How is this achieved?

Inspiring Hope

It has often been pointed out that people consult therapists when their own coping mechanisms prove ineffective. They may be anxious, depressed, compulsive, or troubled in innumerable other ways, but the question, "What can I hope to derive from this treatment?" is always present, explicitly or implicitly. As such, it requires an answer, either explicitly or implicitly, during the initial interview. Generally, I have found explicit, goal-oriented statements most effective. Here is a typical excerpt between client (C) and therapist (T):

C: When I think about my situation I just see a void, a kind of blackness without any light at the end of the tunnel.

T: When you think of everything at once it all piles up. It's kind of overwhelming.

C: (despairingly) Yes. There's just so much. I wouldn't know where to start. . . . It's just too much.

T: Well, what about taking only one specific thing at a time? Like the new job.

C: Oh, God! (puts hands on neck and leans forward) The job!

T: That scares you?

C: (nods head affirmatively)

T: What is the scariest part of it?

C: (shrugs shoulders and shakes head from side to side)

T: Take one step at a time. What will you do at the new job?

C: I don't know if I can cope. (keeps on shaking head)

T: Did you say that you were going to be selling hardware?

C: (distantly) Uh huh. And garden furniture.

T: Fine. Pretend you're on the job, you're at work. A customer says: "I need a hammer and a folding chair." Can you cope with that? I mean can you show him the hammers, and let him choose one? And can you ring up the price on the cash register? And ditto for the chair? Can you see yourself doing that? Well? Can you?

C: Well, when you put it that way. . . .

T: Well, that's the way it is. By taking small steps, by breaking down something terrible like "the new job" into specific actions, it's more than obvious you can and will cope. And that's how we have to handle all the other situations . . . step by step.

C: You make it sound so easy.

T: Some of it will be easy, and some of it is not going to be at all easy. But the same principle holds true. We will take one step at a time. We will take each problem apart and make sure that you can cope with each individual unit.

C: (looking more relaxed) Can we talk about Susan's pregnancy?

T: Sure, let's do that. Step by step.

There are, of course, many different ways of inspiring hope. Much of what is transmitted will be in the form of nonverbal cues. Thus, if the therapist feels negatively about the client's outlook, this pessimistic bias will more than likely be communicated regardless of the therapist's reassuring words. It is therefore important for the therapist to be fully in touch with negative expectations or bleak prognostic indications. I would never tell a client that I regard him or her as a hopeless case. At worst, I would convey that I was not optimistic that I could effect a meaningful change, but I would stress that someone else might possess the talent and the wherewithal to succeed where I might fail.

Let us now touch on a few other important issues that usually arise during the initial interview.

The Single-Word Technique

Typically, I start my initial interviews with small talk and thereby try to put people at ease. My taking down such formal details as name, address, telephone number, marital status and occupation gives the client an opportunity to adjust to the environment of the consulting room, to experience a verbal interchange, and to be primed for the detailed inquiry that soon follows. Thereafter, the following approach is often most illuminating, especially with clients who are either verbose, or somewhat withdrawn.

I ask, *"If you were allowed only one single word to describe your problems, what would that word be?"*

It is interesting to see what specific word is chosen. Anxiety, depression, guilt, detachment, anger, despair, frustration, confusion, bewilderment, tension, fatigue, uneasiness, worry, boredom, grief, bitterness, and unhappiness are some of the more common examples. The person who selects the word "malaise" usually has a quite different clinical trajectory from the person who says "panic." Two extremely "difficult" clients recently chose the word "victim."

Next, one asks the client to use the selected word in a sentence.

"I have a feeling of *uneasiness* in most places, but it is worse when I don't feel well physically."

"There is a lot of *confusion* in my life about men, marriage, and sex."

"I get *depressed* more often than normal."

"I feel very *frustrated* at work and I find myself getting mad at the world."

"I am a *victim;* everyone's scapegoat, everyone's doormat!"

The single word followed by the single sentence then leads into meaningful elaborations. "Tell me more about your frustration and anger." Apart from the verbal content, it is also interesting to note the latency factors. A person who takes two minutes to come up with the word "unfulfilled" is clearly different from the individual who verbalizes it within two seconds.

When not using the single-word technique, I customarily ask, "What seems to be troubling you?" or, "Will you please put me in the picture," or, after taking down formal details, I simply say, "Over to you."

In Search of Antecedents and Maintaining Factors

Presenting complaints need to be placed in some meaningful context. The two main questions in this connection are: (1) What has led to the current situation? and (2) Who or what is maintaining it?

C: I get these horrible feelings, like I'm going to explode—all tense.

T: (She's dwelling on her sensory modality. Let's stay with it for a while.) Can you tell me more about these sensations?

C: Well, it's all tension. I feel it in my neck, my shoulders, and on bad days my head hurts and even my jaws ache.

T: (Let's get a time perspective.) How long have you suffered from this tension?

C: I don't know. It seems like forever. I've always had premenstrual tension, and at that time of the month I can go batty. Then I have cramps on top of it. I start to feel as if my skin's too tight for my body. When I get that way everything goes to pot. I mean I love to eat, but when I'm really uptight, even food doesn't taste right.

T: (She certainly dwells on her sensory inputs. Let's try to obtain a clearer time perspective.) Did you feel this way as a child, or did you first notice these tensions when you went to high school? Can you remember a time when you were not so tense?

C: Well as a child I was described as "high strung," but this tension . . . well, I'd say it's really been bad for the last couple of years. I've seen doctors but all they did was give me pills. They do help quite a lot, but I don't want to rely on pills.

T: (I wonder what's been happening to her in the last two years, but, first, I want to know more about the drugs she takes.) What pills do you take? Do you recall the names and dosages?

C: The one doctor gave me some muscle relaxants. But I take Valium, the little yellow ones, I think they are 5 mg.

T: How often do you take them?

C: Well, before my period the doctor said I should take three a day. But I'm afraid to get hooked, you know. So I never take more than two a day. But usually I take no more than one, and that's often to help me sleep. I figure if I get a relaxed sleep, I'll be less uptight the following day.

T: You said these tensions have been particularly bad over the past couple of years?

C: Uh huh. Yes. . . . It's about two years.

T: Well what could have started it two years ago? I mean what happened around that time? Does anything come to mind?

C: I've thought about that. You can always blame it on anything. I mean, two years ago I turned forty. Maybe I was afraid of growing old. Two years ago, my youngest son left for college. Perhaps I'm a victim of the "empty nest." But quite honestly, I don't think it's got anything to do with any of these things. I don't know.

T: (These factors may be playing more of a role than she admits. They can be looked into later. At this point, let's check her other attributions.) Well, if you had to take an educated guess, what would you say the tensions were due to?

C: Believe me, I've thought about it. I draw a blank.

T: A complete and total blank?

C: Well, like I said, one can always come up with something. I always said that when my kids leave home I'm going back to college. Maybe that scares me and so I use the tension as an excuse. Who knows?

T: (I think I'll check that one out more thoroughly. Let's see how she responds to an imagery exercise.) Let's test something out. Will you close your eyes and imagine that you have decided to go back to college? Picture yourself in class. . . . What do you see?

C: Um, yes. . . . I see myself finishing a tutorial . . . I pick up my books and walk down the hall. . . . There's lots of people, some young, some not so young. . . . But you want to know my gut feeling? I really don't want to be there.

T: Where do you want to be?

C: That's the question. What do I want to be when I grow up?

T: And maybe that's where the tension comes from. Perhaps you're uptight because you have no direction?

C: Do we have to put our finger on an exact reason in order to get rid of it?

T: No. We can try some relaxation, or biofeedback, or meditation.

But if we have some idea of what it's all about, or I should say, what you're all about, we can be more thorough. (We don't seem to be pinpointing precise antecedents, so let's look for possible gains or maintaining factors.) How about just trying something for a minute. I want to do a simple association test. I am going to say something and I want you to say the very first thing that comes into your mind. Okay?

C: Sure.

T: Here goes. Ready? The good thing about tension is. . . . Quick. Say the very first thing. The good thing about tension is. . . .

C: It makes them take notice.

T: When they take notice. . . . Carry on, quickly, say the first thing. . . .

C: They know you exist.

T: Okay. Now, what, if anything, do you make of those two endings?

C: Well, actually I was thinking of my husband.

T: (I'll state the most obvious inference and see where it goes.) You mean your husband pays you more attention when you are tense? Otherwise he ignores you?

C: No, it's not quite as simple. . . . But, come to think of it, in some subtle ways, perhaps I do fall back on my tension, not only with Gary but also with my friends.

T: (This could be important. Let's switch to some specific behaviors.) Can you give me some specific ideas of what you do and how they react?

C: Gee. I haven't thought this through and I'm sort of guessing, but to be perfectly honest, perhaps people are . . . uh . . . maybe say a little kinder . . . um . . . less demanding after I tell them that I have a tension headache. It could be I'm using it.

T: Okay. Going along with that, tell me for what reasons you would need to resort to excuses?

C: Maybe it's a cop out. I don't know. I mean it's often easier to get out of something because you're not feeling well than it is to refuse for no good reason. Do you know what I mean?

Commentary

It is all too easy to leap to fatuous and incorrect conclusions. The client is correct when she points out that "one can always come up with something." Is her tension a function of her fears of aging? Is it connected with the fact that she has too much time on her hands? Does she lack goals and purposes? Are her husband and friends deliberately or inadvertently reinforcing her complaints? Is she so unassertive that she needs to use illness as an excuse for saying no? The foregoing notions are viewed as tentative leads. When multimodal therapists obtain vague hints rather than precise facts, they tend to conduct a BASIC I.D. analysis. Often, a cursory inquiry across each modality (as outlined in Chapter 1) will round out the picture. Thereafter, completion of the Multimodal Life History Questionnaire (see Appendix 1) will further clarify the clinical picture.

In essence, accurate assessment consists of separating pseudoproblems from genuine problems, ferreting out relevant antecedents and the various maintaining consequences, and then choosing appropriate interventions. Let us now address the separation of pseudoproblems from actual problems.

From Calling Cards to Real Problems

Thorough assessment requires the therapist to take careful note of *what* the client says and *how* the client says it. Careful attention to the manner in which people say something is often more revealing than the verbal content of their remarks. People have distinctive ways of *saying* things and of *concealing* them. The therapist's aim is to *evaluate* the person and his or her problems. To reiterate, it is usually best to start with what the client wishes to relate. It is well known that clients frequently present "calling cards" in the form of problems or symptoms they find easy to discuss. If the therapist appears to be someone they can trust and confide in, they move onto more central or relevant issues. This process can readily be expedited by the therapist, as the following excerpt from the initial interview with a 19-year-old woman illustrates:

T: So your doctor said that your headaches are all due to tension. Whereabouts does your head hurt? How often do you get these pains?

C: (covering the crown of her head) Here, and it also goes down into my neck. I get these headaches nearly every day.

T: Do they make you nauseated? Do you get dizzy or see spots before your eyes?

C: No, not really. But I can't read with one of these headaches. And I can't concentrate. I take aspirins but I don't think it's good to keep doing that.

T: When did your headaches first start?

C: During the summer.

T: About two or three months ago? What was going on in your life at the time?

C: Nothing, really. I had a summer job at the boardwalk. I was dating Jamie. I guess . . . (she looked downcast at this moment and grew silent.)

T: Did you break-up with Jamie?

C: No.

T: (acting on a hunch) Had you gone to bed with anyone before Jamie?

C: You may think me stupid or old-fashioned or something, but I don't believe in that sort of thing.

T: Either way is perfectly okay and fine with me. As long as you feel good about it.

C: Don't you believe in right and wrong?

T: Sure, killing, stealing, raping, hurting are all very wrong, indeed. To harm a person is decidedly wrong in my view. But what has this to do with love, with joy, with sex and intimacy?

C: Well, I wasn't brought up that way. I was raised differently and I can't help feeling bad about such matters, you know. I mean, it's not the kind of thing you can discuss over dinner. Well, maybe *you* could. I mean, but, in my home, with my parents. . . .

T: And Jamie's parents?

C: I wouldn't know. But that's his problem. I mean, I just feel bad that I sort of went against my mother's wishes. Sort of like I let down the family, if you see what I'm getting at.

T: You feel guilty because you had sex with Jamie and went against your family's teachings?

C: You wouldn't understand!

T: Who would understand?

C: Maybe a priest.

T: You want me to act like a priest and tell you that you have sinned?

C: (laughing) I don't know what I want. (long pause) Doctor, can I ask you a stupid question?

T: Try me.

C: You're really going to think I'm batty. (pause) Do you think I'd still be able to go to heaven?

T: Sure, if God is a good psychologist and not a nasty clergyman.

I heard no more about headaches from this young girl, but we did manage to focus on areas of central concern. Subsequent sessions were taken up with further guilt feelings and their resolution, and discussions of orthodox morality. The thrust of therapy then moved to social skills training and her desire to loosen family bonds while still retaining satisfying family ties.

To summarize: By starting with what the client wishes to tell, it is usually relatively easy to obtain a description of various problems, their onset and development, and their relationship to general stress factors in the client's current environment.

The Inner Circle Strategy

A simple procedure that often proves effective in eliciting central and significant information was outlined previously (Lazarus, 1971) and is worth repeating here. As we emphasized in the preceding section, many clients are reluctant to divulge personal information, and others are uncertain about the type of information that is best shared with a therapist. Clients often need to be led into personal territory instead of dwelling on the situational and peripheral aspects of their lives. When they repeatedly digress, or focus on matters that have no bearing on their basic problems, or when their tendency to keep the therapist "at arm's length" interferes with the treatment goals, the *inner circle strategy* often proves valuable.

The following figure is drawn for the client:

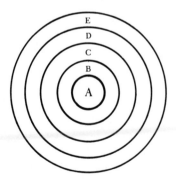

The therapist explains the diagram as follows: "This represents various layers of personal privacy. The little inner circle marked "A" represents the person's most private and personal territory. Some people keep all the information in their A zone entirely to themselves. They do not share these thoughts, deeds, feelings, or wishes with anybody else. Others may share A or parts of A with a very special person who is considered totally trustworthy. Circle B is reserved for one's very closest friends and confidants, while other good friends are permitted only as far as Circle C. One's acquaintances will be taken no further than Circle D (they are not allowed into C, B, or A). The E zone represents a person's superficial contact with the world and includes the sort of information that may be gathered from minimal social interaction."

After explaining the diagram to the client, I emphasize that good therapy takes place within the B and A zones. Telling a client, "I feel that you are keeping me in Circle C," often begins to facilitate the flow of more significant information. Alternatively, it may be helpful to ask the client, "Do you think that you have let me into your B or A zones?"

It is also helpful to point out that some people have large and closely guarded (barricaded) A zones, as depicted in the following diagram,

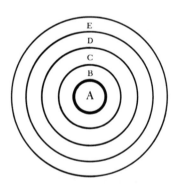

and to discuss the probable repercussions of adopting such an opaque and highly defended position. The net result of these exchanges is generally a greater willingness on the part of the client to take the risk of divulging material that might otherwise have been kept from the therapist.

Beyond Questions and Answers

It is important to attend to the attitude of the client as he or she discusses each event. The therapist must be on the alert for special sensitivities and vulnerabilities. It is imperative to look for the general manner in which clients express themselves (what they gloss over, ignore, and choose to talk about); to observe the rate of speech (hesitation, blocking, confusion) and to note whether the pitch and timbre of the client's voice tends to change when different topics are brought up. Facial expression, body position, posture, movement, and gestures are most significant, as are flushing, changes in pallor, perspiration, moist palms, tears, frequent swallowing, dry mouth, and even pupilary dilation. It is worth noting whether breathing rates increase or decrease at specific times. Sometimes one is alerted to a central clue by noting that head-scratching or the rubbing of eyes, or a tendency to glance away tend to signify that person's characteristic way of covering up anxiety. *The minutiae are important.*

The therapist must also be aware of how he or she is perceived by the client. The therapist's physical appearance, sex, age, manner of speaking, posture, and so forth will all influence the clients' responses. In essence, they will be asking themselves, "What is useful and safe to reveal here?" Also, the role that the therapist adopts will significantly influence the course of therapy. Does the therapist come across as an authority figure, a policeman, a teacher, a coach, a priest, a judge, a businessman(woman)? Bear in mind the obvious fact that we are seldom seen for what we "really" are. I noticed, for instance, that when my hair turned prematurely gray about ten years ago, my "reinforcement value" was clearly augmented for those clients who responded to a "father figure" or who wanted me to play a professorial or avuncular role. I was less effective with younger clients who wished me to fill a fraternal gap, or represent a peer or some other contemporary. It is important to discuss the impact one has on the client, especially when one suspects a role conflict. As one of my black colleagues advised, "Don't be color blind." The white liberal therapist who pretends to be so nonracist as not even to notice that the client's skin color is distinctly different from his or hers, is likely to be hoisted on his own petard. Typically, I will ask a nonwhite client how he or she feels about trusting a white man, because effective psychotherapy is predicated on trust. I will usually discuss this crucial issue within the first ten minutes of the initial interview. Sometimes a client cannot trust someone who is a different color, or who is not fluent in a different language, and so forth. In these cases, appropriate referral is often the method of choice!

In my experience, handsome dividends are paid to the therapist who adopts a "fallibility" stance from the outset instead of trying to live up to an image of compulsive "professionalism." To pose as the perfect healer, the sagacious, self-actualized being, or any other phony role inevitably places the therapeutic relationship in jeopardy. I prefer to establish that I, like every other human being, am imperfect. I have acquired certain facts and skills that can prove effective. But I can err, and when I do, I make an effort not to hide my errors. The fallibility stance obviates face-saving maneuvers by the therapist.

If possible, it is helpful for clients to realize that in therapy they will be offered desiderata not usually available from most social relationships. For example, they can profit from the realization that criticism of the therapist will *not* meet with the usual defensive, retaliatory reactions. It is important that the therapist model constructive criticism, engage in selective self-disclosure, display nonjudgmental interest in and understanding of the client, and show full acceptance (which is not the same as *approval* of everything he/she says and does). In my experience, the very best therapists are essentially kind and gentle people with obvious flexibility and humor.

I generally take notes during sessions (jotting down key words and phrases in addition to any recommendations I might make) but I refrain from doing so if it appears to interfere with the flow of conversation. I do not believe in letting clients bathe in the sweat of tense and protracted silences. I prefer to channel the conversation into areas that are less painful. Subsequently, I tend to steer the drift of the dialogue back to the affect-laden material and usually find the person more willing to disclose information. When it seems important to help the client get over a block instead of steering away from it, it sometimes helps simply to say, "Is something making it difficult for you to talk to me about this matter? If so, can you tell me what it is?" At other times, one may venture an opinion about what lies behind the client's reluctance to discuss the subject. "Perhaps you are afraid of what I will think about you?" On occasion, the following paradoxical question has elicited important information: "If you were able to talk about it, what would you tell me?"

It is important to obtain highly *specific* information. For example, a client says, "My mother was mean to me." The therapist would then ask for specific examples of her meanness. For even greater specificity, this is best followed by the usual what, when, where, who, and how types of questions. "What happened then?" "Who was with you at the time?" "How did you feel about that?" "When exactly did this occur?" "Where were you when this occurred?" The therapist often has to channel the direction of the interview. One of my trainers once told me that interrupting a client was counterproductive. "Whatever the client is talking about is important and significant to that person." Nonsense! Clients often ramble or babble on tediously about irrelevant matters. They may discuss trivial events as a smokescreen, hiding and blotting out the real issues. There are gentle and effective ways of cutting into the flow. "I notice that you spend a lot of time telling me about Donna and Fred. I'm not sure I see why they are so important to you at this time." This type of bridging remark then opens the opportunity to ask for some significant information. "Please tell me something about your marriage." "What has led you to change your jobs?"

The Educational Emphasis

When dealing with behavior, affect, sensation, imagery, cognition, and interpersonal factors (as well as when attending to details about nutrition, exercise, and health concerns in the D modality) the emphasis is essentially educational. Generally, our successful clients are willing to practice relaxation, meditation, and other prescribed exercises; they are also willing to read recommended books and other reading materials; they keep activity charts when indicated; and they openly share their thoughts and feelings with the therapist. In turn, the therapist tries to modify faulty styles, offers guidance, displays caring, provides information, corrects misconceptions, and delivers the support and encouragement necessary to assist the client in reaching his or her goals. We emphasize that most of the responsibility rests with the client to practice between sessions. Often, this educational emphasis is spelled out during the initial interview. The following is a brief excerpt from the initial interview with a bright young author who was having "creative blocks" and who had not derived benefit from previous therapy.

C: Please don't take offense at what I am about to ask you, but I've already seen three doctors. . . . I received therapy from Dr. R for over two years, and I'm still no better. . . . So I guess what I'm leading up to is why you think you will succeed where the others have failed. I hope you're not offended.

T: No, not at all. You seem to be inquiring if I have any special abilities that my colleagues don't possess. That's a legitimate question.

C: It's not that I'm asking for *magic*. . . .

T: (very gently) I really think you are. The way you worded the question made it sound as if I would do, or fail to do, something to you that might solve your problems, or not solve your problems.

C: I don't see that. . . .

T: Let's word the question differently. If you and I work together, if we collaborate and pool our energies, what are the chances that many of your difficulties will be alleviated? If you don't trust me, if you avoid taking emotional risks, find reasons and excuses for not doing homework, miss your appointments, withhold information. . . .

C: Oh, come now, I wouldn't be here if I was going to adopt that attitude. But you make it sound as if *I* have to do all the work.

T: As I tell many people, the therapist is a coach. If you look at therapy as education, you can liken it to someone who wants to learn a new language, or play a musical instrument, or improve his or her tennis game.

C: Hardly! I feel that my life is at stake! This is no picnic for me.

T: I'm merely using an analogy; I'm not minimizing the importance of the situation. Nevertheless, what I'm trying to get across is that the process of change is one of *education*. I can't help wondering how much you tried to assist Dr. R, how much you tried to help him help you. Do you see what I'm asking?

C: I was never uncooperative. . . .

T: But what did you do that was actively helpful? Perhaps you didn't obstruct the therapy, but did you take any responsibility to make it work?

C: I'm not sure I follow you. The approach that Dr. R takes is more traditional. I mean the most homework I had was to write down my dreams.

T: And did you do that?

C: Frankly, after awhile I couldn't see the point of it. I mean. . . .

T: Did you tell that to Dr. R? Did you come right out and say that you couldn't see the point of it?

C: Well, not exactly.

T: Okay. That's what I mean by cooperation, by responsibility. I would expect you to level with me all the way, one hundred percent. If I make a suggestion or a recommendation that you consider irrelevant or beside the point, I want to hear honestly about your feelings, actions, and reactions. You can start right now by telling me exactly how you feel about what I have been saying.

C: It makes sense.

T: How do you *feel* about it?

C: Like I said, I like it. It makes sense. I won't hide things from you.

T: I wish I could believe that.

C: Don't you trust me?

T: Well, you weren't honest with Dr. R, so why should you be any different with me?

C: (laughing) Because you're a son of a bitch.

Comment: In addition to establishing the main thrust of my approach as educational, I was also teaching the client (priming him) to interact with me in a forthright manner. By stressing the need for honesty in our relationship, I was able to use this to good effect whenever I had reason to suspect that he was withholding feelings or information. "Are you leveling with me?" I would ask, and to underscore the point, I would add, "or are you treating me like Dr. R?" Our rapport became excellent and the course of therapy went very smoothly.

A Diversity of Styles

The multimodal orientation emphasizes therapeutic flexibility and versatility above all else. The principle of individuality speaks to the fact that there is no unitary way to approach peoples' problems. The therapist who exudes warmth and empathy with everyone will offend, or at least prove less effective with, those who prefer a more distant, formal, and business-like interaction. One begins the initial interview in an accepting, neutral, and open manner. The perceptive clinician can soon gauge how best to augment the level of rapport. Some people respond extremely poorly to statements of sympathy. A client who snapped, "Don't mollycoddle me!" when I stated, with honest concern, "I really feel for you," responded very positively when I adopted a tough, almost insensitive stance throughout her course of therapy. Sympathetic and empathic reflection only made her feel sorry for herself, whereas the message, "Stop making such a fuss!" inspired her to initiate constructive changes.

Some clients require a clarification of their affective reactions. For them, a client-centered, reflective atmosphere is made to order. Others require direct confrontation, cognitive disputation. Those with obvious response deficits call for active modeling, coaching, and social skills training. In many instances, the therapist is called upon to treat the same client with tenderness and sympathy on some occasions, and with tough-minded pragmatism on others. It is thus more difficult for a therapist to be a multimodalist and display versatility and adaptivity than to follow one method and allow a "natural selection" of clients to ensue.

If several colleagues, unfamiliar with my therapeutic approach, were to observe me with different clients, their views would diverge widely if they were asked to identify my orientation. One might say: "He's a Rogerian. All he did for the hour was reflect back the client's affective statements." Someone else might say: "He combines Alfred Adler with Jay Haley's problem-solving therapy." Another observer might conclude: "He's a gestalt therapist. He used psychodrama and imagery techniques." "I disagree," yet another might say, "he reminded me very much of Albert Ellis." Other observations might include: "He's so eclectic that I can't pinpoint a specific orientation" or, "He's obviously a behavior therapist—the hour was made up essentially of desensitization followed by assertiveness training." It is even possible that someone might conclude: "He's a psychodynamic practitioner. He spent most of the hour merely listening and making occasional comments about childhood events."

Again, it cannot be overemphasized that, when drawing upon Freud, Rogers, Ellis, Perls, or any other personage, one need not accept any of their theories or principles. For example, when I (as a technical eclectic) discuss a client's dreams, I do not rely on Freudian or Jungian symbolism; nor do I believe that dreams are the royal road to the unconscious. On occasion, dreams, especially recurring dreams, yield clues in the imagery modality that can lead to the implementation of behavioral and interpersonal techniques. Thus, when a client reported that she frequently had dreams that involved "being shoved like a sardine in a subway train," we used associated imagery (see Appendix 2) and arrived at the conclusion that she felt "hemmed in" by her boyfriend. Accordingly, behavior rehearsal and assertiveness-training techniques were selected.

The range of clients with whom a therapist can be effective is probably in direct proportion to the degree of flexibility and versatility he or she can muster. Multimodal therapy presupposes a kind of training different from the traditional approaches to psychotherapy. It will also presumably attract a different kind of person. The therapist who prefers to learn how to do one or two things extremely well will probably not be an effective multimodal practitioner. Clinically, we have support for the contention that it is usually better to cover seven areas fairly thoroughly than to deal with one or two modalities in extreme detail.

Another point needs to be covered in this overview of the initial interview: It is vital for therapists to examine their own feelings during and after the interview. In looking at our own "gut" reactions we frequently find clues to central problems that tend to elude other lines of inquiry. In trying to understand our feelings about the client, we can, if we remain honest and objective, tune in to subtle cues that the client emits. When I notice that a client evokes tense or uneasy feelings in me, I divulge these reactions, provided I feel that the client will take my criticisms in a positive spirit. "I want to share with you the fact that I don't feel comfortable and relaxed with you. There is something about you that leads me to feel rather uptight." When I said this to a 26-year-old engineer who had consulted me because of frequent clashes with his co-workers, he said, "I'm not here to entertain you or to relax you. I'm paying you to help me get over some problems." I smiled and said, "Now I know why I feel uneasy around you. It's because I sense that my feelings will be ignored or even trampled on. I wonder if other people also feel that way about you, and I can't help wondering if it has a bearing on your problems at work." He looked thoughtful and then asked, "What is it exactly that I am doing to create these hostile feelings?" I replied, "That's an excellent question. Let's see if we can figure it out together."

Effective psychotherapists are constantly on guard against fitting the patient to the treatment. A primary purpose of the initial interview is to determine how to fit the treatment to the patient. Using the norms and probabilities that we may glean from the scientific literature, we need to tailor our general clinical knowledge to fit a given individual. Consumers are apt to receive what the therapist knows—a biological psychiatrist is unlikely to delve carefully into family dynamics; a psychoanalyst is unlikely to employ behavioral techniques. By adopting a pluralistic stance, multimodal therapists are constantly on the alert for the interplay between biological, psychological, and sociological variables. Instead of viewing the client's problems from one or two perspectives, multimodal practitioners use seven lenses. This avoids dichotomous thinking (e.g., one would not ask, "Is this a systems or an individual problem?" since the multimodal view holds that *personal and interpersonal* processes enter into nearly all of life's circumstances), and it underscores the "specificity factor" (i.e., Who is best equipped to provide the specific therapy for the special problems that this particular client experiences in different situations?). Again, it should be emphasized that a judicious referral is sometimes the definitive choice.

The Assessment (Diagnostic) Sequence

We have presented several important facets of the initial interview. It is crucial to realize that the needs of the individual client will determine the format of the initial (and every subsequent) interview. Nevertheless, in most instances, a fairly typical sequence may be followed.

Phase 1. Evaluate the client's presenting complaints; assess their severity and duration. Be on the alert for dysfunctions across the BASIC I.D. Search for target behaviors (i.e., anything measurable, something that can be counted), as this often provides clues for meaningful homework assignments, which, in turn, reveal more central problems. (For example, by asking a seemingly timid client to count the number of times each day that she said "I can't," I enabled her to realize how she was using passive-resistance as an interpersonal weapon.)

Phase 2. Search for immediate antecedent events; carefully evaluate the presymptomatic environment. Try to establish what immediate factors seem to have brought the client to his or her current plight. Whenever there is a definite discrepancy between the client's apparent presymptomatic stress and the severity of the ongoing disorder, particular attention should be paid to biological factors.

Phase 3. Carry out a careful assessment of the postsymptomatic environment. What other treatment has the client undergone, and with what results? In examining the postsymptomatic environment, a key question is, "Who or what appears to be maintaining the problems?"

Phase 4. When in doubt, perform a formal mental-status examination. The usual mental-status inquiry usually evaluates the client's orientation to *place* (e.g., What is the name of the town we are in?), *time* (e.g., What is today's date?), and *persons* (What is your name?

Who am I?). *Memory for recent* events may be assessed (e.g., What did you eat for dinner last night? What are the newspaper headlines about these days?) A procedure that has had long clinical use is *serial subtractions of 7 from 100* (the examinee is asked to take 7 away from 100, then take 7 from what is left, and so on). It is well to note if this takes longer than 1½ minutes, and to record the number of errors (4–6 errors are marginal). When the mental-status examination suggests the impairment of brain tissue, a thorough testing of the client's comprehension, attention, grasp, reasoning and judgment should be made.

(The student reader may wish to consult Ian Stevenson's chapter on "The Psychiatric Interview" in *The American Handbook of Psychiatry* (2nd edition) Vol. 1, Chapter 53, 1974, New York: Basic Books. There is also an excellent chapter (8) "Examination of the patient" in L.C. Kolb's *Modern Clinical Psychiatry* (9th edition). Philadelphia: Saunders, 1977.)

At the end of the initial interview, I usually hand my clients a Multimodal Life History Questionnaire (see Appendix 1) and ask them to fill it out and return it at their second session. When working with persons who cannot or will not fill out the forms, we use the questionnaire as a guide during the interview to obtain a thorough review of the client's background—early development, family interactions, and educational, sexual, occupational, and marital experiences.

Chapter 4

The Multimodal Assessment-Therapy Connection

Franks and Wilson (1980) typify a large segment of the professional community when they comment, "Necessary as they are, artistic skills are secondary; it is *scientific* acumen which is primary." I disagree. Even if practicing therapists had at their disposal ten thousand times the amount of hard scientific evidence that exists today, artistry would still play an important role in the implementation of therapeutic techniques. Some thinkers have even seriously challenged the value of the scientific model to which Franks and Wilson subscribe. Goldman (1976), for example, called for a revolution in counseling research and referred to the essentially trivial and atomistic information that has been derived from laboratory research. Others (e.g., Koch, 1980; Rausch, 1974) have also argued that the knowledge available from scientific research is of limited value as a base or guide for professional practice. This should not be misconstrued as implying that we should abandon our rigorous search for prediction and control. Nevertheless, there are many aspects of "psychotherapeutic grammar" that science is not designed to elucidate. In stressing the limitations of the experimental method, Wachtel (1980) called for a "greater emphasis on observation . . . [and] a greater diversity of method and mode of thought." Colby (1962) referred to psychotherapy as "a practical art, a craft like agriculture, or medicine, or winemaking in which an artisan relies on an incomplete, fragmentary body of knowledge and empirically established rules traditionally passed on from master to apprentice."

Practitioners need a facility for on-the-spot inventiveness. Unusual cases and challenging problems call for a high degree of clinical acumen and an innovative flair, but even relatively straightforward emotional problems impose a constant series of clinical choices.

Many years ago Erickson (1953) emphasized that "the nature and character of a single finding can often be more informative and valuable than a voluminous aggregate of data whose meaning is dependent upon statistical manipulation." We will not belabor the fact that some therapists are more perceptive, more intuitive, and more insightful than others. Observing a great clinician at work is like hearing a virtuoso violinist. While we can't all have that "special touch" in therapy, by proceeding multimodally, we can at least guarantee a comprehensive coverage that will elicit certain essential features that may otherwise go undetected.

The Use of Structural Profiles

Many therapists whose orientations may be described as multifaceted, or multidimensional, or multifactorial pay at least some heed to problem behaviors, affective responses, sensations, images, cognitions, interpersonal relationships, and biological processes. It is the *precise* and *systematic* perusal of the BASIC I.D. that sets apart multimodal practitioners from other broad-spectrum or multiform approaches. As mentioned in Chapter 3, we find it essential to place presenting complaints within their broader context and to note which modality or modalities of the BASIC I.D. encompass the presenting complaints. "I feel tense, frustrated and unhappy at work and at home," clearly identifies *sensory, affective*, and *interpersonal* factors. As we will show, the multimodal therapist, like many clinicians, investigates and examines presenting problems in terms of their antecedents and consequences, but in addition, he or she assesses each problem for its interactive impact upon the *entire* BASIC I.D. Some presenting complaints are difficult to identify in terms of specific modalities. "I want to get in touch with myself," can hardly be considered a sensory complaint! Typically, upon careful questioning, these vague problems can be reduced to several discrete difficulties across the BASIC I.D. This point will become clearer when we discuss specific cases later in this chapter.

Before commencing with an analysis of *content* across the BASIC I.D., we might mention Ferrise (1980), who has pointed out the value of beginning with a *structural* assessment. In everyday terms, he points out that some people are primarily "doers," whereas others are "thinkers," or "feelers," or people-oriented "relaters," and so forth. He constructs a ten-point scale for each modality and asks his clients to rate the extent to which they perceive themselves as

Doing, Feeling, Sensing, Imagining, Thinking, and Relating. He also asks people to rate the extent to which they observe and practice "health habits"—regular exercise, good nutrition, avoiding cigarettes, drugs, and excessive alcohol, etc. A high D score indicates a health-minded individual. Simple bar diagrams may be constructed.

Cases A and B (see p. 70) are fairly similar. They are both highest on "doing, thinking, and relating," but A is more "health conscious" than B, and the fact that A is a "doer, relater, and thinker," whereas B is a "doer, thinker, and relater," may make for some predictable differences in therapeutic response. For example, both A and B will probably respond well to behavioral, cognitive, and interpersonal techniques, but A might require or prefer interpersonal assignments to methods of cognitive restructuring, whereas B is likely to be more receptive to cognitive interventions. In the case of C, whose lowest modes are "behavior" and "cognition," and whose self-rating reflects a "feeling, sensing, imagining, relating" being, the usual cognitive-behavioral procedures would probably prove less effective than perhaps T-groups (Golembiewski & Blumberg, 1977) and relationship-enhancement therapy (Guerney, 1977).

A brief transcript will illustrate the way one draws up a *structural profile*. The client is a very successful corporate president with "marital problems."

T: Some people may be described as "doers"—they are action-oriented, they like to busy themselves, get things done, take on various projects—whereas others are more inclined to be "thinkers" —they like to plan, scheme, design, reflect, and reason things through. Some people are very high on "feelings and emotions," and some do a lot of daydreaming, have lots of fantasies and vivid imaginations. I'd like you to rate yourself on a ten-point scale in several dimensions. Let's start with "behavior." From zero to ten, how high would you rate yourself on the dimension of being active, a doer, a person who likes to translate energy into action?

C: That's me all right! I like to get things done. Let's face it, I couldn't have achieved all that I have if I were not this way.

T: So what number can we give it?

C: A 9 or 10. Make it a 10.

T: Okay. Now let's rate "feelings and emotions." How emotional are you? How deeply do you feel things?

C: Well, now, that depends. You see, if you are asking me how much feeling I *express*, I would have to rate myself very low. My wife

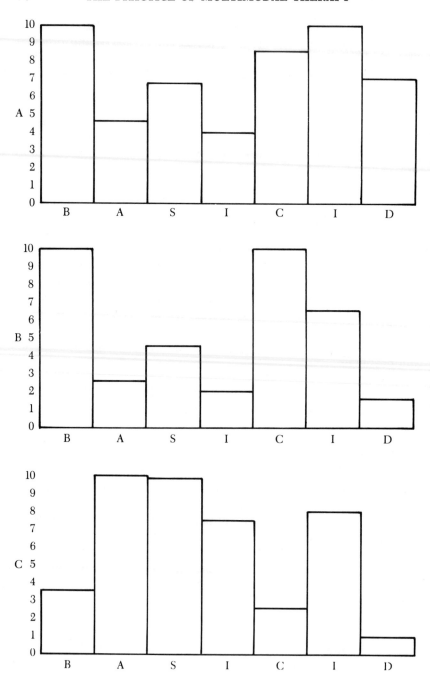

complains that I don't show my feelings, and she's right. I find it difficult to give vent to my emotions, but inside I have strong feelings.

T: Well, let's make two scales, one depicting how much emotion you express, and the other reflecting the full extent of your feelings.

C: I'd give it a 2 and a 7 or 8, respectively.

T: Fine. Now how about "sensation?" Some people attach a lot of value to sensual things from sex to food, music, art, and other sensory delights. They are very tuned into their sensations.

C: I like some music very much and I can enjoy looking at a pretty sunset. I'm not sure how to rate that.

T: Well, in general, how much do you focus on the pains and pleasures that you derive from your eyes, ears, tastebuds, genitals, and so forth?

C: Give it a 5. My brother's a hypochondriac who notices every little ache and pain. I'd give him a 10+.

T: Right, but it doesn't have to be negative. Some people are very tuned into their sensations and derive much joy from bodily functions, esthetic pleasures, and so forth.

C: Let's leave it at 5.

T: Onto "imagery" now. How much fantasy, or daydreaming do you engage in? This is separate from thinking or planning, which we will discuss next. Here I'm asking about dreams, and daydreams, about "thinking in pictures," about mulling over conversations in your head, sort of just letting your mind roam.

C: No, I'm not very imaginative or given to fantasies. I've been described as "down to earth." I like to think things through. I don't daydream as much as plan things out. I'm a definite 10 on a thinking and planning category.

T: Okay, we will rate you as a 10 on cognition, but what figure would you attach to imagery?

C: A 2 or a 3.

T: We have two more to go. Interpersonal relationships. How important are other people to you? This is your rating as a social being. We are talking about close friendships, the desire to gravitate toward people, the desire for intimacy.

C: I have little need for other people. I prefer to keep to myself. I like my own company. I can enjoy reading, or going through my stamp collection much more than partying or socializing. My wife calls me "a loner."

T: That sounds like less than a 5.

C: Give it a 3 or a 4.

T: Finally, I want you to rate yourself on a medical modality. Here I am talking about health and the avoidance of bad habits like smoking, too much alcohol, drinking a lot of coffee, overeating, and so forth. Do you exercise regularly, get enough sleep, avoid junk foods, and generally take care of your body?

C: I'm in perfect health. I don't smoke or drink and I eat sensibly. The only thing I don't get is as much exercise as I would like. So let's give it a 7 or an 8.

It takes a few moments to sketch a bar diagram that serves as an immediate and ready reminder of the client's main proclivities. As we will discuss in Chapter 9, this procedure is particularly useful in marriage therapy.

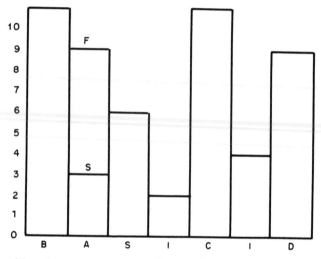

If a man (like the company president) who rates himself as high on Behavior and Cognition, low on Affective Expression, and low on Imagery and Interpersonal Intimacy, has a wife who depicts herself as being low on Behavior and Cognition, but very high on Affective Expression, with a need for close human contact and intimate friends, the degree of incompatibility might make "divorce counseling" a more realistic option than marriage therapy (Lazarus, 1981). In all therapy, the most important considerations revolve around the exact problem content within each modality and their interactive effects. Let us now discuss the way in which Modality Profiles are constructed.

Constructing the Modality Profile (or the BASIC I.D. Chart)

A distinctive feature of multimodal therapy is the BASIC I.D. Chart or Modality Profile, which serves as a compass, a blueprint, and a cognitive map. We are often asked if it is necessary to draw up a Modality Profile or if this is merely an exercise in compulsivity. Writing down the salient features of a client's BASIC I.D. facilitates the systematic processing of information within the therapeutic context. It allows a clear nexus between diagnosis and treatment by integrating the functions of assessment, the setting of objectives, and the specification of therapeutic techniques.

To illustrate the way in which a Modality Profile is constructed, let us cite the case of a 40-year-old man whose presenting complaints are "anxiety and panic attacks" that have been growing progressively more troublesome over the past four or five years. A successful executive, he is good-looking, well-dressed and outwardly relaxed, with no signs of serious aberrations. Initially, antecedent factors and maintaining consequences were difficult to identify. "I started having these attacks about five years ago for no apparent reason. There's no reason for me to feel this way; everything is going well with my life. I have a wonderful wife, two great kids, and a first-rate job." Recently, over the past year or two, he had begun to limit his range of movement. "I was on the road a lot and used to travel anywhere for sales meetings, but now I'm afraid to be more than an hour from home in case I have an attack." As a result, he was losing business, which, in turn, often led him to feel depressed. Moreover, during the past year he had seen specialists for a spate of illnesses, mainly for headaches and stomach pains. He had been in treatment with a psychiatrist for the past three years, but his condition continued to deteriorate. At the end of the initial interview he was given a Life History Questionnaire (Appendix 1) to fill out at home. He completed it diligently and returned it at the start of the second session.

During the second interview I glanced through his completed Life History Questionnaire and asked specific questions about items that were unclear or ambiguous. At the end of this session I was armed with information from our two meetings plus his Life History Questionnaire. Before our third meeting, my own homework assignment was to peruse this material and draw up an initial Modality Profile. The following problem areas emerged:

B. Phobic avoidance
    Loss of control
    Stays in bed when highly anxious (feigns illness)

A. Anxious
    Panicky
    Bouts of depression

S. Abdominal cramps
    Headaches
    Dizzyness
    Palpitations
    Tension
    Numbness
    Tremors
    Dry mouth
    Rapid heart beat

I. Images of helplessness
    Pictures himself not coping, losing control, failing
    Memories surrounding father's death and funeral
    Images of himself dying at age 44 like his father

C. Overvalues Protestant work ethic
    Preoccupied with thoughts of death and dying
    "My life is controlled by outside forces."
    "It is very important to please other people."

I. Overidentified with father
    Wife "mothers" him for somatic complaints and is critical of his "anxieties"

D. Takes tranquilizers
    Spastic colon
    Smokes about 20 cigarettes a day
    Adverse reaction to Tofranil. (Psychiatrist had prescribed it to overcome his panic attacks.)

It took about half an hour to read through the Life History Questionnaire, study the notes I had made during the first two sessions, and draw up the Modality Profile. A review of each item of the BASIC I.D. suggests a fairly typical anxiety-panic state—our client feels anxious, panicky, out of control, with a host of sensory and physiological concomitants. Glancing through the profile to answer, "Who or what seems to be maintaining his problems?" the *imagery* modality, the *cognitive* modality, and the *interpersonal* modality stand out. His overidentification with his father, a high-pressured and eminently successful executive who had died of a heart attack at age 44, when the client was 22 years old, seems most significant. He had followed his father's "script" and was now apparently wondering how faithfully he would emulate him. ("My dad was never too ill to miss a single day's work!") He was now in a quandary. Since his wife viewed anxiety as a "weakness," but was most reinforcing in the face of somatic complaints, his "choice of symptoms" may have been related to this dyadic transaction.

By studying the Modality Profile, we arrive at additional "working hypotheses," which I usually share with the client. Of course, with some clients, clinical perspicacity will lead us to avoid certain issues until a stronger therapeutic bond has been established, but, unlike "interpretations" (where the therapist supposedly knows best), these "hypotheses" will be modified, revised, or strengthened by ensuing discussions. It should be understood that multimodal therapists avoid making "interpretations." They share "impressions," "assumptions," "observations," and "hunches." Can a therapist behave toward his or her clients with humility and scientific reserve, and nonetheless appear competent, confident, and capable? We very much believe so. In fact, dogmatism is bound to offend any but the most passive-dependent individuals who may appear to thrive on absolutes and unassailable "truths."

When the preliminary Modality Profile has been completed, each item is discussed with the client in an effort to eliminate ambiguity. Every specific problem is analyzed in terms of antecedents and consequences so that one can appreciate its functional significance. Before describing this process, let us first discuss another matter— whether clients can construct their own BASIC I.D. profiles.

Clients Drawing Up Their Own Modality Profiles

Is it necessary for the therapist to draw up the initial Modality Profile? How well can most clients draw up their own Modality Profiles? Are there advantages to having the therapist and the client draw up separate Modality Profiles and then comparing them?

We have found that many adult clients are capable of drawing up their own Modality Profiles, and it often proves extremely useful for therapist and client to perform this exercise separately and then to compare notes. To draw up their profile, clients need a brief explanation of each term across the BASIC I.D. My clients are handed a typewritten instruction sheet with the following descriptions of each modality:

Behavior: This refers mainly to overt behaviors: to acts, habits, gestures, responses, and reactions that are observable and measurable. Write down what acts, habits, etc., you would want to increase and which ones you would like to decrease. What would you like to start doing? What would you like to stop doing?

Affect: This refers to emotions, moods, and strong feelings. What emotions do you experience most often? Write down your unwanted emotions (e.g., anxiety, depression, guilt, anger, etc.). Note under "Behavior" what you tend to *do* when you feel a certain way.

Sensation: Seeing, hearing, touching, tasting, and smelling are our five basic senses. Make a list of any negative sensations (tension, pain, dizzyness, sweating, blushing, butterflies in stomach, etc.) that apply to you. If any of these sensations cause you to act or feel in certain ways, make sure you note them under "Behavior" or "Affect."

Imagery: Write down any recurring dreams, and any vivid memories that may be bothersome or troublesome. Include any negative features about the way you see yourself—your "self-image." We are looking for "pictures"—past, present, or future—that may be troubling you. We are also interested in "auditory images"—tunes or sounds that you keep hearing and that constitute a problem. Include any vivid scenes, past, present, or future. If your images arouse any significant actions, feelings, or sensations, make sure these items are added to "Behavior," "Affect," and "Sensation."

Cognition: What sorts of ideas, values, opinions, and attitudes get in the way of your happiness? Make a list of negative things you often tell yourself (e.g., "I am stupid," or "I am ashamed of myself," or "I am evil or guilty.") What are some of your most irrational ideas? Be sure to note down how these thoughts and ideas influence your Behaviors, Feelings, Sensations, and Images.

Interpersonal relationships: Write down any problems with other people (friends, lovers, relatives, employers, acquaintances, etc.,) that bother you. Any concerns you have about the way other people treat you should appear here. Check through the items under Behavior, Affect, Sensation, Imagery, and Cognition, and try to determine how they influence, and are influenced by, your Interpersonal relationships.

Drugs: Make a list of all drugs, whether prescribed by a doctor or not, that you are taking. Include any health and medical concerns, and illnesses you have or have had.

The advantages of a Modality Profile over traditional psychological tests and formal psychiatric diagnosis are clearly seen in the following case.

A 33-year-old interior designer was referred for treatment. She had seen a traditional therapist for several years with some positive results, but both she and the therapist agreed that a different approach was now indicated. In the letter of referral from her previous therapist, the following descriptions were provided: "She is largely a combination of some narcissistic and histrionic personality features, with episodes of bulimia. . . . There are obvious obsessive-compulsive features and an atypical depressive disorder underlies many of her somatic symptoms." Enclosed in the same letter was a detailed analysis of two projective tests. Here is an excerpt: "Her major defense mechanisms include transformation, substitution, and exclusion. Introjection also figures prominently, and her penchant for isolation engenders feelings of loneliness and despair. When threatened by feelings, she resorts to hyperintellectualization and she thereby resists reality testing. . . . Relating back to her own father, most of her interactions with men are based on identification with the aggressor." Compare the foregoing to the Modality Profile that she had drawn up on her own after her initial interview:

B.   Procrastination
      Binging and poor eating habits
      Overtalking due to nerves
      Lack of organization in work

A.   Depression, anxiety, and panic
      Work-related guilts
      Self-conscious of everything I wear, own, do, or say
      Fears of rejection

S.   Tension—especially in face, neck and back
      Only fully relaxed during sex
      Head gets a full, confused sensation at times

I.   Picture myself as fat and dislike my body
      Body image tied into eating and exercise patterns
      Frequently picture myself as old and ugly
      Lots of adolescent romantic dreams and fantasies

C.   I can't do x,y,z—it varies
      I'll never find a solution to my emotional problems
      I must have my father's approval
      I can't afford to make mistakes

I.   Unable to have low-key friendships with men (all or nothing)
      Too hung up on pleasing and impressing people
      Lonely—need friends, but people raise my tension level

D.   Take Valium 5–10 mg daily
      Bad eating habits
      Sporadic, almost negligible exercise

Even this preliminary list provides one with immediate ideas about therapeutic intervention. Information from the Life History Questionnaire and the initial interviews and therapy sessions will readily provide additional material to round out the Modality Profile. This Modality Profile is more detailed than most as the client was "psychologically minded" and had obtained many insights from her previous therapy.

Here is a Modality Profile drawn up by a 22-year-old male nurse whose presenting problems were "shy with women," "fight a lot with my mother," "often feel frustrated and depressed."

B.   Stop smoking
      Start exercising
      Start dating
      I shy away from attractive women

A.   Depression
      Anger
      Fear

S.   Tension
      Blushing

I.   I imagine women snickering behind my back
      Many lonely images
      I often imagine my mother saying: "Who do you think you are?"

C.   I'm not good enough
      Attractive women think of me as ugly and dull
      I'm a loser

I.   My mother thinks I'm 10 years old
      Awkward and shy with attractive women
      Not enough friends

D.   Smoke 1½–3 packs of cigarettes a day

Let us now discuss how additional material is obtained, and how cross-checks and double-checks throughout the BASIC I.D. are carried out.

Rounding Out the Different Modalities

In Chapter 3 it was mentioned that all presenting complaints are subjected to a functional analysis in order to pinpoint (1) antecedent stimuli, (2) organismic (mediating) variables, (3) response (observable) variables, and (4) consequences (cf. Kanfer & Saslow, 1969). One asks: What? Where? When? Who? How? For example: "What happened immediately before the problem arose or the symptom appeared? Where were you at the time? When exactly did you first notice it? Whom were you with at the time? How did you react at first? What did you do next? Where did you go? Whom did you see? How did you cope?" Further what-where-when-who-how questions elicit precise reactions and responses that provide a clearer picture of antecedent events, ongoing behaviors, and maintaining consequences. (Occasionally, one inquires *why* certain factors arose or persist, but why-type questions often elicit "I don't know" responses or can lead to misleading rationalizations.)

Bandler and Grinder (1975) vividly underscored the advantages of asking *what-type* questions during problem assessment. If a client says, "It is necessary to behave properly in public," and the therapist asks, *"Why* is it necessary to behave properly in public?" one is likely to receive a reply that echoes social protocol and pedantries. The question, "What would happen if you failed to behave properly in public?" is more likely to elicit clinically relevant information. Other examples are:

C: I must not get involved too deeply.
T: What would happen if you got involved too deeply?
C: No one can love more than one person at a time.
T: What stops you from loving more than one person at a time?

C: No one is able to understand me.
T: What prevents them from understanding you?

As discussed in Chapter 3, excesses and deficits across the BASIC I.D. are closely examined. Whenever possible, quantitative data are obtained in terms of frequency, intensity, and duration. The main question here is, What needs to be increased and what needs to be decreased?

It is also extremely informative to obtain specific facts about *opposite* reactions. "When don't you react that way?" "Under what circumstances do you feel self-confident rather than self-conscious?" "When are you *not* shy?" These questions tend to bring out the person's *strengths and assets,* which the therapist can reinforce and the client can learn to apply to areas where he or she is less competent. (Many of my colleagues have a column for Strengths and Assets on their Modality Profiles. This is most helpful, although my personal preference is to make a separate note of my clients' positive features and to limit their Modality Profiles to problem areas that need remediation. (Hammond and Stanfield [1977] devised a Multidimensional Assessment and Planning Form that covers the BASIC I.D. and lists Assets and Strengths, Deficits and Excesses, Antecedent Events and Situations, Consequences and Purposiveness, Treatment Goals and Interventions, Priority, and Method of Evaluation. In my view, by packing so much into one instrument, the end product is an overwhelming and formidable document that provides a descriptive collage rather than a strategic guide.) When assessing strengths and assets, it is helpful to gain an overall impression of the client's ability to exert *self-control and self-management* (Thoresen & Mahoney, 1974). Rotter's (1966) concept of "expectation of inner control" versus "expectation of outer control," generally termed *perceived locus of control,* can also be clinically informative.

In essence, "self-control" is closely tied to a person's ability to withstand frustration. Many believe that one's frustration-tolerance threshold is innate. Be that as it may, I have found that clients with poor impulse control are generally most difficult to treat. There is a vast literature dealing with specific methods of teaching clients to achieve better self-control (e.g., Kanfer, 1971; Thoresen & Mahoney, 1974; Watson & Tharp, 1972). For purposes of assessment, however, it is useful to determine which specific self-control techniques are already part of the client's response repertoire. "How have you managed to control that in the past?" "What has assisted you in *not* reacting that way?"

While there are specific tests and questionnaires to measure perceived locus of control, multimodal assessment does not require quantitative indices to determine whether clients attribute what happens to them as being due to their own actions or to external events. (People who lean toward *internal control* are inclined to view positive and/or negative events as stemming from their own behaviors, as being a consequence of their own actions. Conversely, those who regard positive and/or negative events as unrelated to their own behavior think in terms of *external control* and are apt to consider their problems as being beyond personal control.) The perceived internal-external locus of control is readily detected by asking clients to describe the factors they consider responsible for their present plight. Those who see themselves as "victims of circumstance," are usually more difficult to treat than clients who recognize that they are largely responsible for orchestrating their own problems. At the same time, however, those "internal reactors" who take the blame for everything that goes wrong and indulge in self-hate and self-abnegation are as difficult to reach as their extreme counterparts who blame everything on others.

To summarize: All items on a Modality Profile are examined in terms of antecedent stimuli, organismic variables, response variables, and consequences. One tries to determine what needs to be increased and decreased, and one attempts to separate excesses from deficits. Opposite reactions are elicited, and the person's strengths and assets are noted. Let us further clarify these steps by processing the first two items on the forementioned 33-year-old interior designer's Modality Profile—Procrastination and Binging and poor eating habits.

Procrastination: What does she mean by "procrastination?" When did she first start procrastinating? What are some specific examples of her procrastination? What impact does this have on her feelings, thoughts, and images? Is her procrastination tied to other people? If so, how does it affect her relationships? What are the main consequences that she suffers as a result of her procrastination? What benefits does she derive? Under what circumstances does she not procrastinate? Does she attribute her procrastination largely to internal or external events?

Binging and poor eating habits: Let me reconstruct the client-therapist dialogue to elucidate this item.

T: Can you tell me exactly what you mean by "binging?"

C: Every now and again I go crazy and consume just about everything I can lay my hands on.

T: How often is "every now and again?" Do you mean once a month, or twice a week, or three times a day?

C: I have binges at least three times a week.

T: How long has this been ongoing?

C: A couple of years.

T: What set it off?

C: Bill and I broke up. I remember being very good about my weight when I was dating Bill. When we broke up I think I turned to food for solace, and I also didn't give a damn anymore. After all, if by being trim I couldn't keep my man, why bother?

T: What exactly do you eat when you are binging?

C: Oh, I can consume two packets of chocolate chip cookies, a pint of ice cream, a whole box of candy, plus a jar of peanut butter and whatever else is sweet or fattening. When I go to that extreme I force myself to throw up. Sometimes I just binge on a couple of chocolate bars, or a packet of cookies, and then I don't make myself throw up.

T: How is it that sometimes you are able to stop after some candy and cookies whereas at other times you keep going?

C: It depends on what I have planned. Most of my binge eating is at night. If I happen to be feeling low and have no plans and start feeling sorry for myself, I will binge until I burst and then throw up. If I am feeling good and have something to look forward to, I can either not binge or decide to binge up to a point.

T: So it's tied into your feelings and your level of activity.

C: It's also related to my tension level. Actually, having sex or an eating orgy are both powerful tension reducers. Another thing that can lead to binging is when my father criticizes me.

T: Have you ever been feeling low, with no plans in the offing, plus receiving criticism from your father, and yet managed not to binge?

C: Yes. When I have been on a sensible eating program and I have been exercising regularly, and have a good sexual and personal relationship with a man, I can stop myself from binging.

T: How do you stop yourself?

C: Well, for one thing, when I am following a sensible diet, I just don't have any junk foods in the house. And when I'm into regular exercise, I can just go out and jog.

T: Over the next couple of weeks would you keep a special chart. Will you write down: Trigger, Frequency, Intensity, Duration, Result. Under "trigger" note what caused you to binge on that occasion. Under "frequency" just make a check mark so we can count how many binges you had in two weeks. Under "intensity" give a number to indicate if it was a small binge (1 or 2) a moderate one (3) or an extreme orgy (4 or 5). Also would you time yourself so that under "duration" you note how long you binged? Finally, will you record the "result"—in other words if you felt relaxed and/or guilty or whatever else followed the binge? I'll just write down these headings on a card for you. Will you keep a close record for me?

C: Sure.

T: Now in addition to binging, you wrote down "poor eating habits." What exactly does this refer to?

C: It refers to the fact that I eat junk from time to time even when I'm not binging. For instance, I'll eat an ice cream cone and follow it with candy or some other form of sugar.

T: How often does this happen? (The pinpointing of antecedents, behaviors, and consequences is then carried out for this particular item.)

The problem-identification sequence enables the therapist to understand the functional role played by each item on the Modality Profile. While pursuing this line of inquiry, the therapist also obtains clues about the most useful therapeutic techniques to select. For example, concerning the "binge eating" we need to select several strategies that will teach the client to reduce her general tension level (relaxation training, self-hypnosis, meditation, biofeedback, regular exercise regimens, and various positive-imagery excursions are among the best-known tension-reduction methods). The client indicated that she has used a form of stimulus control (e.g., not having junk food in the house) to good effect. She might profit from instruction in a wider array of stimulus-control procedures. One obvious tactic would be for her to budget her evening hours so as to engage in activities that are incompatible with binge eating. Furthermore, the father-daughter relationship warrants further inquiry with an eventual goal of desensitizing her to paternal criticism. While a variety of therapeutic techniques will be addressed in Chapter 8, it might be mentioned at this point that the choice of a particular strategy is made in collaboration with the client. I describe various tension-reducing methods and ask the client to select those having the greatest appeal.

Clearly, the more we know about a person the easier it is to predict which techniques, methods, and strategies are most likely to have positive effects. Entire books (e.g., Hersen & Bellack, 1976; Mash & Terdal, 1976; Ciminero, Calhoun & Adams, 1977; Haynes & Wilson, 1979; Nay, 1979) are devoted to behavioral assessment, and entire journals *(Behavioral Assessment, Journal of Behavioral Assessment,* and *Behavior Analysis)* address this important subject. The average clinician is apt to feel overwhelmed by this mass of literature, especially when many multidimensional systems end up with at least twenty-four categories (Cone, 1978). It seems more advisable to conduct cost-benefit assessments and cost-effectiveness analyses of the various proposed assessment schemas. It cannot be overemphasized that the practitioner needs an assessment schema that is comprehensive and yet easy to understand, easy to remember, and easy to administer. The BASIC I.D., with its discrete and interactive components, affords both quantitative and qualitative information about human functioning, and provides a *vade mecum* for the thorough and specific remediation of psychological dysfunction.

Obtaining Second-Order BASIC I.D.'s

Some distinctive features of the multimodal orientation are:

1. The identification of human personality as comprising the BASIC I.D.

2. The recognition that every modality influences, and is influenced by, each of the other six modalities.

3. The notion that an accurate evaluation (complete diagnosis) requires a systematic assessment of each discrete modality and the interactions among and between the seven modalities of the BASIC I.D.

4. The view that comprehensive therapy calls for the specific correction of every problem across the BASIC I.D.

It should be mentioned that many people seek therapy for some clarification, emotional support, crisis-intervention, or immediate help with situational problems. In such cases, a complete multimodal assessment is neither necessary nor feasible. Nevertheless, a cursory evaluation of the client's BASIC I.D. will often prove helpful, even in acute situational reactions.

Thus far we have been addressing what might be termed the "content analysis" of the BASIC I.D. After conducting two or three interviews, including perhaps the Deserted Island Fantasy Technique (Chapter 6), and perusing the completed Life History Questionnaire (Appendix 1), one is in a position to construct a Modality Profile with or without the assistance of the client. At present, we have in mind the adult client typically seen by private practitioners in extramural settings. The multimodal approach to children, adolescents, and hospitalized patients is dealt with in Chapter 11.

Let us also for the moment put aside those suspicious, noncompliant individuals who are uncooperative or uncommunicative. Even the most cooperative and highly motivated individuals experience gaps in self-knowledge and are not in touch with several facets of their BASIC I.D.'s. Indeed, part of the purpose of therapy is to discover certain hitherto unrecognized factors that fit into one or more categories of the BASIC I.D. (one form of "insight"). Often, as therapy progresses, people make the following sorts of observations: "I never realized how much my brother influenced my career decisions, and still directs much of my life. Let's add that to the list of interpersonal factors." "I've come to see how quickly I picture myself as a loser. That should be added to the other items under imagery." "I've been having these nightmares and waking up in a cold sweat. Does that go under imagery or sensation?" Assessment and therapy are both reciprocal and continuous.

The initial BASIC I.D. or Modality Profile provides a *macroscopic* overview of "personality." When reading through the various items on a Modality Profile and trying to assess their interactive effects, one obtains a good overall grasp of intrapersonal and interpersonal problems and their maintaining variables. By conducting a *second-order BASIC I.D.*, any item on the initial Modality Profile can be magnified or examined in greater (dare we say *microscopic?*) detail. To illustrate: The item "tension headaches" appears on a client's Modality Profile under the sensory modality. Relaxation and biofeedback training have been applied with minimal success. (Our rule is first to treat problems with the most logical and obvious procedures. If these fail to remedy the situation, a reevaluation, such as a second-order BASIC I.D., may be warranted.) As the term implies, a "second-order BASIC I.D." consists simply of subjecting any item on the initial Modality Profile to a more detailed inquiry in terms of behavior, affect, sensation, imagery, cognition, interpersonal factors, and drugs or biological considerations. "When you experience these tension headaches, what do you usually do? How do they affect your behaviors? What emotions do you typically experience when suffering from one of your headaches? Can you describe the type of pain and its location? Apart from the pain in your head, what other sensations do you experience at the time? Are there any pictures or images that come to mind when you have a severe headache? What sorts of thoughts go through your mind when you are having a really severe tension headache? How do your headaches interfere in your dealings with other people? Do you take any medications other than those already listed? Are there biological disruptions such as vomiting or insomnia?

Second-Order BASIC I.D. of Tension Headaches

B.   Withdraws
      Stops working
      Lies down in darkened room
A.   Anxious
      Sad
S.   Head throbs, eyes hurt
      Pain radiates into neck
      There's "an inner trembling"
I.   Tries to picture calm scenes and relaxed muscles
      Vague flashbacks to having measles as a child
C.   "What if it's a brain tumor?"
      "I must relax"
I.   Refuses to participate in social interactions
      Inclined to be short-tempered and irritable
D.   Seldom resorts to more than Excedrin but will take codeine
      and muscle relaxants when the pain is "very severe"

Second-order BASIC I.D.'s often give clues to those factors that tend to support the specific problem under investigation. The degree of self-pampering, the catastrophic cognitions causing further tension and anxiety, and the interpersonal controls are just some of the items that lend a different complexion and meaning to the client's "tension headaches." Is there any connection between tension headaches and the childhood bout with the measles? Was there any talk of encephalitis? Did the client receive undue pampering at the time? Are tension headaches ever used in place of assertive responses (e.g., "I would gladly do xyz were it not for my headache!")? Answers to the foregoing questions can shed a completely different light on the functional significance of the "tension headaches" and explain why relaxation and biofeedback failed to effect improvement. Finally, the second-order BASIC I.D. can point to alternative modes of treatment that are more likely to succeed.

Some of my colleagues have conducted "third-order BASIC I.D. analyses." Theoretically, the process of "magnification" is almost endless. Personally, I have never found it necessary to proceed beyond second-order BASIC I.D. analyses. The additional information obtained from this procedure permits one to follow more central and productive therapeutic avenues. It should be emphasized that, while multimodal assessment has the unique features of thorough BASIC I.D. and second-order BASIC I.D. analyses, we also resort to standardized tests and other instruments when appropriate. For example, the use of projective tests may amplify the understanding of a client's imagery modality; the application of standard intelligence tests (especially with children) may augment the appreciation of specific cognitive deficits. Various measures of "organicity" or brain damage, eye-hand coordination, aptitudes, and special abilities can all be used to good effect with selected individuals. Numerous checklists may be employed for the measurement of different goals and functions—the behavior of children in classrooms (O'Leary & O'Leary, 1972); husband-wife behaviors in the home (Carter & Thomas, 1973); adult-child interactions (Wahler, 1975); heterosexual skills (Barlow, Abel, Blanchard, Bristow, & Young, 1977); and many others. When we have reason to suspect the accuracy of our assessments, we endeavor to make use of observation (in natural environments and in such structured environments as the videotaping of couples trying to solve a conflict). In the treatment of difficult sexual disorders, we have been impressed with the value of combined observation and psychophysiological assessment (Rosen & Kopel, 1978). There is no point in belaboring these additional measures in the present book.

Let us now discuss interactive aspects across the BASIC I.D. and demonstrate how to remove much guesswork from such decision-making processes as (1) the identification of primary and secondary problems, (2) the clarification of goals and objectives, and (3) the selection and implementation of appropriate techniques.

Chapter 5

Determining Basic I.D. Interactions

A client says, "I suffer from anxiety attacks."
A multimodal therapist would first explore the *sensory modality*
to establish exactly what the person means by "anxiety attacks." The
range and variety of sensory concomitants provide important clues
for the development of a differential diagnosis. First, organic factors
must be excluded. The client whose "anxiety" is manifested by palpitations, extrasystoles, chest pains, and breathlessness may simply be
a chronic hyperventilator (Lum, 1976), but this notion can only be
seriously considered after cardiopathy has been ruled out. The usual
sensory concomitants that one associates with anxiety—dryness of
mouth, tachycardia, sweating, lightheadedness, uneasiness in the
stomach, an inner sense of trembling—could be simple "nervousness," the result of a low-grade infection, a sign of hyperthyroidism,
or a manifestation of any number of other organic disorders. How
does the multimodal approach expedite the process of determining
whether the biological (D) modality is primarily or secondarily implicated?

A problem can be considered "psychological" only when clear-cut
indices across the person's behaviors, affective responses, sensations,
images, cognitions, and interpersonal dealings reveal consistent patterns in terms of antecedents and response consequences. In other
words, when one has to labor unduly to account for a client's problems across the BASIC I, organic factors (the D modality) should be
seriously investigated. A brief case excerpt should help to clarify this
important point.

A 42-year-old woman complained of "chronic nervousness."
T: Can you describe exactly how this "nervousness" feels to you?

C: I feel jumpy all over, my insides are quivering all the time, and I can hardly sit in one place. I want to keep moving all the time. (She appeared tense and hyperkinetic.)

T: How long have you felt this way?

C: I'd say it's been getting steadily worse over the past two or three weeks.

T: Has anything changed in your life in the past weeks or months?

C: Well, my youngest daughter left for college about a month ago. I wondered myself if I am an anxious mother suffering from the "empty nest."

T: What did you conclude?

C: Do you mind if I walk around? Sitting and talking makes me feel even more restless and nervous.

T: Go ahead.

C: (pacing up and down the office) What were we saying? Oh, about my daughter. No, not really. I've never been a clinging mother, but when you feel so awful you start looking for all sorts of reasons. I went back to school myself—I'm enrolled in a master's program in social work—and I thought perhaps this is the reason for my anxiety. I just don't know. Look at how restless I am. I can't sit in class.

T: Have you ever experienced similar feelings in the past?

C: Oh sure. I've had the heebie-jeebies from time to time. Who hasn't? But never anything like this. I've tried relaxing and my sister gave me a tranquilizer, but nothing helps. By the way, I discussed this with one of my cousins who is a psychiatrist, and he suggested that I was using this to express anger toward my husband.

T: You are angry with your husband?

C: It must be deeply imbedded in my unconscious mind. I do get angry with him at times, especially when he lets his male chauvinism slip out.

T: And how do you handle it?

C: I'm no shrinking violet! I tell him exactly what's what.

(After this less-than-two-minute conversation, it seemed obvious that unless the client was hiding and distorting a multitude of factors, there was little to be gained by further exploration of the BASIC I modalities. I therefore addressed the D modality.)

T: Are you on any medication?

C: I'm slightly hypertensive—it runs in the family. My mom and dad both have high blood pressure. So does my brother. My doctor put me on antihypertensive medication about six months ago.

T: Did your doctor prescribe anything different in the past month or so?

C: No. I've been taking one Diuril tablet every day.

T: Have you discussed these restless symptoms with your doctor? Does he or she know about them?

C: No, he's not very psychologically minded. I mean he's a good internist but he's from the old school, if you know what I mean. I've been reading about biofeedback. Do you use that?

T: Let me share my thinking with you. What you have told me does not hang together psychologically. Of course, anyone can make a case for your having psychological hangups by inferring all sorts of unconscious forces. I gather that you are a pretty together person with "normal" anxieties, except over the past few weeks you have been restless, uptight, and hypersensitive. Because I don't see an obvious psychological explanation, and because sometimes there are medical explanations for this type of symptom, I think you should ask your doctor to give you a complete examination. Sometimes your type of symptoms can result from electrolyte imbalance due to Diuril. You may simply be having an adverse reaction to Diuril. If we are on the right track, and your doctor agrees, I'd like to see if a course of meditation will normalize your blood pressure without any medication.

The client consulted her doctor, who sent her for blood tests. She discontinued the medication, was given potassium tablets, and her "chronic nervousness" cleared up in a matter of a few days. She received a course of Clinically Standardized Meditation (Carrington, 1977) and she has had neither undue anxiety nor hypertension over the past two years. This is a straightforward case that most therapists would probably have handled very similarly, but it shows the rapidity with which a BASIC I.D. conceptualization facilitates diagnosis and treatment. In less obvious cases, it takes longer to explore ramifications of the BASIC I modalities before concluding that organic factors are probably operative. Of course, any severe somatic complaint calls for exclusion of medical issues before the BASIC I is examined. Let us discuss in further detail how multimodal assessment searches for interactive features that constitute "emotional problems."

What is emotion?

In Chapter 1 we touched on the multimodal view that affective reactions are a function of the interaction among the other six modalities—behavior, sensation, imagery, cognition, interpersonal processes, and biological factors. In his succinct review of several pertinent experimental studies on emotion, Woolfolk (1976) stressed that, while affect can be viewed as the manifestation of interactions among the other modalities, "it must be considered a separate response system." *"Affect" or "emotion" can be worked with only indirectly.* If asked to deal specifically and directly with behavior, we can readily show someone how to act and react, what to do, what to say, and so on. The sensory modality is open to direct intervention in all areas—see this, hear that, taste this, smell this, feel that. Direct and specific interventions in the interpersonal modality are the mainstay of such methods as role-playing, imitation, and modeling. The biological modality, of course, is directly influenced by drugs, surgery, and a myriad of substances that can be introduced into one's body.

How can one deal *directly* with affects or emotions? One cannot! "I arouse emotions directly by getting people to scream while pounding foam rubber cushions," one therapist informed me. "No," I replied, "you are arousing emotions via behaviors (screaming and pounding are not emotions) and by generating sensations and images." Even if one arouses emotions by implanting electrodes into the brain, this is still using direct biological means to evoke behaviors (e.g., rage reactions). Over many years, work conducted by Richard S. Lazarus and his associates (Lazarus, R., 1968; Lazarus, R., Speisman, Mordkoff & Davison, 1962; Lazarus, R., & Opton, 1966; Lazarus, R., Kanner & Folkman, 1980) has underscored the role that cognitive factors and other phenomenological mediators play in affective arousal, especially in response to stress. In multimodal terms, emotion is generated and perpetuated by the interaction of biological processes with ongoing images and cognitions that generate sensory concomitants and a variety of behaviors. Most maintaining factors depend on interpersonal repercussions (attention or punishment from significant others).

The view that affective responses comprise behaviors, sensations, images, and cognitions that often center on interpersonal dealings—all of which rest on a biological substratum—has a specific and direct impact on therapeutic decisions. When dealing with any "emotional disturbance," the multimodal therapist will explore each of the six modalities that feeds into "affect" to determine precisely which modalities are playing a central role in any given instance. We have seen many cases of generalized anxiety treated unimodally. Clients were given tranquilizers, or advised to take up meditation or to undergo a course of progressive relaxation therapy. Again, multimodal theory regards all affective reactions as a product of stimuli and responses within, between, and among the B,S,I,C,I, and D modalities. Relaxation, meditation, and tranquilization cannot be expected to remedy behavioral deficits, negative images, faulty cognitions, or interpersonal games that serve to initiate and maintain "maladaptive emotions." Even in treating bipolar affective disorders where lithium carbonate is considered the treatment of choice, a multimodal therapist would first exclude negative cognitions, sensations, affects, images, and interpersonal reactions that might preclude taking the drug. Thereafter, the impact of ingesting lithium (a potentially lethal chemical that can have several adverse side effects) would be tracked across the BASIC I.D.

Tracking the BASIC I.D., or Talking the Client's Language

Without subscribing to rigid trait theories or typologies, it should be noted that people are inclined to value, rely on, and use some modalities more than others. For example, some are disposed to deal with problems cognitively (intellectually), whereas others lean toward affective ("gut feeling") solutions. The "emotional dreamers" (those with a penchant for affect and imagery) enjoy a different quality of interpersonal interaction from the "thinkers and doers" (i.e., people who favor cognition and behavior). These are not absolute and discrete categories that encompass all situations and remain constant over time. However, people display a discernible and fairly consistent proclivity for specifiable modalities under predictable circumstances. Consider the following examples:

C: I had a dreadful argument with my husband this morning.
T: Would you care to fill me in on the details?
C: Oh boy! I'm so hopping mad I can feel it right here in my gut. I'm still shaking all over. Oh, does he get my goat. My head is throbbing and my whole body feels as if it is going to explode.

Compare the foregoing response to the following one:

C: I can still picture his face, red as a beet. His eyes look as if they are going to pop right out of his head. He's got that bottom lip of his curled down like a baby who is about to cry.

Now let's consider yet another response:

C: The trouble with Pete is that he argues from false assumptions. Apart from obvious syllogisms that just infuriate me, most of his conclusions are vitiated by the elementary logical fault of "petitio principii." In other words, one can never reach a satisfactory conclusion because of this fatal defect in his logical reasoning—his conclusion is implicit in his original assumptions.

The first example represents a *sensory* reactor, the second typifies an *imagery* reactor, and the third example is that of a *cognitive* reactor. One of the main mistakes my trainees tend to make is to introduce a modality different from the one the client is presenting. Thus, the therapist who responds to any of these three outputs with, say, "Let's try some role-playing to see if we can get at the problem" (a behavioral intervention) is likely to meet with resistance. In my experience, it is important to tune in to the client's presenting modality. In response to the "sensory reactor," the therapist might say, "Tell me more about the way your body feels right now." The "imagery reactor" might be asked to, "Picture yourself using a zoom lens to focus in on his eyes and see what messages you can read in them." The "cognitive reactor" could be asked to, "Outline some of the false assumptions and tautological inferences under which Pete labored." If one enters the client's domain, he or she is likely to feel heard, understood, and acknowledged. Thereafter, the therapist can more readily switch to a different modality: "Let's try some role-playing." We may refer to this process as *bridging*.

By referring to "a sensory reactor," "an imagery reactor," or "a cognitive reactor," I do not mean to imply that a person will always respond in a given modality. Clinically, however, we have noted a tendency for people to favor one or two modalities. Bandler and Grinder (1976) point out that there is a crucial difference between the comments, "I *see* what you're saying" and "I *hear* what you're saying." The former tends to reflect a person who responds to and organizes his/her world largely through images—in this instance the most highly valued representational system is visual. Visualizers tend to "make pictures" out of what they hear. In terms of split-brain research (Sperry, Gazzaniga, & Bogen, 1969; Galin, 1974; Kimura,

1973) people who favor the imagery modality are probably right-hemispheric dominant, whereas the cognitive reactors are perhaps left-hemispheric dominant.

Bandler and Grinder (1976) deal only with the sensory modality when emphasizing the importance of tuning into the client's representational system. They refer only to kinesthetic, visual, and auditory reactors. It is important to go beyond proprioceptive, visual, and auditory reactions, and also to take note of gustatory and olfactory responses. Seligman (1972) documented the powerful conditioning effects of stimuli involving taste and smell. Watzlawick (1978) stressed that "olfactory perceptions are particularly conducive to the mental reconstruction and reexperiencing of past events in their totality." Our language relies on metaphors involving gustatory and olfactory reactions no less than kinesthetic, visual, and auditory effects. "That leaves a bad taste in my mouth," and "That smells fishy to me," are two common examples. I have treated individuals whose sexual disinclinations emanated from malodorous encounters and for whom sexual enjoyment required adherence to thorough physical hygiene on the part of their mates. In my experience, there is little point in trying to attenuate a person's exquisite olfactory hypersensitivity. When a woman mentioned to me that her husband becomes "sulky and truculent" when he dislikes her brand of perfume, and added, "I'll be damned if I let him boss me around like that! I'll wear whatever perfume I please!" I explained that she might be making a serious mistake if her husband was a "primary olfactory reactor."

It cannot be overemphasized that a multimodal therapist continually monitors the entire BASIC I.D. There is continual scanning of each modality and its interaction with every other. For example, having established that a client is very "visual" and creates vivid images that precede and accompany virtually every encounter, we would next ask what impact this has on each specific modality. One would also attempt to ferret out the exact sequence in which the modalities are brought into play. Let us discuss this in greater detail.

The Modality Firing Order

Two clients suffer from "anxiety and panic attacks." They are each asked to take special note of the stimuli and events that seem to precede and accompany these attacks. Their own subjective observations plus the therapist's detailed inquiries into the BASIC I.D. reveal the following response patterns:

Case 1: "I can be going along just fine when suddenly I become aware that I am feeling quite together. I then tend to check this out, just to be doubly sure that all's well. That's where the trouble starts. I invariably notice that something is slightly out of kilter—it could be some queasiness in the pit of my stomach, or perhaps a little light headedness. The next thing I know, my heart's beating like a tom-tom."

Case 2: "I get these stupid thoughts and ideas. They just pop into my head. For example, in the supermarket last week, I started to think *what if I passed out?* I then imagined the scene with me lying on the floor, and I started rushing down the aisles to finish my shopping as fast as I could. The next thing I was feeling dizzy and faint and I left my shopping cart in the store and went outside."

In the first case, we see how "anxiety and panic" began with the *sensory* modality.

The second case started in the *cognitive* modality, immediately followed by *imagery.* Cognition and imagery were followed by *behavior* ("I started rushing down the aisles"), which led to *sensory* reactions ("I was feeling dizzy and faint") that culminated in *avoidance behavior* ("I left . . . the store and went outside"). Thus, we have a C-I-S-B modality sequence or "firing order" for Case 2 (Cognition-Imagery-Sensation-Behavior).

If both cases were treated by relaxation training, the second one would be far less likely to derive benefit than Case 1. Our clinical findings point to the need for techniques to be fitted to the initiating stimuli: to treat sensory reactions with sensory techniques, cognitive reactions with cognitive techniques, and so on. Case 2 would probably respond favorably to thought-stopping, coping or positive imagery, and rational disputation. Of course, a multimodal therapist would not stop there, but the point under consideration is how to select an initial technique.

In Case 1, "anxiety and panic" seem to commence with the sensory modality. I will now present a typical dialogue to demonstrate how a more complete range of modality firing orders is uncovered.

T: So you first tune into your sensory responses and you seem to manufacture some unpleasant sensation that starts to escalate.
C: Yes, that's about right.
T: Now what happens right after that?
C: I get anxious and panicky.

T: I would guess that there are a few steps between "unpleasant sensations" and a full-blown panic attack. Let us try to spot the missing links.

C: When I feel my heart pounding I get very anxious.

T: If you ran up some stairs and your heart was pounding would this invariably trigger an anxiety reaction?

C: No. Not if I knew why my heart was beating fast. After running up stairs you expect your heart to go faster.

T: What happens when your heart beats fast when you do not expect this to occur?

C: I think something must be wrong.

T: For instance?

C: Well, perhaps something serious will happen like a heart attack.

T: Ah, so it seems that when you notice your heartbeat accelerating you start thinking that something must be wrong, perhaps seriously wrong. Can you do something right now? Imagine that your heart is racing for no reason and tell me what you start thinking.

C: Oh God! What's happening? Am I going to die? I know it's silly. The doctors have told me there's nothing wrong with my heart, but I still get scared when it starts pounding away.

T: And you think you might be dying? What else happens when you think you might be dying? Do you *do* anything differently, or do you get any *pictures,* or are you aware of other *feelings?*

C: I picture myself getting weaker and weaker, or sometimes I imagine that I will become crazy and run wild.

T: What happens when you picture yourself running wild?

C: My heart is racing, my head is swimming, and I am charging around screaming and knocking into things.

T: So it seems when you get anxious, the first thing that sets it off is some minor sensation, something unpleasant in your gut or in your head, and soon your heart starts racing. When that happens, you start *thinking* irrational things such as something must be terribly wrong and you may die as a result. These thoughts, in turn, evoke *images* in which you may see yourself growing weak or running wild.

C: And by the time I work myself into this state, I am really upset and the only thing I can do is go to bed and stay there.

T: And who takes care of the store?

C: My wife is willing to pitch in at those times.

The foregoing is not an actual dialogue taken from a given case, but it is a typical construction of the "tracking sequence." Whereas

Case 2 was shown to have a C-I-S-B sequence (Cognition-Imagery-Sensation-Behavior), Case 1 seems to follow a different order: S-C-I-B (sensations lead to cognitions followed by images that eventuate in withdrawal). Here, the first line of therapy would aim to control the negative sensations and modify the associated cognitions. Thus, the client might be given the following advice: "When you start noticing unpleasant sensations, start relaxing your body and concentrate on the abdominal breathing that I showed you. At the same time, keep telling yourself that it is not serious or potentially fatal." Let me repeat that we start with the most obvious remedies while further exploring interactive effects across the other modalities. The statement, "My wife is willing to pitch in at those times," for example, might be a central clue to much of the problem. A basic dictum is, "Don't complicate the problem." If the first and most obvious methods fail to work, a more careful scrutiny across the BASIC I.D. is called for, and second-order Modality Profiles may need to be constructed.

The specific use of second-order BASIC I.D. analyses and the tracking of modality firing sequences, are unique to the multimodal orientation. We have found these procedures of inestimable value. They shed light on some of the subtle nuances of emotional disturbance that otherwise seem inaccessible to diagnosis or problem-identification. The following transaction illustrates the clinical significance of these procedures.

After attending a seminar on multimodal therapy, a well-known psychologist in the audience facetiously said, "I didn't realize that I am a multimodal therapist. All this time I thought that I was just a good eclectic psychotherapist." I asked my colleague if he would allow me to observe him in action, and he kindly invited me to attend one of his group therapy sessions. In the group, I watched him doing a splendid job in the behavioral and interpersonal modalities. He was also highly skilled at spotting cognitive errors and in achieving affective expression. One of the group members was a man in his mid-forties who was silent through the first half of the session. When asked why he was not participating, he replied that he felt too depressed to do any talking. Addressing the entire group, the therapist said, "I think that Murray is one of those classic cases of anger turned inwards." Murray shook his head and muttered, "I'm not angry," whereupon my colleague asked him to stand up and simply to say, "I am angry!" ten times, but to utter these words more loudly each time. After some coaxing and cajoling Murray obliged, but each time he said, "I am angry!" the therapist and all the group members chanted, "Louder! Louder! We can't hear you!" and provoked him in other ways. (The group members had obviously been through at least one of these exercises before.) By the time Murray had reached his seventh or eighth count of proclaiming, "I am angry!" he was visibly upset and was indeed becoming irate. By the time he reached repetition number ten, he was shaking with rage and he screamed "I am angry!" with convincing resonance. Thereafter, goaded by the therapist's skillful probing, Murray expressed a great deal of anger about his employer and the fact that his father-in-law interfered with his married life.

When the group ended, I expressed admiration for the clinical skills that had been ably demonstrated throughout the 90-minute meeting, but stated emphatically to the therapist, "Let me tell you how a multimodal therapist might have handled certain matters." First, I pointed out that he glossed over (if not entirely overlooked) important features in two clients when imagery and sensory interventions were called for. Second, a multimodal therapist would not assume that the elicitation of anger was necessarily therapeutic unless it pointed to specific steps that could be taken to alleviate it. (There is no evidence that "catharsis" per se produces long-term therapeutic benefits.) Thus, at the very least, a multimodal therapist would explore the advantages of instituting social skills training vis-à-vis Murray and his employer and his father-in-law. Most important, however, to a multimodal therapist, the term "anger" is a description, not an explanation. A second-order BASIC I.D. would identify the ingredients of Murray's "anger" and point to specific ways of overcoming it. Multimodal therapy is not the same as eclectic psychotherapy.

Observation of colleagues and associates who have embraced multimodal thought and practice for several years reveals certain shared habits. They automatically think in BASIC I.D. terms and almost reflexively track events across each modality. They also adopt pluralistic thinking and rarely ask singular questions like, "What is the problem?" "What is the cause?" "What is the remedy?" Instead, problems, causes, and remedies are addressed in recognition of the fact that all human processes are multileveled and multilayered. Unimodal practitioners will in all likelihood continue to adhere to a particular method, or school, or theory with fervor. This is unfortunate for numerous reasons, but the consumer is the one who suffers by being fitted to a treatment that he or she does not require (Bergin

& Lambert, 1978; Strupp, Hadley & Gomes-Schwartz, 1977). Singularity of thought is one of the greatest impediments to learning and progress.

This chapter has stressed the importance of getting a "feel" for the client in order to "know" the other person, to "talk his or her language," and to "tune in" to the individual's style and preferences. The next chapter describes a technique that often proves most helpful in facilitating these objectives. At this point, it may be illuminating to list some of the main similarities and differences between "behavior therapy" and "multimodal therapy."

Similarities and Differences Between Behavior Therapy and Multimodal Therapy

---

Similarities

1. Target behaviors are usually dealt with *directly* (as distinct from methods that deflect attention away from overt problems onto intrapsychic conflicts).

2. Treatment procedures are individually tailored to different problems in different people.

3. The therapist is primarily responsible for the intervention plan, and the therapist is largely accountable for progress or lack of progress.

4. Most problems are presumed to arise from deficient or faulty social learning processes.

5. One obtains informed consent from the client concerning the use of specific techniques.

6. Antecedent factors as well as the immediate and long-term consequences of behavior are systematically examined.

7. The therapist-client relationship is more that of a trainer and trainee than that of a doctor treating a sick patient.

8. Transfer of learning (generalization) from therapy to the client's everyday environment is not considered automatic but is deliberately fostered by means of homework and other in vivo assignments.

9. Labels, fixed diagnostic categories, traits, and global descriptions are avoided in favor of behavioral and operational definitions.

10. Measurements and evaluations are carried out during the entire course of therapy (e.g., self-reports are studied as well as data from significant others, or readings from physiological instruments and apparatus).

Differences

1. In multimodal therapy, personality is specifically and systematically divided into seven discrete but interactive components (modalities) represented by BASIC I.D.

2. Multimodal therapists deliberately construct Modality Profiles (BASIC I.D. Charts) as a "blue-print" for therapy.

3. Second-order BASIC I.D. Profiles are employed to overcome treatment impasses and to elucidate significant areas of "personality" and "psychopathology."

4. The *goodness of fit* in terms of the client's expectancies, therapist-client compatibility, matching, and the selection of techniques is examined in much greater detail by multimodal therapists.

5. The multimodal therapist determines interactive effects across the BASIC I.D. in order to establish the Sequential Firing Order of specific modalities. (This procedure is called *tracking.*)

6. Multimodal therapists tune into the client's preferred modalities to enhance communication before delving into other areas that seem clinically more productive. (This procedure is called *bridging.*)

7. The amount of depth and detail that is entailed in examining sensory, imagery, cognitive, and interpersonal factors and their interactive effects, goes beyond the confines of the usual stimulus and functional analyses conducted by behavior therapists. (Thoresen [1980] has edited a stimulating and provocative book that tries to answer the question, "What does it mean to be a behavior therapist?")

Chapter 6

The Deserted Island Fantasy Technique

It has often been pointed out that the best way to get to know people is to live with them for a while. The idea of using a *structured, interactive, projective technique* to approximate this end first occurred to me many years ago when working with a particularly frustrating client who was full of contradictions. I said something like, "For me to understand you, I'd need to observe you for 24 hours a day." Her retort was, "Well, let's go and spend a few months on a desert island." Ignoring what I regarded as seductive undertones, I inquired, "What would I learn about you on the island?" She launched into a monologue that proved highly informative. As I listened to her fantasies about our island sojourn, I was able to infer a great deal about many of her qualities, the impact of her moods, her basic hopes, fears, and frustrations. Notwithstanding the subjective nature of this interaction, I felt that I had indeed emerged with considerable knowledge about her significant thoughts, feelings, and actions.

Subsequently, I started using this fantasy excursion with many people and found that it often yielded important clinical information. Initially (Lazarus, 1971) I would ask clients whether they would prefer my company to six months of solitude on the island. Additional experience with the Deserted Island Fantasy Technique led me to make two modifications. First, with many people, the term "desert" tended to conjure up images of an arid and barren wilderness with forbidding prospects, whereas a *deserted* island could be lush and green and eminently habitable. Since the main purpose of the test is to assess the client's capacity for establishing intimate relationships rather than to determine how he or she might deal with the cultivation of dry tracts and parched sands, the island is presented as uninhabited (deserted) but by no means uninhabitable. Because of side-tracking that occurred at times as a result of sexual fantasies about the therapist, I now routinely recommend the presence of another person, not the therapist, on the island. When the therapist is not on the island, seductive, competitive, and threatening aspects are mini-mized; moreover, it permits the therapist to ask more critical questions about the interactions when he or she is not part of the process. Let us discuss the procedure.

Administering the Deserted Island Fantasy Technique

A therapist endeavors to get a "feel" for the client, to "be on the same wave length," to "know" the other person in order to identify with, understand, and help him or her. The Deserted Island Fantasy Technique facilitates this level of understanding. It is worth administering when the therapist feels puzzled by the client as a person, where there are lacunae concerning interpersonal attitudes and conduct. Generally, I apply this procedure during the initial interview or at the second meeting, but the test can be used at any stage of therapy. While there is no need for a set pattern, my instructions usually proceed more or less as follows:

I'd like to ask your indulgence and cooperation while we engage in a fantasy experiment. Just bear with me for about five or ten minutes and really try to enter into the spirit of the fantasy. Please try to use your imagination to its fullest extent; try to put yourself right into the situation I'm about to describe. I'll be asking you some impossible questions to which you may be inclined to say, "How the heck should I know?" but don't answer in that manner. Try to imagine how you think you might react if you really were in the situation.

Okay, here we are sitting and talking. Suddenly the door opens and in walks a magician. Now, for the purposes of this narrative anything is possible. The magician addresses you and says, "When I wave my magic wand you will instantly appear on the proverbial deserted island and you will remain there for six months." Now there's no point in begging or pleading with the magician not to do that, because you have no choice in the matter. He will wave his magic wand and you will be whisked off to the island. Can you picture it so far?

Before waving his magic wand, he explains a few things to you. He informs you that while you are on the island, the rest of the world will remain in suspended animation—time will stand still. In other words, you will live through six months, day after day, week after week, but when you reappear back in this office, it will still be (today's date). The other thing he tells you is that you do not have to worry about your survival. It's a magic island where there will be plenty of food and provisions.

Now, before waving his wand, the magician gives you a choice. In effect, he allows you to choose company or solitude. Would you prefer spending six months alone, or would you rather find a pleasant person of the opposite sex (or, when dealing with homosexuals, a person of the same sex) waiting for you on the island? Some people welcome the opportunity to spend six months in their own company with their own thoughts in peace and solitude. Others definitely prefer company, even though they have never met their island companion. Now please tell the magician whether you would choose company or solitude. (Wait for client to make the choice. In my experience, about 85% choose company over solitude. Assuming the choice was "company," let us carry on with the fantasy.)

All right. The magician waves his wand, time stands still for the rest of humanity, and you appear on the island. You look around. It's a narrow strip of land, green and cultivated, with a little sandy beach. There's a palm tree for shade, an adequate shelter, lots of provisions. But there are no books, no television, no distractions. You and your companion are entirely dependent on one another for entertainment and stimulation. Do you have the image in mind? Your companion welcomes you to the island. He/she seems very pleasant, attractive, warm, and friendly. Picture yourself in that situation. Now, my first question is, How will you occupy your time? Please just run with the fantasy and tell me what happens. Let the story unfold. What happens?

Outcomes and Inferences

The variety of responses one obtains from different people is both fascinating and revealing. Consider the inferences that may be drawn from the following reactions.

"It sounds marvelous. Ah, to get away from the drudgery of reality!"

"Well, the first thing I'd want to do is stake out my own territory."

"Oh, boy! I'd have a captive audience of one to whom I can tell all my troubles."

"Look, I'm not paying you good money to play games."

"The first order of business would be to make it perfectly clear that I have no intentions of cheating on my wife."

"I really can't do this. I have a very poor imagination."

"Well, I'd introduce myself to my companion. We'd have a lot of talking to do because I'm sure we would each want to find out about the other person."

"Knowing me, I'd say that my moodiness would ruin everything. Here is a perfect chance to have a great time, but I'd blow it!"

"I'm trapped there for six months? No books and no TV? I'd probably die from boredom."

"You said there's lots of food? Good, I'd have an orgy—food and sex, not necessarily in that order."

"Everything would depend on the kind of person the so-called companion turns out to be."

"What do you want from me? Can't you ask me straight questions instead of beating around the bush?"

"You told me not to say 'How the hell should I know?' but since I've never been anywhere near such a set-up, how can I know how I would react?"

"You're trying to trick me. You're a sly one, you are."

"First off, we'd have to create work and delegate chores."

"I'd spend most of my time trying to get off the island and back to civilization. Since two heads are better than one, I would hope that my friend would join me in this endeavor."

"God! I'd feel absolutely raw and unprotected in that situation."

"If she's attractive, I'd fall in love with her, and she'd probably feel turned off to me."

"Everything will depend on what happens *after* the six months are up. I mean, am I never to see this person again, or will he be in a position to marry me afterwards if he so desires?"

"Everything would be fine because I'd be on my best behavior."

The variety of responses is almost unlimited. They generate immediate impressions and lead to clinical hunches that can readily be pursued. One deals with the client's questions, misgivings, or objections by urging him or her to try to enter into the spirit of the fantasy, and by coaxing the client to reveal whatever he or she considers most likely to happen over the course of the six months. To assist reluctant clients, one may use prompts such as: "What would you talk about?" "What might go wrong?" "How much would you disclose?" "What would your companion need to be like to make certain that you have an enjoyable time?" "Would you prefer a sexual or a platonic friendship with your companion?"

The presence or absence of the ordinary give-and-take of personal interaction emerges quite clearly from this fantasy test. Narcissistic individuals are apt to construe the situation as one in which all their needs will be satisfied. The companion exists solely to satisfy their whims. Others, while not so extreme, nonetheless betray an inability to consider other peoples' needs. At the opposite pole, the "people-pleasers" denigrate themselves and end up acting as the companion's slave. It becomes evident that some people lack social graces and have other interpersonal deficits. A number of clients indicate that coercion is their major interpersonal contribution—they would assume dictatorial leadership and control their companion. Life with some would be reminiscent of the parallel-play of young children. They would exist side-by-side with the companion without sharing any basic thoughts or feelings.

Some clients are unable to picture themselves suspending their hostility, aggression, or depression, and talk of committing murder or suicide on the island. These reactions should alert the therapist to the threatening potential of close relationships per se, in addition to other aspects of "psychopathology." One easily detects those instances where people are especially afraid of close contact with the opposite sex. Feelings of inferiority are also readily brought to light. Evidence of autistic or overinclusive thinking may emerge.

Direct questions concerning the evolution of friendship on the island can provide important clues about the way in which the therapeutic relationship should be structured. The presence of rebellious, anti-authoritarian themes may steer the therapist away from an overt pedagogical role. One is on the alert for such statements as, "I would never open myself up to someone who did not share some of his own shortcomings" or, "Ideally, my companion would let me do most of the talking." The foregoing may indicate a desire for therapist self-disclosures in the former instance and for a willingness to be a patient listener in the latter. Of course, it would be naive to take these statements at face value, and each of them may warrant further exploration in its own right. However, they can provide the therapist with important information concerning the necessary do's and don'ts for establishing and maintaining rapport.

Therapeutic Implications

This simple fantasy procedure can be used for more than assessment; it also has specific therapeutic applications. When self-defeating patterns of thought and action are revealed in the fantasy, for example, the therapist can present the client with better coping strategies. Here is an excerpt:

C: Well, he'll probably think I'm bitchy and moody, and he'll end up wishing that somebody else would have come to the island.

T: Why is that?

C: Because I can be really nasty some of the time. . . .

T: Some of the time. How much is "some of the time?" I mean are you negative and nasty 90% of the time? Is that what you mean by "some of the time?"

C: No. Um, I'd say about less than half. Oh, let's put it at 40%.

T: You'd be unpleasant about 40% of the time?

C: That's about right, although when I'm premenstrual it will be more like 90% or even 100%.

T: So how will you be the other 60% of the time?

C: Easy to live with; easy to get along with. . . .

T: It sounds like a pretty good deal to me. Nobody's perfect. Who is a sheer delight 100% of the time? A 60-40 ratio doesn't sound too bad. But it depends how you handle the negative 40. For example, there's a difference between someone who attacks, gripes, whines, and behaves like a pain in the neck when they are feeling negative, as compared with someone who handles it maturely by saying something like, "Look, I'm feeling very crabby right now. I want to be off by myself, just sitting with my feet at the edge of the water, alone."

C: I'd never say that.

T: Why not?

C: It sounds so self-indulgent. Why make speeches when you can just as well go off and be by yourself? It's so pompous.

T: There's no problem if you can go off by yourself and be left to your own devices. But what if your companion comes over and joins you and tries to have a conversation?

C: I'd just turn him off!

T: Most people would prefer to have been clued-in beforehand. I, for one, would most certainly appreciate it if someone took me into her confidence, told me where she was at, instead of letting me walk into an unpleasant response.

C: Hmmm. (pause)

T: What's going on?

C: I'm just thinking over what you said. You know . . . well . . . it certainly gives one food for thought. I see what you're getting at.

T: Good. Now let's get back to the island and see what else transpires.

The main purpose of the Deserted Island Fantasy is to examine the client's capacity for developing and maintaining close, genuine relationships. Can the person picture himself cultivating a friendship. How would she go about it? Is he or she likely to relate honestly and openly? How much manipulation, deception, and one-upmanship will be evident? Whenever asocial, antisocial, and other maladaptive patterns emerge, the therapist can insert a variety of corrective experiences. The transcript of an initial interview that used the Deserted Island Fantasy test for assessment and therapy will demonstrate how this might be done. But first, there are a few other considerations that need clarification.

Dealing with the Choice of Solitude

A relative minority choose to go alone to the island for six months. It is necessary in such instances to ascertain the reasons. Generally, the choice of solitude is a poor prognostic sign. It implies that other people, especially strangers, are viewed as potentially obstructive rather than as facilitative. It suggests detachment and a penchant for aloneness that amounts to withdrawal. There may indeed be peace and comfort in solitude. It has been argued that the eloquence of silence provides answers to one's problems. But the "loner" who elects six months of solitude would have to reside in the cave of his mind without the benefit of a sounding board. (This, however, may be the norm in Far Eastern cultures.) The inability or unwillingness to establish rapport with an island companion often portends a similar difficulty in relating to a therapist. The decision to go to the island alone also tends to reflect an unwillingness to take emotional risks. Schizophrenic patients often elect to go alone.

After finding out why the person elected to go alone (often very revealing), one may ask how the person will occupy him- or herself during the six-month period. "What will you do with the time?" "What sorts of thoughts will you think?" "What kinds of decisions or conclusions may you reach?" When these and any other relevant issues have been covered, the therapist alters the conditions of the island sojourn by restructuring it so that the person is no longer offered a choice in the matter.

Now let's change the condition. This time you have no choice. The magician says, "There will be a young (man or woman, as the case may be) on the island whether you like it or not." There is no point in pleading with the magician not to do so. He waves his magic wand and there you are on the island with a companion. Now look around. You are both on a narrow strip of land, green and cultivated, with a little sandy beach. There's a palm tree for shade, an adequate shelter, lots of provisions. But there are no books, no television, no distractions. You and your companion are entirely dependent on each other for company and stimulation. Your companion welcomes you to the island and says: "The next six months can be a complete horror, or they can be most enjoyable. This will depend on the kind of people we are. It's up to us. We can make each other thoroughly miserable or we can have a ball." Now please tell me what problems you see; what's going to happen; what's going to develop?"

Other Variations on the Theme

When applying the Deserted Island Fantasy Technique, therapists may have reasons to alter the foregoing structure. In some instances, (e.g., when the client is gay, or when one suspects that the client may have homosexual conflicts) the island companion may be presented as someone of the same sex as the client. Another variation is to structure the island situation around a group of people (e.g., when one has reason to evaluate the client's potential for broader social interaction rather than a one-on-one relationship). When family dynamics are a central issue, it is often illuminating to structure the island scene around the entire family constellation. When the client and his or her family are removed from the exigencies of day-to-day transactions in the real world and placed in the cloistered island environment, it is often revealing to see what transpires.

Some of my associates have tended to vary the time factor. While I have always used the arbitrary but convenient six-month period, my associates tell me that they have tried using a range from one week to as much as one year.

It is also quite informative to conduct a postisland inquiry. Assuming the person has described the evolution of a close bond, a veritable A-to-Z friendship with the island companion replete with loving and gratifying sexual intimacy, the following question may be presented:

Let's assume that at the end of the island sojourn, you return home and soon discover that your island companion lives fairly close to you. How would you deal with this?

Here are some typical responses:

"That would be dreadful! It would create terrible conflicts. I don't know what I'd do."

"I'd just carry on having a delicious affair."

"If I knew that to begin with, I'd have made sure that we did not get too close on the island."

"Well, a lot would depend on whether he was married and how he felt about his marriage."

"What happened happened, and I would keep it in the past as a beautiful experience, but I would not cheat on my wife."

"There's no question that I would want to get a divorce so that I could marry my island companion."

"I'd want to try and carry on a friendship but without sexual involvement."

A verbatim transcript will now be presented in the hope that it will clarify the interactive quality of the Deserted Island Fantasy Technique. I have selected a "difficult case"—it is the initial interview with Ms. A, a 29-year-old woman who chose solitude rather than companionship.

How to Derive the Most Benefit from Reading Ms. A's Transcript

When supervising my students and trainees, I point out the value of *response-couplets*. The client says or does something (i.e., emits a response); now the therapist *must* react to the client's response. Let us assume that the client says, "Doctor, I feel particularly annoyed with you!" The therapist may burst into tears; the therapist may laugh, or simply remain silent, or get up and walk out of the room. The therapist may respond by saying, "You are angry with me," or "Please tell me more," or "I'll bet you're not half as annoyed with me as I am with you." The range of possible responses is almost unlimited. The question is whether the therapist's response may be regarded as *positive, neutral,* or *negative.*

A positive therapeutic response facilitates the realization of therapeutic goals; a negative response diminishes the treatment objectives. By thinking in terms of response couplets and rating each therapist-reaction as positive, neutral, or negative, the trainee becomes better attuned to the intent and impact of his or her interventions. Typically, my students present tape-recorded sessions to a group of four or five other therapists-in-training while I am present as discussion leader. We listen to the tape and often switch it off at what seems to be a critical point. Thus, the client may ask a pertinent question, make a specific observation, express a basic feeling, and so forth. We stop the tape and then discuss a variety of responses that could be considered positive, neutral, or negative. Thereafter, we continue listening to the tape and pay special attention to the trainee's actual response.

Apart from providing a specific method for elaborating the interpersonal side of a client's life, the interview with Ms. A will enable the reader to "observe" me at work. The transcript can provide a medium for provocative clinical class discussions if the specific response couplets are critically examined. The reader is bound to find several "negative responses." There is no such thing as a perfect session. I would hope that most would agree that there are a fair number of positive and neutral responses.

INITIAL INTERVIEW WITH MS. A

Age: 29
Marital Status: Single
Occupation: Interior designer, advertising executive, but currently unemployed.
The therapist made a note of the client's address and telephone number. He then asked for her permission to record the interview.

T: Okay. You said you had been referred by Dr. B.

C: Well, every time I see him he wants to use tapes or techniques and they just don't work. We've tried this desensitization . . . where you use office work . . . and we just go through it time and time again and it just hasn't worked for me . . . he admits this. He still feels that behavioral therapy is the right direction. He says he knows the problem, but he just doesn't know how to get to it. He's lost.

T: Now, what would you say is the central problem?

C: Well I think Dr. B. put it very well. He said that I hadn't been nice to *me*. I don't respect *my* feelings. I think of other people. I think that's the main problem. This is really a big problem. . . . It hurts me very much . . . I just could sit here and cry about it because I just can't believe that I can't accept the fact that I haven't considered myself first, so to speak, and it puts me into shock almost.

T: Now, you weren't always that way I gather. Is this of relatively recent origin?

C: No, I think I've always been that way.

T: Always been that way, sort of programmed to always put other people's needs before your own, to put yourself down. Where did you learn that?

C: I guess it's from my parents, my background. I can't say that one person taught me that because as far as I've ever known this is the way I've reacted and been, so I guess it goes as far back as my childhood.

T: So it seems you were raised with the belief that the way for you to be is inconsiderate of your own needs because you're not *entitled* to have your needs satisfied. You must consider other people's needs. You must be passive, submissive, put yourself down, build up other people, and then you will find the way to love, happiness, and fulfillment. You've been following that program more or less, but it hasn't worked. Is that correct?

C: Right, especially in the male/female relationship. . . . When I try to come into contact with someone and try to have a relationship it doesn't work. I set myself up for abuse . . . I don't respect myself so how can they respect me?

T: And how does this lack of self-respect come through?

C: Well, it doesn't happen with my girlfriends; it's not so much in a business situation. It's mainly with the male/female relationship thing. I would say that is primarily the problem. It's an assertiveness problem. And maybe like a new acquaintance or something, like meeting you for the first time, there's a certain amount of nervousness. It depends upon the person, really. I guess inwardly something would bother me, but I don't really say anything, but inside it's really building up to something.

T: Let us assume that I had some kind of special psychic x-ray machine and I held up this particular psychic x-ray machine so that I would get a scan of your make-up. "I see from this x-ray machine that you really are a horrible, worthless, useless, depraved human being; you are not like other people; you do not deserve happiness and fulfillment. You are made of bad stuff, poor material, poor protoplasm. You are just an inferior creature." How would you react?

C: (laughs) Well, that's not really it. I don't feel that I'm a bad person. In fact I feel that I'm a good person—too good. In other words, I'm to the point where there's no one out there that could give me what I really want to be happy—as far as marriage goes.

T: There's no one out there to give you what you want to be happy. . . .

C: As much as I could give, in other words. . . .

T: You would always be giving much more than the other person?

C: Right. From my experiences, I don't feel as though anyone is willing to do that.

T: Now what is the "that"? It sounds like, "Gee, she wants so much."

C: Nothing comes between me and a person I like; they're on my mind all the time. Like if I'm in a store and I remember that so-and-so said they needed this I'll stop and go out of my way and get it, or if someone mentions something I'll surprise them with it. I always want to do things for someone that I'm fond of, and I don't seem to get that in return. No one thinks anything of it. They say "thank you," but they don't really get excited or show any emotion, whereas I'm different. Maybe I expect too much in return. I don't really know, it's hard to explain, I sort of get lost there.

T: Okay, perhaps you have certain unrealistic expectations. You might be an unusually giving person. You might discover that you are a bit extreme. Even though other people might be givers, compared to you they seem like takers, so you end up feeling short-changed. We can work on that. Can we digress for a while into a fantasy experiment. If you would just bear with me. Here it is, 10:25 on April the 15th and you and I have met for the first time and we're sitting here talking and suddenly the door opens and in comes a magician. Now for purposes of this narrative, anything is possible. The magician comes in and says to you, "I'm going to wave my magic wand and the result will be that you will instantly appear on a proverbial deserted island; you will be there for six months." In this exercise you can't say no. He's going to wave his magic wand and off you go, whisked off to the island. But he explains a few things to you before doing so. He says, "Time will stand still, which is to say that the world is in suspended animation, but you are going to have six months, real months, on this island. Don't worry about your survival, you'll be fine. There's plenty of food, plenty of provisions." But there's one question that he asks: "Do you wish to go alone or do you wish to find a most decent and pleasant young man whom you have never met waiting on the island for company?" Now some people choose solitude, saying, "Who wants to get into a hassle with a guy I really don't know who may be a real royal pain in the neck." Others say, "No, I'd like company." Now that's the question. He says, "You can't choose your boyfriend or your favorite film star. It's either him or go on your own." Solitude or company is really the question. Now, what do you choose?

C: To go alone.

T: You choose to go alone. Okay, so be it. Now the question is: Why do you choose solitude? What's the reason for that choice?

C: Well, six months is a long time and maybe it would be good for me to be by myself and think things out rather than have someone there to talk to. In other words, maybe within myself I'll be able to work things out and I probably wouldn't feel comfortable with a perfect stranger . . . I really have to know someone to really feel comfortable . . . to go with for six months rather than say we'll get to know each other within the six months or just remain perfect strangers—I don't know. I prefer to go alone.

T: Okay, so the reasons that you give for choosing solitude seem to be:

(1) This will give you a protracted period to think things through clearly and that might be very helpful—a kind of resorting of your own thinking might give you some answers.

(2) You seem to be saying that you don't want to take the risk of going with a perfect stranger which may or may not turn out to be good and, therefore, you elect to go alone. Now, let's just change the condition slightly. This time the magician says, "You have no choice. There will be a young man on this deserted island for six months whether you like it or not." Now for you to say, "No, let me go alone or choose somebody I know" is out of the question. He's waved his magic wand and there you are, you are on the island with the man. Now look around. There's a narrow strip of land, green and cultivated with a little sandy beach. There's a palm tree for shade, there's a hut for shelter, plenty of food and provision but no distractions—there's no television, no books, nothing, which means that you

and this man are now entirely dependent on one another for company and stimulation. He turns to you and says, "The next six months can be a living horror or they can be very nice, depending on the kind of people we are, depending on the way we handle the situation. If we handle it intelligently, in years to come we may look back upon this with nostalgia rather than horror." Now please tell me what problems you see; what's going to happen; what's going to develop? Can you just run with the fantasy for a bit?

C: Well, right away I'll start worrying about feelings, my feelings, what we would say to each other, and I'll start worrying about what he thinks of me, what do I think of him. Right away I'll form a conclusion as to whether or not I want to swim away . . . I really don't know . . . I'll start forming conclusions about what he thinks of me and putting myself outside myself and saying, What is he thinking, What am I thinking, and probably also thinking about what I'm going to say beforehand . . . watching things . . . being very, very cautious and unrelaxed.

T: This notion of "what is he thinking of you"—what would you want him to think of you?

C: I don't know. It would depend on what I started to think of him, whether or not I started to have any feelings.

T: Are you saying that if you felt positively about him, then it would be important for him to feel likewise about you? But what if you started out feeling pretty negative toward him? Then what?

C: I'd get very uneasy and get probably hostile. I don't know, I'm not really hostile. I'd probably start thinking of ways of getting away from him or the island.

T: That's interesting and I'll tell you why. As I see it, the ideal for both of you would be if you discovered that you really liked each other. If he would say to you, "Gee, I really think you are a fine person and I have a high regard for you" and you felt that same way about him, your six months of friendship would be smooth and enjoyable. Would you agree that would be the best?

C: Most comfortable.

T: The worst would be if you both hated each other's guts. Now, you make it sound almost predestined. Either you're going to like him or not, either he is going to like you or not. Surely, it's going to depend on the way you interface. For example, let's assume that you can't stand people who pick their toenails and there he is sitting on the beach talking to you and picking his toenails and this is really turning you off, it's getting on your nerves. . . .

C: Okay, but that's putting me at a low tolerance level and I'm not that way, but I'm just putting myself in a position where I'm going to make up my mind immediately, the way you pose the question. It seems like "Make up your mind, now, what are you going to do?" That type of thing. I wait for the person to react and so I don't have a low tolerance, I'm willing to put up with a lot if I first decide that I really want to be with that person. If that person shows me they like me and I like them, okay, that's fine, I really don't care what he does. He could climb the walls and I wouldn't care, but I'm happy because he likes me and I like him and I don't really care.

T: It almost sounds as if your need to be liked is so great that you are willing to put up with a lot of things, too many things.

C: Right, and I use material things as well. I'll run out and get things.

T: The need to be liked at all costs.

C: Exactly.

T: Okay, in this forced choice on the island, your companion says to you, "One of the things that is going to make life a lot easier for both of us is if you are willing and I am willing to be really above-board and honest. I will tell you if you do things that annoy me, if you tell me the things that I do that annoy you. In this way, we can keep out of each other's hair and really maximize the pleasure." How do you respond to that?

C: Well, I've never known anyone that has done that with me. I don't feel that any of my male friends have been totally honest with me so I can't relate to that. This is why I feel the way I feel.

T: What has happened in the real situation? When you say, "They have not been totally honest," what has been the pattern?

C: My wanting them and in the end them not really wanting me.

T: So you feel rejected. I wonder about the level of honesty you would risk in a relationship. You see, if you have this all-pervasive need to be liked, then you're going to be putting up with a great deal of discomfort and saying nothing about it, but I bet you're going to feel it.

C: Right, that's basically what happens every time. That's exactly what I do each time and that's the way it ends. We've sort of come to the conclusion that I set myself up for these things. In other words, I don't show them that I respect myself so they're going to abuse me and put me down.

T: Let me see if I understand the process. The way it might go is as follows: You might be involved with some guy whom you like very much. It's terribly important for him to like you if you like him. In order to maintain his level of liking, you seem to go above and beyond the call of duty. You are unusually considerate and helpful and so on, and that is all very well and good and nice, but this is not reciprocated and when the other person does things that are perhaps inconsiderate, uncaring, you become hurt, deeply hurt. But you don't say anything because you don't want to alienate the person, you don't want to lose his affection. But, nevertheless, that has an impact upon you. The old cliche "what goes in must come out" implies that if you are feeling hurt, it's going to come out in some way, in a way that you are not in control of. You might show a certain coldness, a certain aloofness. You might even be a little passive-aggressive because you're feeling hurt. You're not really coming out and saying to the other person, "Hey, you know, I really feel bad about the fact that we seem to have such an unequal relationship. What I would like you to do, Charlie, old boy, is mend your ways." But, no, you don't do this sort of thing. It accumulates, and you begin to withdraw, and they begin to say, "Gee, what's with this woman? She's a royal pain in the ass." Then they withdraw. Am I right, half-right, wrong?

C: You're right! But it doesn't come to grips. I usually just disappear. Like the last situation, I just got on a plane and left because I was unhappy and I couldn't verbalize it, so I just left.

T: You avoid confrontations. It seems the major error there is not nipping it in the bud.

C: Well, I'm afraid of causing any bad feelings because I don't want to lose the person.

T: But you *do* end up losing the person. With your pattern the inevitable outcome is loss. You don't want to precipitate the loss, therefore you don't take the chance of expressing the feeling as soon as you have it. I think that after a while, if you haven't expressed a half dozen feelings, it's very difficult for you to express number 7 because number 7 now has the accumulation of 1, 2, 3, 4, 5, and 6. So if you express the pent-up feeling it's going to come out pretty strong, so you'd better shut up. By the time 8, 9, 10, and 11 come around, you hop on a plane and say "bye-bye." From what you've told me I would say to you, "If you want to have a good relationship you had better not remain silent about things. You had better learn to speak up fast and take the chance and discover that by expressing your feelings and stating your needs, far from producing antagonism, you will be helping your companion to understand you as a person." He doesn't have to abide by your wishes. He can say to you, "I think that demand or request is unfair, so let's talk about it and come to a compromise." Now, I'm saying I want you to respond differently on the island, like you've never responded. Your male companion is going to be totally honest with you and I'm saying that with total honesty in return, something new will be gained, and you will not be sorry that the magician forced you onto the island with this man. You will learn a lot more in those six months than you would on your own. How do you feel about that?

C: I can't imagine that. It's never happened to me. I don't believe it could happen.

T: Are you saying "I don't believe that human beings can really function that way?" I'm not sure what the disbelief is about.

C: Well, there are people I have in my life that I've known for a long time that function that way, but it wasn't that way in the beginning. It took a lot of years . . . five years, ten years . . . people I've known a long time. I know they are capable of doing these things, but somebody that just came into my life, I could never see that happening.

T: You seem to be saying something like this: "Social protocol in general follows a certain pattern. When people meet and they are strangers, they are guarded, on their best behavior, kind of phony. Certainly you're not willing to be straightforward, open, and honest. This is not ordinarily done." Is that the sort of thing you mean?

C: I think it's more of a trust thing. Like I wouldn't trust them, they wouldn't be honest with me. They might say they'll be honest with me but I won't believe it.

T: We're onto something important . . . trust . . . tell me more about trust.

C: Well, I guess I have to trust someone to really be that way. For them to say to me they're going to be completely honest, they have to trust me and I have to really trust them. Do I really know them that well? Do they really know everything about me and do I really know everything about them and do we have a good relationship? But if I've just met someone and they say that to me, I'd be very skeptical about it, I won't believe it.

T: So, trust seems to mean that you've been able to test out over a period of time that this person says what he means as opposed to someone who might deceive you.

C: But if I don't know them, how can I trust them?

T: Let me see if I understand your point. Trust means that you really need to be able to be sure that this person is telling the truth, and this is impossible to know for sure on a first, second, or third meeting. It is consistency over a period of time that leads you to say you can trust the person. Going back to the island, your companion says, "Trust me. I'm going to level with you and I want you to level with me. Take the chance. I am playing it straight." How would you react?

C: I still wouldn't believe it.

T: All right, then you have an interesting view. "Most people are guilty until proven innocent. Chances are, he's lying, he is putting me on, he will not come through as promised. If I believe in him I'm going to be let down and hurt so I'm going to keep my distance."

C: I don't think it's that final. I think it's just a precautionary thing with me—the hurt feelings within. I don't make judgments that quickly. I don't say that you're no good because. . . . I just have the feeling that I have to be careful. We have to prove it to each other somehow. Time has to go by maybe. If you read my mind the way that I want you to because I don't express my feelings and you prove to me that you're willing to give as much as I am, then fine.

T: But you do realize that once you set up a mind-reading condition, it's doomed to fail because there are no mind-readers? What you are saying is true in this respect: There are a lot of dishonest people in this world and there are a lot of people who take advantage and say one thing but mean another. How are you to know that a person means what he says? But your solution seems to be: "I'm going to be cautious; I'm going to be very disbelieving; I'm going to have this person on test, on trial, under the microscope until I can determine if there is truth." Now if that is your path, it's not a good path, because life's too short.

C: There's a certain amount of hurt feeling, a certain amount of despair that has been built up in me which I cannot compromise. I think that has more to do with it than with what you have just said. You make me come on very strong when you say that I put people on trial. I'm more sitting there in my tears hoping someone is going to come and rescue me rather than putting them on trial. It's not that direct.

T: In some ways if it were that direct you might be better off. Let me make my point by referring to the island situation again. Here is what your island companion says to you: "I hope that a good friendship, a good relationship will develop because it would be so much nicer than if it were a horrible relationship. It would be so much nicer if you liked me rather than hated me. So, I'm most eager to make it positive rather than negative. But let's not waste time. We've only got six months here, so for us to sort of get to know each other over a couple of years is impossible given the time limit. Let's take a chance. I'm going to assume that you are what you say you are —that you are a person with kindness and compassion and generosity and sensitivity. You might be lying about it; you might be the bitchiest, most vicious and negative human being on earth. For all I know, when I'm asleep at night, you might bash in my head with a rock. But, I'm going to take the chance because if I don't, I just end up being anxious and negative in the relationship. I want you to take a similar chance that I'm a pretty decent guy as well. I mean it is possible that I may wind up being the most rotten bastard in the world but let us both think positively and take the chance."

C: I can't—it's really tough. . . . I have to think of him in terms of someone else. I have to put someone else's face in front of his, someone I already know and trust.

T: What thought comes to mind when he says to you, "Take the chance and trust me?"

C: Well, what are we talking about? Are we just discussing things. . . . I'm just going to sit down in six months and start discussing my problems. . . . just a day-to-day thing?

T: Well, look. . . .

C: In other words, I'll start saying, "Okay, I'll go along with it." But I'll keep it at a very trivial level, like, "how's the weather" type of thing. In other words, I don't intend to get involved with him emotionally and I'm not really going to tell him how I feel.

T: You're not going to tell him how you feel about what?

C: Well, what are we talking about?

T: If this relationship is going to be trivial and you are just going to talk about the weather, as you say, or "Isn't the sunset pretty," or "Should we get some scallops for lunch," and that's just about the extent of it, you have just guaranteed a very miserable six months.

C: But why? I don't understand.

T: Why? Because friendship, I think, is predicated upon knowing one another, and disclosing, and revealing. Most people would ask: "Who is this person I am here with for six months? What kind of a person is she? What has she done? What has she felt? What is good, bad, or indifferent about her?" You cannot have growth without that kind of sharing. And if people are willing to take the chance to share they grow emotionally.

C: So, what you're saying is he's there to discuss my problems.

We're there on this island for six months to try and get to the bottom of me.

T: Well, that could be one thing you might do, but if you treated your friend as a psychotherapist for 24 hours a day, it would be pretty lousy. What about his needs? Maybe he views you as an intelligent person and would like to chat with you about some of his feelings and thoughts and hang-ups. Does he get a turn? Or is it a one-way street?

C: No, but it's just not there. It has to come in time, maybe after a month, two months. But initially I don't think I could sit down and have a conversation like that.

T: Now, let me ask you something. Here you are meeting me for the first time and we are sitting and having a conversation. Now we are not talking about the weather. How do you feel?

C: I feel, well, I really don't know how I feel. I'll probably know when I leave. Right now I feel there's a certain amount of tension . . . there's so much . . . we're talking about 29 years of my life. It's so hard to cram it all into a time limit, and I sort of feel you have certain feelings as to what is in my head . . . so that we can get to the bottom of this thing. Other than that, I really don't have any. . . .

T: But let's say you are sitting on the island having this same conversation. You are now talking about trust and about basic feelings and you were saying something quite honest: "Hey, look, I'm really having great difficulty in trusting you. It would be easier if I imagined you being somebody else whom I know." Now there you are expressing an honest feeling. Your companion replies: "I understand the difficulty, but it would be to your advantage as rapidly as possible to by-pass all the suspicion and take the chance of trusting me." You turn to him and say, "But this is very difficult for me." Now you are not talking about the weather, you're talking about some basic feelings.

C: I can't express my inner feelings with a person I don't know. I can't sit down and talk about those things . . . I don't want to get too involved . . . he might not understand . . . he might slough it off and say, "Oh, she's a fool." I want somebody to understand and give me the feeling, compassion, the understanding. Not just to shrug it off and say, "You're stupid or you're foolish, go away!" I don't want to be rejected in that way . . . hurt further.

T: Now, why does that have to hurt you? If another person is insensitive enough to put that kind of construction on your feelings, why must you allow yourself to feel so upset? If some silly ass says: "You're just hypersensitive, you're just a silly woman, now pull yourself together," why upset yourself? Why not answer by saying something like, "I'm disappointed that you are so shallow that you cannot understand." You could add, "I'd hoped that you had more depth and understanding than that." Why do you shake your head?

C: Because I'd never say that.

T: But would you think that? Could you think that?

C: No, I'd probably think they were right—that I was stupid and I'd say I'd have twice as much hurt now because, first of all, if I like him and he's telling me that I'm stupid and he's not willing to understand my problems, I would focus on my problems even more because he's not willing to understand and that would be twice as much grief. I would not say, "You've disappointed me."

T: Therein lies a very important solution.

C: It's an assertiveness problem.

T: It's an assertiveness problem and it's a definitional problem. It seems to me you can only be assertive once you have defined something correctly. This is what I'm thinking. You are probably an extraordinarily sensitive person. This can be good and this can be bad. Good in the sense that there is warmth and caring, and bad in the sense that your nose can get out of joint too easily if someone doesn't give you the caring you desire. In a close relationship, somebody might be in a bad mood, into his own agonies and lash out angrily instead of acting compassionately, and you are so sensitive that you start bruising and withdrawing and then more problems come in. So the thing that you need to do, I think, is not simply look at how you are doing all the time, but ask what's with the other person. To take an extreme example, if I say: "Come with me to a back ward of a mental institution, we're going to go see some patients," and some poor psychotic individual comes out and says to you, "You are an idiot," and you say, "Oh, mortal wound!" I would ask "What's with you? This guy is talking crazy, how can you take him to heart?" But you don't need extremes like that. Your beloved boyfriend could be in a bad mood and, therefore, inclined to react in a most inconsiderate way. If I saw you overreacting to his mood by bruising and bleeding, I would say to you, "Can't you see where his head's at? He's not in any position now to give you strokes and love even though you need it. . . ."

C: You see, they're right all the time. If I like them . . . whatever they say or whatever they want to do . . . that's it. Once I make up my mind that I like them or I want to be with them it has to be their way. Otherwise, I won't tell them what I really want. I'll leave them, if I find they're putting me down. I won't try to work it out because I'm too hurt—they just don't understand.

T: Give me some idea of the put-downs you have received, some of the things they might have said.

C: One time this guy said to me, "You've lost your flair," and I didn't say anything. . . . Different things like that.

T: What did he mean by that?

C: He meant it in a sexual type of thing, like I wasn't jumping all over him. . . . I was waiting for him. So he would say something stupid like that. I wouldn't say anything on my behalf.

T: Why had you lost your flair?

C: Because I was terribly bruised and wallowing in my misery and I was feeling rejected and getting very uptight and very upset, wishing I were back home because he's not reacting the way I thought he would react.

T: Let me just leap to the blackboard and try to put visually on the board what I think is happening and tell me if this hangs together for you. We're talking now of male/female relationships. Here's the point where you meet the person. Now if you kept going on this path, it would be beautiful and rosy. But what happens, typically, is that something occurs somewhere along the line. At this point he has made an act of omission or commission that displeases you. If at that very point, the instant it registers with you, you're in the habit of making an assertive response, it would be erased. In other words, without attacking him as a person, you would say, "Gee, I wish you wouldn't do that," or, "That really hurts me," or whatever. Then what would happen is that, if this guy is one of the people not worthy of trust, which is to say that he's not willing to modify his behavior, you could cut the relationship at that point.

C: But I can't do that; that's where it stops. First of all, it's not easy to find nice people. So when someone comes along who seems decent, I want to hold onto him. I want to keep going even though it's misery for me.

T: You need to express your feelings immediately and you also need to make your own desires known. How are we going to get you to take certain risks to be able to do the things you know you need to do?

C: So, what you're saying is more assertiveness or is it more of a risk-taking?

T: It's a risk-taking and assertiveness and more. Now, I'd like you to take a chance. You said you went to see some good therapists, but after one session you knew that you were not going to be able to work with this person. Since it is your life, your happiness, and your finances, you are fully entitled, at any time, to fire your therapist. Now, someone says to you: "You've spent a session with Arnold Lazarus, tell me about it. What's he like?" The risk I want you to take is level with me and tell me what you would answer. For instance, if you are thinking that I should be incarcerated in the State Home for the Bewildered, Nervous, and Confused, please tell me.

C: (laughs) I really can't; I'm embarassed. It's hard for me to sit here and tell you what I think of you.

T: Start by taking that risk and then you've already made progress.

C: I can't do that.

T: What you mean is you won't do it. That word "can't" is a killer. You're saying it's very difficult for you to do. And I'm saying, "I know it's difficult, but try."

C: What do I think of you or what do I think of how you've tried to analyze this situation.

T: Either way; whatever is easiest for you.

C: Well, it's hard to say . . . at the very first meeting. I feel like I would like to work with you if you're willing to work with my situation. But as far as getting to the core of these things. . . . I have to have reasons and I have to be convinced of everything. Like if anybody says anything to me, I say, "I wonder what the reason is." Dr. B was always saying, "Well, go home and use the tapes and call me or come back in a week," and I'd get crazy because I'd use the tapes and not get anywhere, and I'd sit there memorizing these things, trying to apply them to my life and it's not working and it was a constant 'round and 'round. So I'm starting to go off in all kinds of crazy directions, and every article or book I pick up—"It's me!" And it was an awful ordeal trying to find someone to work with when I was desperate. It's really a difficult situation and I'm just going around and around and I'm not getting anywhere, I'm getting worse. I don't want to do anything now. I'm not working. I'm afraid to take a trip. I'm afraid to go here and there. I don't want to do anything because I don't want to make a mistake and do anything wrong that's going to hurt me or upset me, so I'm just standing still.

T: You feel the need to understand yourself better? You don't want tapes and homework exercises?

C: I think I need both. I just got your book "I Can If I Want To."

T: Well, that book is not something merely to read. It is a work book. I hope you might carry out some of the exercises. What I'd like to do is give you a life history form to fill in if you would. It will overlap with a lot of things we discussed today, but it will also help us to see things in a kind of sequential order. I will do my own homework by listening to the tape of this session before we meet next week.

Drawing Up a Modality Profile

The reader might find it instructive to draw up a BASIC I.D. profile outlining the specific problems that emerged in Ms. A's transcript. This may be compared with the profile I drew up after listening to the tape of the interview.

MODALITY PROFILE

Ms. A, aged 29

PROBLEM AREAS

B   Not working
Avoids expressing negative feelings
Does not take "emotional risks"—overcautious
Spends excessive time worrying over and dwelling on small incidents
Tends to run away from unpleasant situations
Appears to be stubborn and resistant
Inclined to wallow in her misery
Compulsive
A   Negative feelings build up inside her
Unexpressed feelings of resentment
Hypersensitive, insecure; feelings easily hurt
Terrified of criticism and rejection
Anxious about traveling; afraid of working
S   Tension (specific details will be obtained by further inquiry)
I   Poor self-image (inclined to view herself in the light of others' deprecatory statements)
C   Lacks self-respect
Suspicious, nontrusting
Unrealistic expectations of others
Believes that she gives more than she receives
Prone to excessive cogitation, seeks reasons for everything
Jumps to conclusions
Perfectionistic, must not make mistakes

I Inclined to put others' needs before her own (especially when
romantically involved)

Passive-aggressive

Unassertive

Goes out of her way to please others

Appears to be a "loner" (chose solitude in the Deserted
Island Fantasy Test)

Overwhelming need to be liked by others

Continually tests people to determine if they are trustworthy

D ——————

After spending one hour with Ms. A, I discerned twenty-nine problem areas. This initial draft of her Modality Profile may undergo several changes as more facts come to light. After the second session, and after we study her Life History Questionnaire, many additional items will undoubtedly be added. An assessment of her positive attributes across the BASIC I.D. could also be added to the profile. Next, with her cooperation, specific strategies will be selected to deal with each problem area. A logical starting point will also have to be found. Each of these points will be covered by subsequent chapters.

One point that should be mentioned is that some therapists waste time determining where exactly to place a given item. Would "avoids expressing negative feelings" be more accurately placed under Affect rather than Behavior? Is "suspicious, nontrusting" a Cognitive attitude rather than an Affective response? Clinically, it is counterproductive to waste time over "perfect fits." As long as a relevant problem appears somewhere on the profile, it will receive the necessary therapeutic attention.

Chapter 7

Relationship Factors and Client-Therapist Compatibility

When therapists try to legislate fixed rules of conduct they destroy initiative for the sake of security. "Don't answer the client's questions; seek to determine the meaning behind them. Don't reveal anything about yourself; try to remain inscrutable. Don't socialize with clients. Don't engage in pleasantries such as helping clients with their coats or putting your arm around them. Don't give the client gifts and don't accept gifts from clients." Therapists who adhere to these and many other don'ts are certainly spared the inconvenience and the threat of thinking for themselves. They know how to respond and how to relate as if clients all came from identical molds. By contrast, multimodal therapists approach each client de novo and try to determine the depth and type of relationship that best suits the needs and expectancies of that individual. The only don'ts to which we subscribe are (1) Don't be rigid and (2) Don't humiliate a person or strip away his or her dignity.

I develop formal relationships with some of my clients. They call me Dr. Lazarus and I refer to them by their surnames. With a few clients, I would not answer the simplest question without first examining their intentions behind it. At the other extreme, some clients come away from therapy knowing almost as much about me as I know about them. The very act of dining out with certain clients, inviting others to a party, playing tennis with some, and even going as far as to offer free board and lodging in my home to one young man, served to promote favorable treatment outcomes. Since there are no clear-cut, objective criteria to help one decide what type of relationship would best be developed with each individual, I have erred on more than one occasion. Nevertheless both therapist and client can profit from mistakes and can modify the relationship accordingly. Fixed rules and standardized procedures may augment therapists' levels of confidence, but how good are they for the clients? Frank (1970) alluded to the caricature of the young psychoanalyst who remarked, "The wonderful thing about psychoanalysis is that even if the patient doesn't get better, you know you are doing the right thing."

Person-Centered versus Multimodal Considerations

The best-known clinician whose treatment orientation is perhaps the antithesis of the multimodal approach is Dr. Carl Rogers. A film in which Rogers conducts an initial interview with Gloria, a 30-year-old divorcee ("Three Approaches to Psychotherapy," 1965) provides what is considered "a typical example of the person-centered way of working" (Meador & Rogers, 1979). Two films in the same series contrast Rogers' therapeutic style and tactics with those of Perls and Ellis. Subsequently, Rogers was filmed with a different client for an updated series ("Three Approaches to Psychotherapy II," 1978), in which a young woman, Kathy, also worked with Everett Shostrom ("Actualizing Therapy"), while I demonstrated "Multimodal Behavior Therapy" in the third 48-minute reel. I endeavored to obtain an initial overview of Kathy's BASIC I.D., but I would not refer to it (or to any single session) as "typical" of the multimodal approach. With another client, my entire pace, content, and interaction might have been quite different. However, in viewing Rogers with Gloria in 1965 and with Kathy in 1978, one observes that the cadence and format of their transactions are virtually identical. There are hardly any discernible differences in style, tactics, or strategies of intervention. Not only is there no change in Rogers from one client to the other, but there is no change from 1965 to 1978. Hence my conclusion that we are at the polar opposite from the "person-centered" orientation of Carl Rogers and his followers (Meador & Rogers, 1979). The multimodal position emphasizes that people have diverse needs and expectancies and call for a correspondingly wide range of stylistic, tactical, and strategic maneuvers from the therapist. Having one "unimodal" manner of approaching all clients makes life a lot easier for the therapist and probably accounts for a good deal of the popularity that Rogerian therapy has enjoyed.

Rogers Revisited: Releasing Blockages and/or Remedying Deficits

A truly "person-centered" approach would be geared to individual and personalistic differences and would not rest on a tripartite basis;

namely, that the necessary and sufficient conditions for therapeutic growth and change are (1) the therapist's genuineness or congruence, (2) the therapist's empathy and understanding, and (3) the therapist's unpossessive caring. These facilitative conditions would be regarded as useful (not essential) but quite insufficient for covering the BASIC I.D. The multimodal view stresses the need for a therapist to be *more* than a decent human being. In addition to warmth, caring, compassion, and empathy, the therapist needs to master a wide range of specific skills and techniques. It is the properly executed and well-orchestrated application of appropriate techniques that often determines the difference between therapeutic failure and success (Goldfried & Davison, 1976; Kazdin & Wilson, 1978; Walen, Hauserman & Lavin, 1977; Wilson, 1980; Wilson & O'Leary, 1980).

While using different terms, many therapists seem to subscribe to the Rogerian view that an "actualizing tendency" becomes truncated through various inimical experiences, and that the emotional relationship that develops between client and therapist can *release* these barriers or blockages. This is clearly conveyed in Rogers' (1959) definition of psychotherapy as the "releasing of an already existing capacity in a potentially competent individual" (p. 221). Other therapists will refer to "the lifting of repression," "the removal of character armor," and so forth. The following diagram depicts the Rogerian or so-called person-centered view of emotional disturbance.

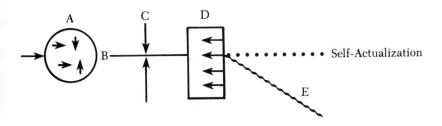

A. The person at birth is a product of a genetic endowment and the impact of intrauterine and other environmental influences.

B. The life trajectory proceeds along a path toward "self-actualization."

C. Various events create conflicts between organismic needs and self-regard needs.

D. A barrier against self-actualizion arises.

E. The person moves off the self-actualization pathway and is now characterized by incongruence, distortion, a lack of awareness, and self-defeating action.

According to the Rogerians, the proper therapeutic relationship will release the person's inherent potential and again enable the client to traverse the pathway toward self-actualization.

The foregoing schema makes no provision for those problems that do *not* stem from conflict, traumatic events, impositions from significant others, and restrictions on organismic urges. Many people suffer emotionally because their learning histories failed to equip them with essential coping responses. They do not have barriers or blockages that, if released, will enable them to utilize their prior knowledge; they never possessed the requisite knowledge or skill in the first place. The latter etiological view of emotional disturbance may be depicted as follows:

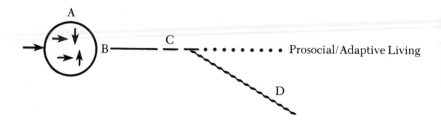

A. The person at birth is a product of a genetic endowment and the impact of intrauterine and other environmental influences.

B. The life trajectory proceeds along a path toward "prosocial-/adaptive living."

C. Gaps or deficits in experience and social learning (due to poor role models or the happenstance of missed opportunities for acquiring necessary information and skills) create lacunae.

D. Due to these response deficits, the person moves off the adaptive pathway and displays incongruence, distortion, a lack of awareness and self-defeating action.

Teaching, coaching, training, modeling, shaping, and directing are necessary. No amount of empathy, genuineness, or unpossessive caring is likely to fill the hiatuses. In the multimodal view of personality development and problem-solving, *both* of these models are valid. Most clients suffer from conflicts, the aftermath of unfortunate experiences, *and* various deficits in their social and personal repertoires. Hence unimodal remedies are bound to leave significant areas untouched.

The powers of influence and healing that certain therapists attribute to themselves and to their therapeutic relationships tend to deflect attention away from the fact that the generalization of skills from the consulting room to the outside world is not automatic. The transfer and generalization of these skills call for specific, preplanned interventions. In my early years of practicing therapy, I assumed that when formerly hostile, withdrawn, and belligerent clients became consistently friendly, talkative, and assertive rather than aggressive during therapy, they probably adopted similar adaptive behaviors with significant others. I soon learned that new and adaptive behaviors within the relationship were usually confined to the relationship unless I specifically prescribed homework assignments that were designed to encourage particular response generalizations (Shelton & Ackerman, 1974).

A Continuum of Feelings and Investments

Many years ago, Franz Alexander (1932) described the mainstay of therapy as "a corrective emotional experience," which involves the contrast between the therapist's helpful and objective attitude and the original (presumably pathogenic) parental attitudes. Alexander (1950) later wrote that "to experience such a novel human relationship in itself has a tremendous therapeutic significance which cannot be overrated" (p. 487). More recently, Arlow (1979) echoed these views by stating that "emotionally, the person of the analyst assumes major significance in the life of the patient." Multimodal therapists espouse a very different view.

Certainly, it is essential for the therapist to be respected by his or her clients, to establish sufficient trust for them to confide personal material, and to create an atmosphere whereby clients can freely disclose embarrassing, distressing, or anxiety-provoking information. But this essential rapport is not necessarily predicated on the development of strong affection, transference, dependency, or the like. In keeping with the pluralistic philosophy of the multimodal tradition, we see the client-therapist relationship on a continuum extending from a rather formal, business-like investment at the one end, to a very close-knit, dependent bonding at the other. Most therapy relationships fall in the middle. Some clients vacillate between liking and loving the therapist, while others remain ambivalent and manifest love-hate polarities. It is my contention that many therapists deliberately or unwittingly foster dependent, romantic, or other deep attachments in their clients. Since multimodal practitioners are largely task-oriented, so-called transference factors rarely intrude or erupt. Most of my clients regard me as a skillful professional who has the wherewithal to help them combat their negative emotions, maladaptive behaviors, interpersonal deficits, and so forth. They like and respect me and find they can relate to me, but they are not in love with me. They depend on me but are not dependent on me.

Of course, there are exceptions. Some people, because of their own peculiar needs and perceptions, are bound to misinterpret, distort, and overidentify. They will develop elaborate fantasies and act out scenes that emanate from their own conscious and nonconscious desires. Childhood feelings may be projected and a transference of attitudes may occur whereby the client directs upon the therapist certain feelings that are applicable to a significant other, usually a parent or close family member. This, however, is the exception, rather than the rule. When it does exist, it has to be dealt with and may well become an important therapeutic focus, tantamount to resolving the "transference neurosis" that psychoanalysts espouse. However, whereas analysts state that "the transference neurosis, its gradual unfolding and its eventual resolution, becomes the central concern of the analysis" (Freedman, Kaplan & Sadock, 1980), the central concern to a multimodal therapist is to eliminate as many specific problems as feasible across the client's BASIC I.D.

In multimodal therapy, the client-therapist relationship is examined or discussed only when there is reason to suspect that it is impeding therapeutic progress. When therapy is proceeding well, why waste time analysing the dyadic transactions between client and therapist? But when progress halts or falters, one factor worth questioning is whether issues or feelings vis-à-vis client and therapist may account for this lack of improvement. Sometimes misunderstandings arise that are readily corrected when straightforward communications and metacommunications are examined. Here is dialogue that occurred toward the end of the second session with a 32-year-old man.

T: Well, it seems quite clear to me that you tend to be very tough on yourself. While you appear to be quite tolerant of shortcomings in others, you have lots of must's and should's for yourself.

C: I'm a perfectionist.

T: You seem to say that with such pride.

C: Yeah? Well, I guess I am rather proud of myself when I do something really well. . . .

T: Ah! Doing something well, striving for adequacy or even excellence, is different from trying to be perfect. Being a perfectionist means that you will feel frustrated most of the time because you will seldom, if ever, attain your impossible standards. You know, I want to recommend a book by Albert Ellis. He has written extensively on the subject of how one's excessive demands, one's perfectionistic strivings create emotional turmoil. . . .

C: (looking out of the window) I'm glad it's stopped raining.

T: Me too. Here let me write down the name of the book. (I notice that the client seems uneasy.) What's wrong? I'm picking up something sort of, um, kind of tension in you.

C: Well, (pause) I don't know. I'm not really tense.

T: Something seems to be bugging you.

C: Okay, well, it's like when you say to me, "Go read a book," I feel that you, um, I mean I feel sort of rejected . . . I mean like you're telling me not to come to you with trivial details but to go away and read about it instead.

T: I'm really pleased you shared that with me. I had no idea you would see it that way. I want to talk some more about your feelings.

We examined some of his expectancies and feelings and I pointed out how important "bibliotherapy" can be as part of a psychoeducational retraining. At the end of the session he jokingly asked: "If a picture is worth a thousand words, how many sessions is a good book worth?" I answered, "Oh, give or take a dozen," and a potentially volatile situation had been dissipated. He stressed the importance of feeling accepted by me, and I enabled him to appreciate that homework assignments (especially reading prescribed books and other materials) was not an indication of lack of interest on my part. I now make a point of exploring my clients' feelings and perceptions whenever I make specific recommendations. Instead of merely saying, "Here, borrow this relaxation cassette for a week, use it twice a day, and let me know if it eases your tension," I will follow this with, "How do you feel about this suggestion?" If I detect hesitation or a less than positive response, I examine the client's reactions to determine if specific expectancies are not being met.

In addition to procedural misunderstandings that can compromise the relationship, one encounters more central and subtle affective investments that can impede progress. For example, when treating a 35-year-old woman for agoraphobia, I had accompanied her on several in vivo excursions—walking longer distances, driving during peak-hour traffic, waiting on line in a supermarket. I then arranged for some paraprofessionals to assist her with these behavioral assignments while I devoted our sessions to her irrational ideas and her lack of assertiveness with certain people. Although she had been making steady progress, she started to experience more anxiety and began complaining that she had become "very weepy" and that she was having difficulty falling asleep. My paraprofessional helpers found her uncooperative. What could account for this negative turn of events? A plausible assumption was that she felt rejected by me since I was no longer present during her "field assignments." It appeared necessary to examine her attitudes and feelings toward me as the probable basis of her treatment impasse or regression.

I opened the discussion by saying, "I feel you're angry with me, but instead of expressing it, you're holding it in." After some initial denials and evasions, she acknowledged a variety of factors that were having a negative impact on the therapy. The fact that I had stopped accompanying her during (what she termed) "outings" led her to conclude that I had lost interest in her case. As we discussed allied feelings, it became evident that she was not one of those clients who responded to me merely as a professional. She entertained elaborate sexual fantasies and, from time to time, tended to project attributes onto me that more accurately belonged to her father, or her husband, or her oldest brother. In her case, my major therapeutic inputs amounted to a fairly traditional "clarification of affect" while my paraprofessional helpers continued their in vivo excursions with a now highly motivated subject.

Whenever positive outcomes are not achieved, some therapists beg the question by attributing their failures to the patient's "resistance." Instead of labeling all noncompliant behavior "resistance," it would be illuminating if clinicians would attempt to ferret out the specific antecedent and maintaining factors that generate uncooperative behaviors in specific contexts. For example, one client may countermand a therapist's endeavors due to anger, disrespect, or mistrust, whereas another's genuine desire for help may be undermined by "emotional saboteurs" within the client's social network. A systems or family therapy approach may be indicated in the latter instance, whereas in cases of incompatability between client and therapist, I recommend referral to a colleague whose methodology and personality seem better suited to the client's needs and expectancies. (This point will be amplified later in the chapter.)

The Seminar Client

The manner in which psychoanalytically oriented clinicians tend to overvalue the significance of the therapist in the treatment dyad was poignantly illustrated in one of my classes. I was treating a woman in front of a group of some fifteen advanced doctoral students. First, they would observe me conducting a 50-minute therapy session, after which they would ask questions of the client or me, volunteer opinions and suggestions, and make other comments about the process and procedures. One of my psychoanalytically oriented colleagues also served as an observer on a couple of occasions. After one of these sessions he made some accurate observations. First, he noted that the client had positioned herself with her back toward most of the class so that she sat looking directly at me while effectively blocking out a majority of the students. Second, she appeared to be unusually tense and uneasy throughout the session. Finally, my colleague remarked that she seemed to be withholding significant feelings from me and from the class as she probably felt unsafe and too embarrassed to reveal them.

I agreed with each of these observations. During the session I had in fact remarked to the client that she seemed more uncomfortable than usual, and I shared with her the fact that I felt "shut out." The students, my analytic colleague, and I discussed some probable reasons for her behavior, whereupon a distinct bifurcation took place. Those with an analytic bent hypothesized that her behavior in the session was directly related to her feelings for and about me. They alleged that I was being responded to (1) as a father figure and (2) as a sexual object, and that these two conflicting feelings and perceptions were reenactments from her past. We knew from the client's history that, as a child, she tended to withdraw from and reject her mother and gravitate toward her father. Thus, according to my analytic colleague, the class members symbolized her mother, whom she was excluding so as to draw closer to me (her symbolic father). She was unwilling to admit her sexual feelings toward me in front of the class (the symbolic mother), which kept her hiding behind trivia for much of the session while growing more tense and uneasy.

Some of the more venturesome and imaginative students began offering deeper dynamic interpretations, at which time I called a halt to the discussion and issued a challenge for them to substantiate any of their hypotheses. My most pointed question was, "What data have emerged in any of the sessions to suggest that the client is even remotely interested in me sexually?" I was provided with no facts or any supporting evidence, but instead was accused of being naive.

Later that evening the client called me at home. She opened the conversation by telling me that she had felt tense and upset during much of the session. I told her that I had been aware of her discomfort. She inquired whether I had noticed how she had kept her back to most of the students and had avoided looking at the class. I shared with her the fact that we had all been aware of it. She then said that she had had some strong feelings that she had very much wanted to talk about. After a pause she mentioned that they had to do with sexual desires that she felt too embarrassed to bring up in front of all the students. At this point I had vivid images of the smug looks that would adorn several faces if they were privy to this conversation.

She then narrated how, over the past several sessions, she had grown increasingly aware of one of my young, good-looking male students, whom she described as "the type of man I really go for." She found herself becoming more and more sexually turned onto him and developed elaborate fantasies about him. "I feel so foolish," she told me, "like a schoolgirl with a crush." Seeing him prevented her from concentrating on her therapy. Consequently, she resolved to sit with her back to him to derive more benefit from the session.

The way in which this was handled is beside the point of this narrative. Rather, the point is that many therapists are perceptive and make lucid and accurate observations about peoples' behavior, whereupon they tend to apply Procrustean interpretations to accommodate these phenomenological data, thereby distorting the realities of the situation. In this case, my colleague had read the cues correctly, but had misinterpreted their locus of intent. He was generous enough to capitulate, although he did point out that his more dogmatic counterparts would call upon the mechanisms of displacement, projection, and denial to bolster their case.

Affection versus Respect

Is it necessary for a client to like a therapist or feel affection for the therapist in order to derive benefit? In the early sixties, I was consulted by approximately twenty people who had been in therapy with the most ineffective therapist I have known. When I listened to these people recounting gross deficits in his clinical understanding and a veritable absence of therapeutic acumen, I was amazed that he was a licensed practitioner. Yet, without exception, every person who had consulted him told me how much they liked him, what a warm and wonderful person he was. Men and women both lauded his kindness and human decency, but in the many treatment failures I saw, affection and caring were obviously not enough. While these positive feelings may be insufficient to effect significant change in many people, are they nevertheless necessary? Most therapists will say "yes!" but I maintain that the client's *respect* rather than his or her affection is a sine qua non for effective therapy. Let me cite a case where a mutual lack of affinity characterized the relationship but did not impede therapeutic progress.

I was consulted by an academic professor of international preeminence in his field. He was a most impressive-looking man, about five or six years my senior, whose voice, manner, and bearing were very much in accord with my stereotype of a "brilliant scientist." He informed me that he and his wife were having marriage problems and that he was examining and interviewing a number of therapists in the area to determine their suitability. Thus far, he informed me, his mission had been unsuccessful. Each therapist had been rejected "out of hand" because he found them deficient. "What were they lacking?" I asked. He replied, "Cerebral wattage!"

During the interview I found myself straining to give the impression that I possessed cerebral wattage. I dredged up polysyllabic words and, when questioned about my theoretical stance and academic background, tried to give a sterling performance reminiscent of a doctoral candidate during a dissertation defense, or a job applicant being interviewed for a key position. (I withheld any interpretations about his pompous and intimidating style, partly because I was in awe of the man, and partly because I realized that this would truncate the development of a working relationship.) I must have passed the examination because he arranged to bring his wife with him for a visit.

She was renowned in her own right, a lawyer who was also active in local politics and government. A fiercely competitive person, she constantly insisted that she could have been as famous as her husband were it not for the fact that she had elected to devote years to the upbringing of their children. She complained that her husband looked down on everyone and often made disparaging remarks about her, her friends, her work, and her basic intelligence. He denied all this and said that he only resorted to these put-downs in retaliation for the love and sex she was inclined to withhold. It became evident that they both used passive-aggressive tactics and that they both possessed brilliant intellects to supply their arsenal of weapons.

Initially, I attempted to intervene with specific suggestions for achieving interpersonal harmony, but this merely put me in firing range of their big cannons, and I rapidly retreated to the safe sidelines of Rogerian reflection. From time to time I would put down my shield of reflective echoing and hazard an opinion or venture to suggest alternative modes of interaction. On one occasion, they got into a shouting match and, with their permission, I switched on my tape recorder. Subsequently, I listened to the tape and was able to identify some significant errors and irrational ideas in several of their transactions, whereupon I wrote a letter to them outlining and analyzing these processes and recommending specific steps for constructive change. A few days later, I received a photocopy of my letter in the mail with a "C–" written in red on the upper right-hand corner and a memo from the professor with "For your information" in his handwriting. I was furious! Ordinarily, I would be amused by this sort of tactic, but coming from him, my archetypal professor, this touched off my own insecurities. They had an appointment with me later that same day.

Initially, I decided to explore his feelings in as open and nondefensive a manner as I could muster, but rapidly, I found myself growing angry and started saying things like, "I'm surprised that someone with your intellectual prowess harbors such a deep lacuna in his understanding" and, "In a similar situation, I wonder how many of your less esteemed colleagues would have failed to grasp the subtle implications behind each one of my specific recommendations." We both grew more angry, our voices became loud, and his wife kept pleading, "Stop it! Will the two of you please stop it!" I realized that I had lost control, and, to try and save face, I turned to her and inquired, "Would you say that the interaction between your husband and me in any way mirrors the battles you enter into at home?" She affirmed that the similarity was unmistakable. "Did you notice how my display of anger merely escalated matters?" I asked. She nodded and then described a recent interchange between them that parallelled what had transpired in the consulting room. I managed to capitalize on our aggressive encounter, and the remainder of the session was devoted to emphasizing the virtues of assertion versus the destructive impact of aggression.

There were no further shouting matches inside or outside the therapy and they appeared to derive benefit from my ministrations over the next few months. They still continue to consult me intermittently when certain problems arise. The main point of this narrative is the following: I do not like this couple—individually or as a dyad —*and they don't like me.* I regard him as pompous, arrogant, intolerant, somewhat grandiose, with a paranoid flavor to his interpersonal perspective. But he has learned to contain his anger and to display open affection to his wife. She, in turn, is condescending, an intellectual snob, no less critical than her husband, and hides most of her own insecurities behind a veneer of sophisticated disdain. (In my view, to tamper with these personality issues would be worse than playing with plutonium!) But she no longer tends to use sex as a weapon and seldom resorts to passive-aggressive tactics with her husband.

Their dislike of me was confirmed by one of their sons, who consulted me about some uncertainties over his choice of career. In his view, I had "done miracles for Mom and Dad." In advising their son to consult me, they had told him that, while I am not their type of person, I am competent at what I do professionally. They both respect me, but they have no special affinity for me. I am laboring the point because I see as counterproductive the widespread notion that to be liked by one's clients is essential for effective therapy. Therapists who endeavor to be *liked* will behave differently from those who require nothing more than *respect* for their capabilities. Setting out to be or to appear "likeable" can lead one to use charm as a cover for incompetence. While it is best to be liked *and* respected, the point I am trying to underscore is that if and when a choice arises, it is more important for a therapist to be respected rather than liked by his or her clients.

Expectancies and Compatibility

Many clinicians contend that people enter therapy with implicit (if not explicit) expectations and that the effectiveness of therapy is often linked with these expectations. If the therapist's personality and approach are very much at variance with the client's image of an effective practitioner, a therapeutic impasse is likely to ensue. This, however, should not be construed as a passive and inevitable process. Clients' expectancies can be modified by the therapist. Many clients, for instance, expect the therapist to "cure them" and are quite unprepared to take any responsibility for the treatment process and outcome. In these instances considerable therapeutic skill and artistry may be required to elicit the client's active cooperation. In this regard, role expectancy may be restructured by providing the client with a "role-induction interview" or an "anticipatory socialization interview" (Orne & Wender, 1968). In essence, the client is told what to expect from therapy and how to behave during the therapy in order to derive the greatest benefits. Goldstein (1971, 1975) has carried out some of the most significant studies dealing with therapeutic attraction and relationship-enhancement methods.

Goldstein (1975) comments that "research convincingly shows that the greater the structured similarity, the greater the attraction to the other person" (p. 19). In multimodal vernacular, the most elegant treatment outcomes often depend on a reasonable degree of similarity between the client's BASIC I.D. and the therapist's BASIC I.D.[1] To take a clear-cut example, therapists who function predominantly in cognitive and behavioral modes (thinkers and doers) will have problems communicating with clients who dwell on affective and imagery modalities (emotional dreamers). Other obvious examples include instances where client and therapist come from divergent cultural backgrounds, have antithetical political, religious, and other fundamental ideologies, or where antipathetic reactions are evoked for a variety of reasons. When inappropriate matching results in an absence of rapport, it is often advisable to effect referral to a more compatible resource instead of insisting that the client-therapist difficulties can or should be "worked through."

Here is a blatant example: Several years ago I was consulted by a wealthy widow. About ten minutes into the initial interview I became aware that I was feeling progressively irritated by her. As I

---

[1]In case it is not self-evident, let me stress also the importance that *differences* play in promoting growth. Matching and some fundamental similarities are usually necessary for initial rapport, but outcome is as much a function of creative differences as a product of comforting agreement.

listened to her personal complaints and problems I felt unsympathetic, unsupportive, and even hostile. This "negative countertransference" perturbed me. Why was this woman eliciting these negative responses in me? It was most unlike me to respond this way, especially to a person in obvious distress. What was I telling myself? What images did she evoke in me? Why was I blocking my characteristicly compassionate and caring side? What was going on with me? Suddenly insight dawned. She reminded me of a male colleague whom I had good reason to dislike! As I watched her more closely, I became aware of a physical resemblance, a tonal voice quality, certain mannerisms, and other features that she had in common with him. Since I was now aware of how I was overidentifying the two people and projecting his attributes onto her, could I dissociate the two and deal with her as an individual? No. Listening to her constantly brought to mind numerous grievances that could not be resolved with my colleague. Consequently, I made what seemed to be an ethical and professional choice—I referred her to him. (At the end of the session I said, "When treating your type of problem, I'm not nearly as good as a certain colleague and I strongly recommend that you see him.") They evidently effected a near-perfect match. Knowing my negative feelings, he was puzzled that I had referred a wealthy client to him, and telephoned to thank me for recommending this "delightful lady." Subsequently, she thanked me for referring her to this "wonderful and charming doctor," whom, she said, helped her immeasurably. If I had kept her in therapy, I doubt that I would have been as effective.

Other reasons for referring clients to one's colleagues need not be so subjective. Recently, while working with an adolescent boy, I sensed an impasse and referred him to a young therapist in the community. As I had suspected, the lad admitted that he had difficulty relating to me because I reminded him of his father. "What sorts of things would you have trouble discussing with Lazarus or with your father?" the young therapist inquired. "Well, for one thing, I could never bring myself to admit my homosexual feelings or talk about drugs with either one of them," was the answer. In other instances, it may be fairly clear that a female therapist will do better than a male; someone younger or someone older may be required; a Spanish-speaking therapist would be needed; someone with a Southern accent would be made to order; and so forth.

In Search of Idiosyncratic Relevance

Sometimes, it is essential to transcend all the foregoing considerations to ferret out more subtle and poignant expectancies. A woman I had seen many years ago had complained of "anxiety" that was chronic and persistent for over fourteen years. Apart from psychiatrists and other physicians, she had been treated by a lay analyst, a hypnotist, and several psychologists. She consulted me at a time when I was still practicing a fairly orthodox "behavior therapy." Accordingly, I administered a variety of antianxiety procedures— relaxation training, desensitization, assertiveness training, thought-stopping, and even flooding, all to no avail. I also arranged for her to receive inhalations of carbon dioxide, and with the help of an anesthesiologist, I tried to elicit an abreactive response under sodium pentathol. Her anxieties persisted. Subsequently, I learned that she had consulted a "nature doctor cum chiropractor" who had x-rayed her spine and examined her colon. He concluded that her problems emanated from two specific physical causes. First, there was a nerve ending under pressure in her spine, and, second, her system was in a toxic condition due to poisons in her colon. The recommended treatment consisted of spinal manipulations and colonic lavages or "irrigations." She received these treatments twice weekly over a period of six weeks and experienced lasting relief from her suffering. As a maintenance strategy, she continued having a manipulation and an irrigation twice yearly.

How can we account for this outcome? Competent physicians have assured me that there is no physiological connection between spinal manipulations, enemas, and "anxiety." One plausible hypothesis is that she responded to a placebo that activated her significant images, cognitions, and affective processes to arouse the expectation of help, the hope of relief, and faith in the outcome. Or perhaps this was a so-called spontaneous remission. Was she at a stage in her life where she was able to "give up her symptoms?" If so, would virtually any therapy have produced a similar outcome? It is my contention that the "nature doctor" and his treatment were in line with her expectancies, her personal constructs, and her own perceptions of her illness and its treatment. She first consulted reputable physicians and underwent numerous tests—blood work-ups, endocrinological investigations, neurological examinations, and additional medical procedures—and was proclaimed in good physical health. One doctor prescribed tranquilizers, while another recommended several good psychiatrists in the area. She was plied with more tranquilizers, and, as she put it, "I also learned some interesting things about myself, but nothing helped my anxieties." Could an astute diagnostician ever have concluded: "This woman will not respond to psychoanalysis, or drug therapy, or hypnosis, or behavior therapy. She needs someone to manipulate her spine and to insert a tube up her rectum and wash out her colon." While it is unlikely that anyone would be that precise, could I, or another multimodal therapist, after conducting a BASIC I.D. analysis with a similar case conclude that a medical or pseudomedical procedure was likely to prove more successful than any form of psychotherapy? Conceivably, provided that we were able to listen carefully and create an associative network out of the recurrent cues that tended to underlie the client's expectancies.

For instance, a 22-year-old man was referred to me by his family doctor. The young man had been on drugs; he had dropped out of college, and his wealthy parents were in a state of turmoil over their only child. Initially, it appeared to be largely a "system" or family problem, although the client's BASIC I.D. profile also showed several personal zones of conflict and anxiety. His Life History Questionnaire (Appendix 1) suggested a very different theme. He described his main problems as "a need for spiritual identification," yet he stressed that he was "antagonistic to orthodox religions." He was searching for "a sense of belonging" and expressed a desire for "group affiliation." During the course of several sessions exploring these avenues, it seemed that his bout with drugs had been an unsuccessful attempt to "find himself." He had hoped that hallucinogens would expand his consciousness and self-awareness; he imagined that by achieving an altered state of consciousness he would enter a different plane of discourse that would prove spiritually enlightening. As I listened to him, I realized more and more that this young man was not interested in acquiring a wider range of social skills, in examining his irrational cognitions, or in improving his study habits. A Fritz Perls poster had persuaded him that he was "not in this world to live up to anybody's expectations," and he therefore rejected the idea of family therapy and added that he would "no longer march to old parental drums."

Because in many ways he was overly meticulous, keeping elaborate lists and diaries, some therapists would be inclined to label him "an obsessive-compulsive personality." It was obvious that he welcomed precision and structure. I was convinced that our accomplishments would be limited for many reasons, one of which was the fact that he regarded me as too establishmentarian for his tastes. What therapeutic approach was most likely to resonate with this young man's expectancies?

I pieced together the words he had used—"spiritual identification," "antiorthodox religion," "belonging," "affiliation," "self-awareness," "enlightenment," "different plane or level," "precision and structure." Instantly, I recognized a pattern that was in keeping with the claims made for Transcendental Meditation (Bloomfield, Cain & Jaffe, 1975). While the pundits of TM often go out of their way to emphasize the secular, basically nonreligious orientation of the movement, there is nevertheless a "high priest" (the Maharishi Mahesh Yogi), a formal ceremony performed in Sanskrit, a secret "mantra," and other aspects that emanate from the Vedic tradition that antedates all modern religions. I recommended TM to my client with the hope that it would be congruent with his expectancies.

He attended the lectures, applied for the training, performed the ceremony, received his secret mantra, and started practicing TM twice daily. He met with his trainer several times to evaluate his performance and attended a lecture given by the Maharishi in person. He was enthused. He continued to see me a few times a month in a supportive capacity, and his attention was focused on the wonders of TM and the pure goodness of the Maharishi Yogi. He was determined to become a TM trainer and eventually to study further in India. He claimed to have obtained a serenity and a clarity of vision beyond his expectations. He was now opposed to drugs, and he realized that it was in his best interests to return to college and complete his studies in accountancy. This was over five years ago. Today, he is a Certified Public Accountant and has continued to find viable outlets in TM and other movements.

The point of the foregoing illustration is not to laud the alleged virtues of TM. I am, in fact, extremely critical of this cult and have published a paper on "psychiatric problems precipitated by transcendental meditation" (Lazarus, 1976a). However, in seeking to answer the question, "Who or what is best for this individual at this particular time," the multimodal orientation stresses open-mindedness in fitting the person to the appropriate set of procedures. Nothing is good for humankind; there is no panacea. But if Mr. or Ms. X will derive benefit from standing on their heads, having sitz baths, and ingesting brewer's yeast, so be it! Let us hope that therapists will become less hidebound by their favorite theories so that they may fully appreciate how methods that lie outside their "school" affiliations can prove more helpful to certain people.

Chapter 8

The Selection of Techniques

After compiling a Modality Profile that encompasses the specific excesses and deficits in a client's behaviors, affective reactions, sensations, images, cognitions, interpersonal relationships, and biological functioning, how does one select appropriate techniques? Specifically, how do you decide which problems and which modalities to address first and which particular procedures to evoke? *I recommend starting with the most obvious and logical procedures.* Watzlawick (1978) emphasizes that, by carefully observing clients' previous unsuccessful attempts to solve their problems, we may avoid problem-engendering pseudosolutions. We want to eschew push-button panaceas, but we also want to overcome any penchant for making straightforward problems needlessly complicated. If a client is "tense," the obvious antidote is "relaxation therapy"; if a person is timid and unassertive, "assertiveness training" is called for; if faulty cognitions and erroneous beliefs abound, the "correction of misconceptions" will be the first avenue of intervention. As discussed in previous chapters, the Modality Profile will place specific complaints within a more general framework. Thus, if there is evidence of psychotic or delusional thinking of which erroneous beliefs are a part, phenothiazines rather than "rational disputation" might be the first line of interposition. If the most logical therapeutic tactic proves ineffective, a closer perusal of the Modality Profile, or the construction of a second-order BASIC I.D. will point to alternative strategies. A case illustration should clarify these points.

147

Case Illustration: How Techniques Follow Logically and Blend

with Each Other

Mr. W, aged 32, complained that he had been suffering from "anxiety, compulsive habits, and medical problems" since being promoted as a factory foreman two years before. According to his doctor, the "medical problems" were largely related to "stress and tension" (he suffered from severe headaches and frequent bouts of colitis). He was recently married. "You can add sexual problems to the list," he said.

During the initial interview, Mr. W was obviously so tense that we devoted fifteen minutes of the session to relaxation training. In addition he was given two cassettes for home use. One was for general relaxation, and the other was specifically aimed at overcoming tension headaches. At the end of the session he was given the Life History Questionnaire to complete at home (Appendix 1).

The second session was devoted to discussing items on the Life History Questionnaire that required clarification, and relaxation training was continued, centered particularly on his neck, shoulders, jaws, facial area, and abdomen.

Before his third session, the following Modality Profile was drawn up:

MODALITY	PROBLEMS	PROPOSED TECHNIQUES
Behavior	Compulsive checking (stove, doors, work, etc.)	Self-monitoring; response prevention
Affect	Bottles up or blows up Anxiety attacks	Assertiveness training; calming self-statements; slow abdominal breathing
Sensation	Tension Premature ejaculation (seldom exceeded two minutes of coital stimulation)	Relaxation training Threshold training
Imagery	Pictures of ridicule as a child and as an adolescent	Densensitization

Cognition	"Should's," internal self-demands, self-downing, perfectionism	Cognitive restructuring
Interpersonal	Competitive most of the time; too involved with power and control	Friendship training; relationship-building
Drugs	Valium 5 mg. daily Darvon for headaches Lomotil for colitis	Teach relaxation skills Attempt phasing out of medication

The profile reveals a tense, anxious, overly competitive man with perfectionistic demands, compulsive habits, and somatic complaints. Ridicule from peers figured prominently during his elementary and high school years (in elementary school he was the only Jew in an anti-Semitic neighborhood, and, in a sports-minded high school, he was disparaged for his lack of athletic ability). These experiences may have encouraged his overcompensatory tendencies as reflected by his demanding and controlling ways. The fact that he tended to suppress or "bottle up" his angry feelings, and would finally explode or "blow up" at the slightest provocation, called for assertiveness training that would teach him to express his feelings in an open, immediate, and forthright fashion (Salter, 1949; Lange & Jakubowski, 1976; Alberti & Emmons, 1978; Lazarus & Nieves, 1980).

In glancing through the Modality Profile, one might ask why the item "bottles up or blows up" appears under Affect rather than Behavior. Similarly, one of my trainees pointed out that I had placed "premature ejaculation" in the Sensory modality, whereas in another case it had appeared in the Interpersonal modality. It is a waste of time trying to decide on the "correct" area in which to place a given problem. Since Mr. W had been somewhat tearful and upset when discussing his inclination to suppress or overexpress his feelings, I included these elements under Affect. Premature ejaculation (his "sexual problem") was placed in the Sensory modality because of the manner in which he presented this problem. Mr. W described his subjective reactions and how it felt when he reached the point of ejaculatory inevitability. Other people may gloss over their own sensory reactions and dwell on interpersonal repercussions. "This upsets my wife very much." "I feel' like a worm even though my partner never complains." The important point is not that each problem be placed in the proper or most appropriate modality, but rather that every significant problem be listed somewhere in the schema.

In multimodal therapy, it is not uncommon for specific interventions to be made during the initial interview. One does not wait until the full assessment procedures are completed before commencing to alleviate distress. As discussed in Chapter 3, during the opening phases of the first meeting with a client, it is advisable to approach him or her in an accepting, neutral, and open manner and then to augment the level of rapport by tuning in to the client's expectancies. About fifteen or twenty minutes into the initial interview with Mr. W, I commented that his posture and body movements seemed to be exceedingly tense, whereupon he described himself as feeling "tight as a drum." As the interview proceeded and Mr. W showed no signs of "loosening up," I asked him if he would like me to show him some relaxation exercises. He responded positively to my suggestion and, as already mentioned, we devoted some fifteen minutes to preliminary relaxation training. The second session was largely one of further fact-gathering and additional relaxation training. Thereafter, we were ready to add another mode of intervention.

The third session began with Mr. W describing an incident at work in which he had been unfairly criticized by a fellow employee. He had managed the encounter by being apologetic and by suppressing his own feelings. Paradoxically, Mr. W considered his behavior quite appropriate; he said that it gave him "the upper hand." Further discussion revealed several deficits in Mr. W's social and interpersonal skills, his general nonassertiveness and intermittent passive-aggressiveness being particularly evident. Accordingly, we commenced assertiveness training. We engaged in role-playing where I modeled alternative responses he might have made to his critic at work. I advised him to purchase and carefully study the paperback edition of Fensterheim and Baer's (1975) *Don't Say Yes When You Want To Say No.* Toward the end of the third session the client and I discussed his Modality Profile. I specifically solicited his comments, especially about areas of omission. He added "depression" to the affective modality, as he frequently felt "down in the dumps" when things went wrong at work and when his compulsive checking was out of hand. "By applying assertive skills, you will probably notice marked improvement in your work situations," I opined. I then asked whether he would also like to start working on his compulsive checking habits. "Do you think we could first try to do something about my sexual hangups?" he inquired. I suggested that he invite his wife to the next session so that we could add "threshold training" (Semans, 1956) to the relaxation therapy and assertiveness training.

In multimodal therapy, the selection of techniques and the focus on different problem areas is not based on intuition and random guesswork, as Franks and Wilson (1980) have averred. The choice of techniques often follows logically from issues and points of emphasis that arise during the course of therapy. For example, when Mr. and Mrs. W were being instructed in the "stop-start" technique for delaying ejaculation, Mrs. W commented that her husband's compulsions were more upsetting to her than his lack of sexual staying power. While his priorities differed from hers, he nevertheless agreed that his compulsive checking was extremely disruptive. We therefore agreed to deal with his compulsive checking at our next session. (A Modality Profile was constructed for Mrs. W because we find it a useful and systematic way of identifying areas of mismatching and specific dyadic struggles that may undermine the therapy.)

In the treatment of obsessions and compulsions, research has shown that in addition to cognitive restructuring and various stress-reducing methods (e.g., relaxation, distraction, thought-stopping), *response-prevention* is one of the most effective strategies (Rachman, 1978; Foa & Goldstein, 1978). Since Mr. W had a highly developed sense of integrity and strong motivation, response-prevention was implemented on a self-management basis. He was in therapy when it seemed that President Nixon was about to be impeached. Mr. W had expressed strong moral outrage at the President and his administration. I asked, "Will you agree to send Mr. Nixon a $100 donation every time you engage in any compulsive checking?" We discussed the implications of this *contingency contract* and finally entered into it, replete with a "signing ceremony," in which he attached his signature to a typewritten agreement. Thus, the choice of techniques, in order of selection, included relaxation training, assertiveness training, threshold training, and contingency contracting to achieve response-prevention.

Setbacks are seen from time to time even in straightforward cases. After his seventh session, Mr. W suffered a severe anxiety attack that seemed to have been precipitated by an argument at work and also linked to a fight with his wife. In my view, this called for the incorporation of "friendship training and relationship-building" into his general assertiveness training. In addition to role-playing various interpersonal styles with him (e.g., submissive approaches, assertive approaches, abrasive approaches), I embroidered the theme that love and friendship are predicated on sharing and confiding, not on winning and on being right. Since Mr. W was an avid reader and appeared to derive considerable benefit from "bibliotherapy," I loaned him a copy of Jourard's *The Transparent Self* (1971). Subsequently, he undertook the assignment of engaging in greater *self-disclosure* and allowing certain vulnerabilities to show. Conjoint sessions with Mr. and Mrs. W stressed the desirability of more mutual self-disclosure while reducing their use of "categorical imperatives." This led to methods of *cognitive disputation* for the elmination of "should's" and "must's" (Ellis, 1977a).

After about twelve sessions over a period of some three months, every proposed technique on Mr. W's Modality Profile had been implemented, with the exception of *desensitization* in the imagery modality. I asked whether the recollection of these memories still bothered him. "Yes, when I think about it, it upsets me very much." By this time, most of his presenting complaints had diminished. Since he was especially adept at relaxation, it seemed logical to capitalize on this capacity and desensitize him to his images of past ridicule so that he would develop a fitting indifference to his previous tormentors. We constructed a hierarchy of insults starting with some very mild ethnic aspersions and progressing to scenes of blatant mockery. Following a classic systematic desensitization procedure (Wolpe & Lazarus, 1966) Mr. W was deeply relaxed and asked to visualize the mildest scene on his hierarchy. If he felt unduly anxious or otherwise disturbed, he was to signal by raising his right forefinger. We could proceed no further than the initial item, as Mr. W continued to signal that he felt emotionally disturbed. Deeper levels of relaxation were ineffective in neutralizing his discomfort. Given this impasse, a second-order BASIC I.D. was conducted.

T: If you picture yourself being ridiculed, how do you see yourself behaving? What do you *do?*
C: I guess I withdraw.
T: Now can you get a really vivid image of someone putting you down? Take your time.
C: (after a few seconds pause) I've got it.
T: What exactly do you feel?
C: Rage!
T: What sensations go with that rage?

C: A surging heat. I can feel it right here in my head and down to my feet. It's like seeing red and feeling flames.

T: What other images come to mind?

C: Attack! I picture myself going berserk!

T: How would you go beserk? What would you do?

C: I don't know. . . . Beat them up perhaps.

T: Would you use any weapons?

C: Just my bare hands.

T: You'd beat them up?

C: Right. That is to say, I wouldn't kill them or anything like that.

T: Apart from images of attack, what *thoughts* come to mind? What are you telling yourself?

C: Mother was right! That popped right out, but it makes perfect sense. My mother was always very critical of me and often put me down and told me that I would get into trouble.

T: It's interesting that none of this came up before.

C: Well, it was sort of buried in the background until I really started to think about it.

T: What are the implications regarding you and other people?

C: How do you mean?

T: When you picture yourself expressing all the anger.

C: I'd say *utter rejection.* If I went beserk and beat them up, who'd want to associate with me?

T: Would you first need a stiff drink or anything?

C: Are you kidding? I'd want to be sharp as a tack.

The following second-order BASIC I.D. was drawn up:

	B.	Withdraws
	A.	Rage
Ridicule	S.	Surging heat
	I.	Attack
	C.	Mother was right
	I.	Utter rejection
	D.	_____

It was no wonder the desensitization procedure had failed. I had erroneously concluded that Mr. W was *anxious* about being subjected to derisive or critical remarks, whereas he was exceedingly *angry,* if not enraged. Given this more accurate view of the situation, the most logical step was to augment the assertiveness training, and to draw special attention to the differences between assertion and aggression. I had planned to explore the mother-son relationship and to examine the full extent of his hostility and rage, but Mr. W received a substantially better job offer and moved out of state. I recommended Ellis' book *How To Live With and Without Anger* (1977b) and gave him the name and telephone number of a therapist whom he could consult. After a total of seventeen sessions conducted over a four-month period, Mr. W rated himself as 85% improved. He seldom had headaches or symptoms of colitis, and he reported being far less compulsive, anxious, and tense. He also stated that his marital relationship was significantly better, not only sexually, but also in terms of emotional closeness (an observation with which his wife concurred).

This relatively simple and straightforward illustration shows how the selection of specific techniques follows a logical sequence and is largely a collaborative enterprise. The client's most pressing needs received priority and alerted me to focus on particular problems across the BASIC I.D. The case of Mr. W also shows how a specific error (the implementation of an inappropriate technique) was corrected by conducting a second-order BASIC I.D.

We have referred to Mr. W's case as "relatively simple and straightforward." It may be well to ask what is meant by a "complex case?" Are complex cases those with entrenched habits that are compounded by primary and secondary gains? Does complexity imply the existence of psychotic features? Is the mere presence of a client's ambivalence, uncertainty, and limited motivation sufficient to qualify any such case as complex? Does complexity enter the picture when individual problems are confounded by disturbed family dynamics? Will the presence of organic impairment render a case complex? Are those instances complex wherein inimical life circumstances and environmental hazards are mainly responsible for psychological dysfunction? When confusion, denial, and a lack of self-understanding constitute the clinical syndrome, does this qualify as being complex? Are phobic reactions necessarily less complex than "identity crises?"

In my view, *complexity* denotes a case characterized by a multitude of discrete and interlocking problems across a client's BASIC I.D. Complex cases need not be difficult to treat; difficult cases are not necessarily complex. We have been stymied by some straightforward habit disorders and "simple" phobias, notwithstanding our diligent application of well-documented habit-control techniques (e.g.,

Azrin & Nunn, 1977). Conversely, some exceedingly complex and multifaceted problems with subtle representations and interactions throughout the entire BASIC I.D. have responded rapidly and gratifyingly to our ministrations. The selection of techniques is probably the least difficult aspect of multimodal therapy. The BASIC I.D. analysis takes vague, general, and diffuse problems (anxiety, depression, low self-esteem, frustration, unhappiness, marital problems, family conflicts, etc.,) and reduces them to specific, discrete, and interactive difficulties. Thereafter, the selection of techniques is rather straightforward. If asked, "What is the best technique for the treatment of low self-esteem?" we would say, "This general problem has to be dissected into its component parts before we can provide an answer." If the Modality Profile of a person who suffers from "low self-esteem" reveals (1) deficits in social skills, (2) false cognitions about other peoples' competencies, (3) failure to take emotional risks, (4) negative self-talk, and (5) persistent images of failure, it is fairly evident that the prescribed techniques will include (1) social skills training, (2) the correction of misconceptions, (3) risk-taking assignments, (4) positive self-instructions, and (5) coping-imagery exercises. While the selection of techniques is reasonably straightforward, the *implementation* of techniques is quite another matter.

To say that a person who lacks social skills will usually profit from social skills training says nothing about the manner in which such training will be administered. The assessment, evaluation, and implementation of social skills are neither simple nor unitary (Hersen & Bellack, 1977). Researchers have not reached consensus about a general definition of social skills. For instance, the notions of interpersonal competence set out by Argyris (1968), both overlap and differ from Eisler, Hersen, Miller, and Blanchard's (1975) situational determinants and components of assertive behavior. In the clinical setting, the social skills trainer may fail to make headway with a client by overlooking a subtle but pivotal point, such as rates of eye-contact or adequate voice-projection. Or a client who had been instructed to be less compliant may have required desensitization, or behavior-rehearsal, or participant-modeling before being able to achieve this end. The particular procedures that will yield significant changes across specified component behaviors have not been isolated or identified. This is the point at which clinical experience and a degree of artistry enter the equation.

I have been impressed by the fact that skillful therapists, especially great psychotherapeutic artists, share certain features regardless of their backgrounds, school affiliations, or professional identifications. They are responsible and flexible individuals with a high degree of respect for people. They are essentially nonjudgmental and firmly committed to the view that infringement on the rights and satisfactions of others is to be strongly discouraged. They will not compromise human interests, values, and dignity (cf. Ullmann & Krasner, 1975). They bring warmth, wit, and wisdom to the therapeutic situation, and, when appropriate, they introduce humor and fun. They seem to have an endless store of relevant anecdotes and narratives. They are good role models (they practice what they preach) and are authentic, congruent, and willing to self-disclose. Why am I bringing these issues into a chapter on the selection of techniques? Mainly to stress that the final orchestration of successful therapy depends on what techniques are selected, how they are implemented, and by whom they are delivered. As surgeons are apt to point out, it is the person behind the scalpel who can wield it as an instrument of destruction or of healing. In psychotherapy, it is even more difficult to separate the specific technique from the person who administers it.

Imagery as a Bridging Modality

It is usually not difficult to select techniques for specific problem areas. How does one proceed when the client is unable to furnish the therapist with specific problems? What about the person who experiences generalized unhappiness and distress but who cannot pinpoint any specific clusters of identifiable excesses or deficits? Initial exploration of cognitions, behaviors, affective responses, sensory concomitants, interpersonal repercussions, and biological factors may lead nowhere. Contradictory, ambiguous, and confusing information point in several directions at the same time. In these cases we have found that the *imagery modality* often provides the missing information. As mentioned elsewhere (Lazarus, 1976a), out of hundreds of images at our disposal, trial and error has shown that three particular images tend to yield important clinical (diagnostic) information.

1. Please picture your childhood home. You might have lived in several places as a child, but nearly everyone thinks of one particular place as his or her "childhood home." Will you concentrate on that image? Close your eyes if that helps. Try to *see* your childhood home.

(Pause of about ten seconds). Now tell me, where is your mother in that scene? What is she doing? And where is your father? What is he doing?

2. Now will you take a tour in imagination from room to room, look around carefully. See the furnishings. Try to feel the atmosphere. Do you notice any odors? What sounds do you hear?

3. I want you to picture a special safe place. Any place will do, real or imagined, in which you feel completely safe. (Pause of about ten seconds.) Go to that specific place. Picture it vividly. (Pause of about ten seconds.) Would you care to describe it to me?

Since the nuclear family so often provides the breeding ground for emotional problems, exploration of the *childhood home scene* usually yields significant information. The *tour from room to room* in the childhood home often unlocks memories and strong feelings that have a bearing on the client's ongoing problems. The image of the *safe place* provides clues about important escape and avoidance behaviors. "My safe place is at home with my husband and our two dogs." "A desert island far away from civilization would be the only safe place for me." "My safe place is an indestructible, self-sustaining space ship far away from this galaxy." "My safe place is tucked away in bed with a good book." "My safe place is the arms of my lover." "There is no such thing as a safe place." (There are innumerable imagery techniques, both for diagnostic and for therapeutic uses. See Appendix 2 for a description of seven other imagery procedures.)

In treating a 23-year-old woman whose Life History Questionnaire was mainly left blank as she allegedly "did not know what to write down," and whose first two sessions were equally uninformative (she complained that she felt frustrated and unhappy most of the time), I used the foregoing imagery techniques. Her childhood home scene was unrevealing—her mother was in the kitchen preparing breakfast while her father was shaving in the bathroom—but as we proceeded to take a tour of each room, she voiced strong feelings about being locked out of her older brother's bedroom while he had friends whom she wanted to meet. She then went on to describe a "dining room scene" in which her father accused her of being a prostitute (she was 17 years old at the time). She had locked herself in her bedroom with one of her boyfriends. "I did this to get back at my brother because I knew that he wanted to meet Tony." By dwelling on more images in and around her childhood home, we arrived at a central theme—her father's disapproval and her exaggerated need for his approval. In this way, the imagery modality had revealed a significant interpersonal problem that subsequently led to related difficulties in other areas.

How does one select the most appropriate techniques for dealing with a client's excessive needs for her father's approval? Shall we recommend family therapy and treat the family system? Would it be more productive to see the father alone and/or with his daughter? Shall we use role-playing in which the client could learn to stand up to her father? Would the imagery technique of going back in time and picturing herself confronting her father in the past prove helpful? Might there be value in a desensitization procedure designed to render her less reactive to her father's real or imagined criticisms? Could the best technique be that of cognitive disputation wherein she would be taught to alter her irrational demands and realize that her father's approval is not essential for her sustained happiness? Would a deep exploration of the father-daughter interactions prove therapeutic?

The decision to pursue a certain line of inquiry or to favor a given procedure is usually best made in consultation with the client. "We both seem to agree that you are too dependent on your father's opinion and that you are especially vulnerable to criticism and disapproval from him. Do you agree that it would be in your best interest to become less concerned about his approval or disapproval of you?" If the client does not regard this as a viable treatment objective, one would wish to examine her attitudes, expectancies, father-daughter images, and interpersonal dealings more thoroughly. When client and therapist agree about the desired outcome, the therapist provides a description of the different pathways toward the specified goal, and the client is asked to state which particular methods appear most likely to produce the best outcome.

T: I can think of about seven different ways to overcome this problem. Let me briefly outline each one, and will you tell me what you think? The first alternative is for us to embark on family therapy. If we invited your parents and your brother to join us, we could deal with the whole family unit and try to change some of the communication patterns.

C: Oh, God! I don't like that idea one little bit! Are you kidding? That's no option.

T: Will you give me some ideas as to why you feel so strongly?

C: First of all, wild horses probably couldn't drag my father to see a psychologist, but even if you did persuade him to come, *I* am the one who needs to change. I don't need you to convert him into a good, all-accepting daddy.

T: That's not exactly what I had in mind, but let's not dwell on that. How do you feel about role-playing procedures where I would act the part of your father and would come on with a variety of put-downs and implied criticisms. I would be more and more disapproving and rejecting. You, in turn, would be asked to deal with each situation in a calm, secure, and appropriate manner. If you were at a loss for words, we would reverse roles—you would play the critical father and I would model the secure, mature, and effective you.

C: Are you saying that by putting on a good act, I'll end up *feeling* differently?

T: Up to a point. As I understand it, your present mode of behavior is to become defensive and upset, even tearful, whenever you receive negative messages from your father. If your actual behavior is not that of a 23-year-old woman, your father is bound to think of you and react to you as a child. But that's only part of the picture. The main objective as I see it is for you to realize that you don't have to have your father's approval, that it is not awful or dreadful if he disapproves.

C: I agree with that intellectually, but how can I get to *feel* that way?

T: Okay. There are several avenues. We could explore exactly what you are telling yourself, all the negative self-talk and the mental pictures you form that lead to your feelings of anguish and fear whenever your father, or anyone else for that matter, gives out disapproving messages. By changing what we call your cognitive and perceptual appraisals, you can alter your emotional reactions. Another method we could use is called systematic desensitization.

C: Can any of these things be used together, or do we have to choose one at a time?

T: We could make use of one or more procedures in each session, as we saw fit. For example, we could devote fifteen to twenty minutes to role-playing, followed by cognitive restructuring, and end up with ten to fifteen minutes of desensitization. How does that sound to you?

C: I like it! What's this desensitization?

T: Well, first you learn to relax . . .

It would be naive to assume that one is always guided by the client's predilections. When dealing with emotional saboteurs, one would be led right into cataclysmic outcomes. Manipulative people, especially those with passive-aggressive tendencies often cannot be taken at face value. In most instances, however, it pays to consult the client about those methods and procedures he or she would prefer. The previous example showed that with a young woman who was initially somewhat uncooperative and taciturn, the use of imagery opened specific vistas of therapeutic communication. Thereafter, rapport was facilitated by exploring therapeutic options. She liked the idea of dividing sessions into segments that would focus on different techniques. Other people find it too fragmenting and prefer to concentrate on one aspect at a time. Several years ago (Lazarus, 1973a) I reported a small clinical study that showed the value of meeting the wishes of those clients who ask for hypnosis. In some cases, clients requesting hypnosis were told that relaxation training is superior to hypnosis and they were treated by "relaxation" instead of "hypnosis." These cases were less successful than those in the "request granted" group. The only procedural difference between the "relaxation group" and the "hypnosis group" was the use of the word *hypnosis* in the one and *relaxation* in the other. The point is that meeting expectancies tends to yield more positive outcomes.

Theoretically, the number of techniques is virtually limitless. In my opinion, any good clinician requires many dozens of different techniques at his or her disposal. I am constantly on the lookout for new methods and techniques. Frequently, I have found it possible to help seemingly intractable individuals by inventing or discovering a tactic, a strategy, a method, or a procedure that appears to ignite a positive "chain reaction." After surveying my case notes and discussing specific techniques with my colleagues and associates, I compiled the following list of most frequently used techniques.

Techniques Most Frequently Used in Multimodal Therapy
(See Appendix 2 for a description of each of the following techniques.)

Behavior	*Imagery*
Behavior-rehearsal	Anti–future shock imagery
Modeling	Associated imagery
Nonreinforcement	Aversive imagery
Positive reinforcement	Goal-rehearsal or coping imagery
Recording and self-monitoring	Positive imagery
Stimulus control	The step-up technique

Systematic exposure

The empty chair

Affect

Anger-expression
Anxiety-management training
Feeling-identification

Sensation

Biofeedback
Focusing
Hypnosis
Meditation
Relaxation training
Sensate focus training
Threshold training

Biological

Encouragement of health habits—
good nutrition, exercise, recreation

Referral to physicians when organic
problems are suspected or biological interventions are indicated

Time projection (forward or backward)

Cognition

Bibliotherapy
Correcting misconceptions
Ellis' A-B-C-D-E paradigm

Problem-solving

Self-instruction training
Thought-blocking

Interpersonal

Communication training
Contingency contracting
Friendship training

Graded sexual approaches

Paradoxical strategies

Social skills and assertiveness training

When To Use Unimodal or Bimodal rather than Multimodal Interventions

The pluralistic philosophy that underlies multimodal therapy stresses that successful adjustment to the demands of our complex society requires a wide array of coping strategies. Consequently, the majority of our clients are treated by many different procedures aimed at remedying excesses and deficits across each parameter of personality. Yet some individuals respond poorly to multifaceted interventions. In these instances it is advisable to focus on one or two major problems and to apply only one or two basic procedures. I have had clients who strongly resisted any maneuvers outside of the imagery modality. By exploring associated images, we uncovered a fascinating and complex mosaic of interrelated memories, feelings, and insights. Is an in-depth and exclusive exploration of imagery a form of multimodal therapy? No, but nothing prevents a multimodal therapist from pursuing this line of therapeutic activity. Similarly, some

162   THE PRACTICE OF MULTIMODAL THERAPY

clients have the mental set that only a detailed exploration of their early childhood memories and relationships will benefit them. Again, it seems preferable for a multimodal therapist to conduct this highly focused exploration instead of referring the client to a committed Freudian, Jungian, or any other doctrinaire therapist who may provide the client with specious insights that happen to fit the framework that the therapist espouses (it is well known that Freudian analysands acquire Freudian insights, Jungian analysands emerge with Jungian insights, and so on). Apart from those *individuals* who favor unimodal interventions, a narrow and highly specialized focus of therapeutic attention will tend to achieve better results than multimodal therapy in certain *conditions* or problem areas. For example, in weight loss, McReynolds and Paulsen (1976) have provided data that favor a specialized stimulus-control procedure over multidimensional treatments. Instigating clients to adhere to treatment prescriptions seems to be a key factor in the achievement of positive outcomes (Wilson, 1979). With some clients, the introduction of more than one or two tactics may cause them to feel overwhelmed and confused. Problem areas that may respond better to specialized procedures include some phobias, compulsive disorders, sexual problems, eating disorders, some cases of insomnia, tension headaches, and the management of oppositional children (Agras, Kazdin & Wilson, 1979). Assessment should always be multimodal, but treatment may sometimes be narrowly focused—especially when a BASIC I.D. profile reveals no significant network of interrelated problems.

Multimodal assessment unravels global and diffuse problems into specific entities across the BASIC I.D., thereby pointing to particular techniques to remedy each excess and deficit. When one of my colleagues was bewildered by a family replete with game-playing collusions, triangulation, dyadic struggles, and internecine feuds, I asked him to focus on discrete problems across the BASIC I.D. Four clearcut goals emerged:

1. The father needed to assume more authority. (Logical treatment =assertiveness training; modeling.)
2. The parents needed to cooperate as a team. (Logical intervention=dyadic instruction; role-playing).
3. The parents wanted more cooperation from their children. (Logical strategy=contingency contracting.)
4. The children wanted more freedom. (Logical consequence= cooperation in household earned specific degrees of freedom.)

He stated: "Thinking in multimodal terms quickly showed me some key problems and their most logical solutions. Previously, I was getting lost in a jungle of double-binds and miscommunication." (In order to prevent an "information overload" I refer the reader to the glossary of techniques on pages 229–242.)

Self-control Procedures and Self-help Techniques

Many people who wish to stop smoking or overcome other undesired habits adopt a unimodal or bimodal approach. One man had read about "stimulus control" and applied this method to his smoking behavior. "I tried to kick the habit by restricting my smoking to particular times of day and in specific settings. Thus, I could only smoke at odd-numbered hours—9 A.M., 11 A.M., 1 P.M., and so forth —provided I was sitting in my own office in my own chair at my own desk." Another would-be former smoker relied exclusively on aversive imagery. "I pictured myself becoming sick, and I imagined the smoke causing cancer cells to enter my lungs." Compare this with a client who, after reading *Multimodal Behavior Therapy* (Lazarus, 1976a) and other books on self-control, devised his own "Modality Profile to Stop Smoking."

Behavior:	Gradually cut down by waiting 15 to 30 minutes when the urge to light up a cigarette arises. At the end of each day, count how many cigarettes were smoked and estimate the amount of tar and nicotine. Wrap each pack in aluminum foil with rubber bands so that the cigarettes are relatively inaccessible. Reward yourself for compliance by purchasing a record album every 3 to 4 weeks.
Affect:	Watch out for anxiety, anger, and other emotional triggers that lead to smoking. Deal with the source whenever possible instead of hiding behind a smokescreen.
Sensation:	Use relaxation to overcome tension. If the urge to smoke gets overwhelming, inhale smelling salts between puffs of smoke.
Imagery:	Picture emphysema, heart disease, cancer, and other illnesses caused by smoking. Rehearse positive images of good health associated with not smoking.

Cognition:	Concentrate on the facts about the dangers of smoking. Look up statistics and memorize them. Obtain information from the American Cancer Society. Catch yourself in self-deception, e.g., "Everyone doesn't get cancer."
Interpersonal:	Tell others about the dangers of smoking. Declare yourself to be against smoking.
Drugs:	Get into a physical fitness regimen.

This client stopped smoking three packs of cigarettes a day in less than a month, and he has not smoked in more than three years.

I have edited and changed the language of the client's self-constructed Profile, but the techniques were all independently culled from his own readings. By attacking the problem from seven strategic points, we render it likely that each one will amplify the positive effects of the others. Garson's (1978) controlled study clearly showed the superiority of broad-spectrum therapy in smoking reduction. His research also confirmed the power of imagery techniques.

As already mentioned, some individuals prefer to concentrate solely on one or two modalities. Clinically, our follow-ups point to the greater durability of multimodal interventions. Even obese individuals whose initial weight loss may best be achieved by a concentrated behavioral and stimulus-control program, will more than likely regain weight if related problems across the BASIC I.D. are not corrected.

The self-help potential of multimodal methods is largely untapped at present although most clients have had no difficulty in understanding, remembering, and applying the BASIC I.D. as part of their homework assignments. Nieves (1978a) has provided a multimodal self-assessment procedure in a manual dealing with self-control systems for minority college students, and, in a related publication (1978b), has described a multimodal self-help program for college achievement.

Chapter 9

Multimodal Marriage Therapy

"Most therapists are about as poorly prepared for marital therapy as most spouses are for marriage" (Prochaska & Prochaska, 1978). Until fairly recently, the emphasis in nearly all approaches to psychological malfunctioning was aimed at the individual, at exploring conflicts and forces within the patient. Interpersonal processes were considered entirely dependent on the workings of individual psyches. The psychoanalytic preoccupation with intrapsychic pathologies was clearly apparent in the earlier writings on marital therapy in which couples were treated individually (Mittleman, 1948).

The leap from individual spouses to the marital unit calls for a "wide angle lens," different from the magnification of individual pathogens. Although some therapists were treating couples in joint therapy sessions in the 1960s (e.g., Brody, 1961; Haley, 1963; Satir, 1965), most therapists continued to rely on *concurrent therapy* rather than *conjoint marital therapy*. Virtually every possible variety of combinations has been applied to distressed couples—one partner is identified as the patient and enters therapy; each partner goes to a different therapist; both see the same therapist separately; both see the same therapist together some of the time, most of the time, or all of the time; co-therapists treat the couple; spouses attend separate groups or join the same couples group; couples attend groups with unmarried members. Many other combinations have been tried. Prochaska and Prochaska (1978) comment: "There have been no adequate experiments which have tested whether working with both spouses, either concurrently or conjointly, is more effective than working with only one troubled spouse in individual therapy." From a multimodal perspective one would be less concerned with data about the general effectiveness of different strategies than with specific indications for their application. Some couples may benefit more from being seen separately; others may require conjoint therapy as well as individual attention; time-limited therapy may benefit some and discourage others; and so forth. A multimodal assessment endeavors to fit the client to the therapist and the specific therapy that he, she, or they may require.

Proceeding Multimodally With Couples

"Marriage" or "marital" is used in this discussion in a generic sense to identify an *intimate relationship* wherein two people live together and form a bond, whether or not the relationship is legally institutionalized. I have seen many unmarried couples for "marriage therapy" and have treated a few homosexual couples for "marital discord." The multimodal principles involved are the same.

In recent years, the bulk of my practice has consisted of married couples seeking help for their unhappy relationships. The majority have requested therapy *as a couple,* but, in several cases, one partner entered individual therapy that changed to marriage therapy when the *interpersonal modality* revealed significant dyadic problems. The usual course of multimodal marriage therapy starts with an initial interview in which the couple is seen together and the main presenting problems are discussed. Each partner is given a Life History Questionnaire (Appendix 1) to take home and to fill out independently. An individual session is then arranged with each one for the purpose of examining the completed questionnaire and constructing an initial Modality Profile. Thereafter, the treatment processes are tailored to the individuals and their unique dyadic requirements.

Throughout this book I have emphasized the virtues of flexibility and versatility in meeting the idiosyncratic needs of diverse individuals. These are no less apparent in marriage therapy, which meets an extremely wide range of different needs, lifestyles, habits, and conjugal practices. Therapists must take special care not to impose their own metaphors, or to rely on their personal views or images of marital bliss as a basis for determining the viability of other peoples' marriages. For example, one of my trainees, a feminist with a thorough conviction that nonegalitarian relationships were doomed to failure, could not conceive of a successful marriage in which one partner (especially the wife) was subservient. On the other hand, I have heard male colleagues voice the idea that any man married to a dominant woman lives with constant castration anxiety. In fact, some men appear to thrive in a relationship in which the woman is clearly in charge. Conversely, there are women who blossom and grow in a relationship with a man whom they can admire, respect, and serve. The therapist's task is not to project his or her prejudices but to find out exactly what will best suit a given dyad.

Marriage therapy requires the clinician to design and monitor three programs simultaneously—one for each individual and one for the partnership. This formidable task is rendered fairly straightforward by the construction of Modality Profiles, as the following case illustrates.

The Case of Mr. and Mrs. R: From Combat to Caring

When Mrs. R telephoned for an initial appointment she said, "Frankly, I think we should be seeing a lawyer, but I'm willing to give my husband one final chance." Mr. and Mrs. R were 38 and 34 years old, respectively. He worked as a building contractor, and she taught high school arts and crafts. They were both large, overweight, and extremely loud individuals. In the first minutes of our initial meeting, Mr. R proceeded to impugn the entire profession of psychotherapy and became personally insulting. Mrs. R then started screaming at her husband in my defense. To disrupt their initial game and break the triangulation I said: "You two really are a gruesome twosome! I take it we're doing divorce counseling and not marriage therapy."[1] The moment of refreshing silence was soon shattered by Mrs. R, who proceeded to yell at Mr. R to the following effect: "I've wanted to get the hell out of this marriage for years and you know it! We're wasting time and money here. Maybe Dr. Lazarus can steer us to a good matrimonial lawyer." Mr. R slouched down in his chair looking very uncomfortable and quietly murmured, "Oh, sure. Yes dearie. Uh, huh. Sure thing." Mrs. R's tone escalated. "I'm not joking. I'm dead serious. I don't need you in my life." Mr. R regained his strident voice and said, "Look how well off your friend Phyllis is. And how about Evelyn?" Turning to me, Mr. R added, "She thinks that men will be lining up for her; that she'd soon be married to a foreign prince who would take her away from all this." Mrs. R's fury grew more compelling. "I've told you a hundred times that I'd never want to marry

---

[1]When I am attacked by one or both partners in the first session, I have found it helpful to adopt a tough-minded and strongly nonsentimental position. Combative couples tend to regard the therapist's empathic reflection as weakness.

again. Once has been enough to last me a lifetime." I looked at Mrs. R and said, "I gather you've played this let's-get-divorced game many times." She replied, "What did I tell you on the phone?" I answered, "You said that you thought that a good divorce lawyer is what you need." Looking at Mr. R, I added, "Perhaps she's right," whereupon he launched into a filibustering excursion into his wife's unreasonableness.

In searching for positive features, I came up with the fact that each acknowledged that the other was a loving and devoted parent and that their three children constituted a nucleus of caring and binding attention. On the Marital Satisfaction Questionnaire (See Appendix 3) Mr. R scored 58 "satisfaction points" out of a possible 120, and Mrs. R scored only 51. (I have found that a score of 60 or less signifies a poor level of marital satisfaction.) Yet it was evident that despite Mrs. R's threats and protestations, neither one of them desired a divorce. Mr. R was clearly threatened by the idea, and Mrs. R tended to retract when she felt that she had gone too far. Notwithstanding the degree of turbulence and their low marital-satisfaction scores, I felt that they had a potentially workable marriage if most of the negative games and collisions could be excised. I shared this impression with the couple in more or less the following words: "I'm no sentimental slob who sees marriage as a sacred entity that must be preserved for its own sake. Quite the contrary. I do not hesitate to urge a split-up of marriages that, in my professional judgment, cannot enhance the happiness of the respective partners. In your case, despite some very rough edges, it is my view that the marriage is worth saving. Let me add, nonetheless, that if you disagree with me and really want out, I will be glad to help you achieve an amicable divorce." My speech won over the formerly hostile Mr. R, whose antagonism was based on a fear that I would destroy his marriage. Mrs. R softly and approvingly asked, "Do you really think we can make it?"

Mr. R resisted completing the Life History Questionnaire, but he became fairly diligent when I hinted that his lack of cooperation might lead me to reconsider the viability of their marriage. Mr. and Mrs. R were each seen individually on two occasions before I felt that I had gained sufficient information to construct Modality Profiles. In essence, Mr. R, although generous with money and material belongings, had little idea about emotional togetherness or intimate sharing. He was basically insecure and had images of abandonment that were tied to notions of maternal rejection. (His mother had walked out on his father when Mr. R was 12 years old.) He used food as a healing balm, which, in turn, aggravated his poor body image. He had acquaintances but no friends, and his interpersonal skills were limited to the men who worked for him and with whom he enjoyed good rapport.

Mrs. R was raised in a household in which both her parents were artists and lived in relative poverty. A woman given to violent temper tantrums and depressive moods, she admired and welcomed Mr. R's financial earning abilities but had images of making love to "artists, writers, musicians, and intellectuals." She had had a brief affair with one of the educators in her community but was so consumed by guilt and anxiety that she developed persistent gastrointestinal disorders during this period.[2] She had a few close friends with whom she socialized and played tennis and bridge.

At this juncture, vague and general indications had been gleaned regarding their personal and interpersonal dissatisfactions. By perusing their Life History Questionnaires and constructing Modality Profiles, would a clear-cut treatment regimen become evident?

Modality Profiles

	MR. R	MRS. R
Behavior	Increase exercise and leisure activities	Decrease shouting and attacking
	Reduce overeating	Increase amount of praise and compliments given to husband
	Increase amount of pleasant and relaxed time with wife	Stop using sex as a weapon
Affect	Anxiety (uses anger as a cover-up)	Hostility (a cry for help); depressed from time to time
Sensation	Uses fatigue and tension to avoid obligations	Very concerned with artistic delights— a visual person
	Does not appreciate	Enjoys vigorous exercise

[2]Some therapists consider it unwise to keep confidences of this kind. They appear to have a compulsion to confess and urge their clients to tell their partners about any acts of infidelity. I have seen enormous harm emanate from this "compulsive confession."

	art but very visual re buildings and architecture	
	Limited sensual and sexual awareness	Limited sensual and sexual awareness
Imagery	Themes of maternal rejection	Romantic fantasies
	Poor self-image (overweight)	Fantasies of being a famous artist
Cognition	Stereotyped thinking— rigid ideas about what a wife should be and do, the duties of a mother, the role of a successful contractor	A tendency to confuse husband and father roles—a strong belief in being pampered
Interpersonal	No friends, no confidants	Has close friends and confidants
	Unable to deal with wife except by withdrawing or attacking	Uses moods and temper tantrums to control husband
Drugs	Need for better nutrition	Wishes to quit smoking

After a discussion of these detailed Modality Profiles, the couple elected to begin dealing with three specific and clear-cut goals: (1) to find activities they could pursue together, (2) to improve their sexual functioning, and (3) to overcome their cognitive discrepancies and differing expectancies. Merely showing the couple the tentative and preliminary profiles afforded an opportunity to open some constructive channels of communication. For example, Mr. R said, "It is hard to pamper someone when they are yelling at you," whereupon Mrs. R burst into tears and Mr. R became very solicitous. It is assumed that increasing the observable range, frequency, and duration of a positive balance within a marriage, will deepen subjective satisfaction and mutual affection. The amplification of desirable and rewarding behaviors tends to undercut such processes as undue competition, power struggles, and other aspects of coercive control. The fundamental purpose of marriage therapy is to promote greater happiness and less pain from the married state.

Initially, the conjoint sessions followed a repetitive pattern. Mrs. R was the accuser, the attacker, and Mr. R defended his position, then grew angry and counterattacked. The use of simple homilies often proves helpful. Thus, I handed them three copies of a typed page with the heading "Seven Basic Ground Rules," under which the following instructions appeared:

1. Never criticize a person; only criticize a specific aspect of his/her behavior.
2. Don't mind-rape (i.e., do not tell the other person what he/she is thinking or feeling).
3. Avoid saying, "You always . . . ," or "You never. . . ." Be specific.
4. Avoid right-wrong, good-bad categories. When differences arise look for compromises.
5. Use "I feel" messages instead of "You are" messages. For example, say, "I feel hurt when you ignore me!" but do not say, "You are selfish and inconsiderate for ignoring me."
6. Be direct and honest. Say what you mean, mean what you say.
7. I'm okay, you're okay. I count, you count.

After discussing each item, I gave one list to Mr. R for his wallet, one to Mrs. R for her purse, and one to be placed on their refrigerator door at home.

They complained that it was virtually impossible for them to have any discussion without almost coming to blows. On some occasions Mrs. R had slapped, kicked, bitten, and punched Mr. R, and once or twice he had retaliated in kind. Consequently, I instructed them in the use of *time-limited intercommunication* (See Appendix 2) and advised them to practice it at least three times per week. I also arranged to see Mr. and Mrs. R separately for a few sessions. I wanted to train Mr. R to hear his wife's anger as a signal of pain, and, through role-playing, I hoped to enable him to develop a range of emotionally supportive statements and nondefensive reactions. I wanted to ascertain the full extent of Mrs. R's depressive affect (and decided against referring her for antidepressant medication, as she seemed to have no explicit affective disorder, showed none of the stigmata of a biological involvement, and was opposed to drugs). I also spent several sessions conducting *assertiveness training* to modify her aggressive outbursts. Here is a typical, verbatim therapeutic interchange:

T: Let's take the scene where it is that Sunday when you have been rushing around. You are harried, exhausted, and strung out from having done all sorts of things. You have served. . . .

C: Oh, yes, I had a great big breakfast to serve.

T: Right, you served the breakfast. . . .

C: And I cleaned up, and I just finished cleaning up from the night before.

T: Right, you've been extremely busy.

C: And I've been at Quakerbridge Mall!

T: Right. You've gone to the mall and you've done all those wifely and motherly chores and you feel rather put upon. Now you come home and what does your husband say?

C: That this Bob from one of the architect's offices is bringing this kid over to meet our oldest daughter.

T: And your feeling about that is?

C: My feeling is, Jesus Christ, I mean, you know, he's enhancing his self-image. He's going to use this kid to curry favor with the architect. I mean why lay it on me at 7:30 on Sunday night when I've just walked into the door at 6:15. I'm tired, I just dropped ninety million hundred dollars, which, you know, that fries my ass, and the mall stunk, and I was pushed around by peasants, and I'm annoyed, and the dinner hasn't been started yet—nobody set the table, I mean, God forbid anyone would think of doing anything like that—and he lays this on me!

T: Now, you know, if you came across this way, that would be an aggressive reaction likely to produce a defensive response in him. In other words, if you said "Jesus Christ! Why the hell are you laying this on me, blah, blah, blah. . . ."

C: I didn't say that!

T: I know that. . . .

C: I tried to be relaxed. . . .

T: I'm just making the point that if you had said that, it wouldn't have been too productive. I want to role-play the assertive you and I want you to be your husband. Okay? I'm you now.

C: All right.

T: (role-playing) Ah! You know dear, I'm feeling so put upon that I really wish I didn't have this extra task to perform right now. I sort of really feel strung out.

C: (role-playing) Well, I don't know why you feel like that. For Christ sake, what have you done all day? You know, I took care of Peter at the train, and all you had to do was go to Quakerbridge Mall and you bought Michael some stuff, you know, what the hell?

T: (role-playing) Let me tell you something. You know, when you put it that way, I really feel put down and minimized. I strongly feel that you are giving me a message that I don't count, particularly when you imply that I have done nothing all day. I'm sure you realize that I've had a very busy day.

C: (role-playing) But you're supposed to do these things. You're a mother. You've got to grow up and accept the fact that when Michael is home and he wants to get some stuff, that's your job. You're a mother.

T: (role-playing) I feel that what you are now doing is lecturing to me and you are really missing my feelings, that somehow you are not attending to the message I'm giving you. I'm trying to convey the way I feel right now, which is that I've done all my motherly duties, I haven't shirked any of them, nor do I ever think I do, but nevertheless I am feeling resentful and put upon.

C: (role-playing) You shouldn't feel that way. It's just that this is a chaotic period. I mean, I'm tired, I've got all that crap at the office. I mean, you know about Dave's insurance exam and all that stuff and the added pressures on me, and I mean, you know, we're all under pressure. So, I mean, you'd make it easier if you just wouldn't say anything about it.

T: (role-playing) You know, when you say I shouldn't feel the way I do happen to feel, and you tell me that you're also under pressure, as though that's going to make me feel less under pressure, that isn't very helpful. Do you know what would be really helpful? If you would have said to me: "Honey, I know that it's been a tough day for you, and you do cope superbly, and I'm sorry to add this extra burden, and what can I do to make it up to you? I feel that I owe you a special favor. You'll be doing this for me and it has been a tough day and I truly appreciate it. If you could talk to me that way, boy, I would probably polish your shoes for you and smile about it."

C: (pause) I don't know what he'd say. (laughs) I have no idea.

T: But, you see, what I'm getting at here now is very very important. Observe this special component. You not only delivered the feeling message, which is part of your assertiveness, but when your partner did not respond the way you wanted him to, you told him how you would like or wish him to respond in the future.

C: In other words, you're leading him almost.

T: Right. You are saying, "Boy if you had only said this, or if you had expressed it this way, I would be able to hear you and then I would be more than willing to cooperate. But when you give me this, 'Come on, it's only your duty as a mother,' or when you give me this, 'I've also got plenty of pressure,' or when you hand me this, 'What the hell do you do with your time all day?' I can't put my head in a good place. And if you want me to come to you from a good place, this is what you would need to say." So you've clued him in.

C: I see. Uh, well, I'll really have to do that. . . .

T: Well, let's reverse roles now. This time, let me act like your husband, and you try to handle me assertively, not aggressively. . . .

A most useful tactic in the treatment of Mr. and Mrs. R was what Palazzoli, Cecchin, Prata, and Boscolo (1978) call the *principle of positive connotation*. When using this strategy one endeavors to find a positive or benevolent reason for *all* behaviors. In examining Mr. and Mrs. R's respective cognitive and imagery modalities, it was evident that they both heavily invested in the belief that, at base, they were each very fine human beings. Thus, when they would sabotage the dialoguing exercises or undermine any other aspect of the therapy, I would say, "Let us search for the benevolent reason behind this action. I have come to the realization that when either of you resorts to seemingly nasty or uncooperative behavior, it is because of a good but misguided intention." This therapeutic double-bind (Watzlawick, 1978) seemed to elicit their full cooperation when we introduced sensate focus exercises to improve their sexual functioning (Masters & Johnson, 1970), and also when we discussed specific activities and interests that they could follow together.

Finally, a most helpful realization that arose out of their regular time-limited intercommunication was that they each tended to misinterpret the other's nonverbal cues. I stressed: *"Just because a person appears to be sad, or angry, or tired, or bored, does not mean that the person is actually feeling that way."* They were given explicit instructions to verbalize their feelings and always check out what the other person was feeling rather than leap to false conclusions.

The foregoing procedures involved Mr. and Mrs. R in twenty-seven sessions over a period of ten months—thirteen conjoint meetings, eight individual sessions with Mrs. R, and six sessions with Mr. R. Significant benefits were derived—they both stated that they had achieved a personal and sexual togetherness—and these gains are well in evidence some three and one-half years later. I have outlined the case of Mr. and Mrs. R in some detail because it typifies multimodal marital therapy. Thinking in BASIC I.D. terms tended to facilitate the identification of pivotal differences and crucial conflicts that then became the main focus of therapeutic attention. Since the couple had a sufficient emotional investment in the relationship and a strong element of caring for one another, correction of the main disturbances put them back on the track and enabled them to develop their own self-correcting and self-propelling tactics. Sager (1976) stated that "disharmony within a marriage is usually characterized by a few major issues in the relationship." As always, the multimodal approach is carefully individualized. We do not ask whether couples should be seen individually or together, whether co-therapists should be included, whether couples should be seen in groups, whether other family members should be interviewed; we ask only when and whether any or all of these strategies will prove useful in a given case. In my opinion, general questions are irrelevant. Is marital therapy in a group superior to conjoint therapy? We would better ask, When and for whom is marital group therapy better than conjoint therapy? Thus, Gurman (1973), in comparing the improvement rates for a wide array of approaches to marital therapy, found no evidence that co-therapists obtained better outcomes than single therapists. We would rather ask: "Under what circumstances do co-therapists obtain better results?" With some couples I have worked with, the wife has explicitly requested the presence of a female co-therapist. In other cases, I have suggested eliciting the aid of a co-therapist when progress was faltering. Many years ago, Allport (1937) stressed that in the psychological field there is no "generalized mind," but that "there are only single, concrete minds, each one of which presents problems peculiar to itself."

Several couples whom I have taught to track the sequential firing order of specific modalities (Chapter 5) have found it particularly effective in achieving a deeper understanding of one another. One woman reported: "When John was in a bad mood I used to take it personally. Now I ask him to share his thoughts and mental pictures. . . . You are so right that he starts upsetting himself by thinking negative thoughts and by picturing horrible events which make him uptight and put him in a bad mood. Now I am able to help him break the cycle, and he can do the same for me when I feel one of my headaches coming on." Similarly, a couple who had complained of "Communication barriers" told me that the BASIC I.D. format provided them with a most productive vehicle for sustaining relevant and satisfying conversations. "Before we came to you, we often ran out of conversation. I might have expressed an idea to Mildred or she may have shared a feeling with me and we would each acknowledge the other's remarks and let it go at that. Now, when we tell each other something, and we really want to explore it together, we talk about all the behaviors and feelings and the thoughts and images, and we really end up understanding ourselves and one another."[3]

Contracts and Other Tactics

Marriage therapists, no less than individual therapists, are most effective when they are equipped with a range of methods, from mechanical tricks to phenomenological profundities. Some couples respond well to the use of specific rewards. For example, spouses may give each other differently colored poker chips to signify pleasure or displeasure in response to specific actions (Stuart, 1969). If a spouse is especially pleased with something his or her partner does, a red chip may be given as a token of esteem. A yellow chip might signify somewhat less approval, and a blue chip would denote disapproval or displeasure. Every 48 hours, or perhaps at the end of the week, the partners tally up their chips. A predominance of red and yellow tokens can then be traded for some significant reward (e.g., a special treat out on the town, an extravagant picnic lunch, etc.), whereas a predominance of blue chips would call for reparative consequences (e.g., attending to household duties, having further therapy sessions, etc.). Many people find these mechanical procedures offensive, but I have worked with couples who found them most useful. As mentioned in Chapter 8, one way of determining whether to employ a particular strategy is to outline it first to the clients.

In some couples one or both partners may be strongly opposed to any form of contracting. "Entering into an *agreement,*" one husband asserted, "is necessary and understandable, but *contracts* are intended for strangers, not lovers." A woman lawyer said, "A firm contract with rewards and consequences is essential for business deals but hardly belongs in a marriage. . . . It takes the concept of 'partnership' away from love and caring and places it in a coolie

---

[3]Peterson's (1977, 1979) work also ties in well with the multimodal approach. He has developed and validated an extensive multidimensional method of identifying meaningful response units that characterize interpersonal, especially marital, interactions. He examines overt behavior as well as cognitive-verbal and affective components.

market." In my view, the explicit use of contracts within a marriage won't solve basic problems but it can be a vehicle for setting a benevolent response pattern in motion, after which more fundamental issues may be addressed. To specify when the dishes are to be done and by whom will not begin to remedy a problem that rests on an absence of basic trust, but these picayune details can sometimes serve as useful starting points for cooperative interaction. Basically, I agree with Postman (1976), who asks, "Can anyone plausibly imagine an overburdened wife, having failed to persuade her husband that she needs his help, pulling out a contract from the bureau drawer and insisting he live up to its terms, on pain of legal sanctions? This is not marriage; it is the end of marriage."

When drawing up contracts, it is generally better to aim for an increase in positive behaviors rather than for reductions in undesirable behaviors (Weiss, 1978). We want to eliminate coercive control and other aversive strategies and emphasize instead the virtues of positive reinforcement in interpersonal dealings. "All too often, distressed spouses are quite skilled in punishing each other for the occurrence of undesirable behaviors" (O'Leary & Turkewitz, 1978). Many marital contracts are based on a *quid pro quo* (Jackson, 1965), which means "something for something," or, "I will try to please you since you are trying to please me" (e.g., Azrin, Naster & Jones, 1973; Liberman, Wheeler & Sanders, 1976). This results in a positive trade-off: (1) "If Mike hangs up all his clothes and cuts the grass, Liz will pay the household bills and wash the car," or (2) "If Liz pays the household bills and washes the car, Mike will hang up all of his clothes and cut the grass." Of course, couples can easily sabotage these trade-offs. "You go first!" is the most common subversion.

Unlike the marital quid pro quo, the "good faith" contract (Weiss, Hops & Patterson, 1973) results in a reward that is independent of the spouse's behavior. "If Mike hangs up all his clothes and cuts the grass, he is entitled to watch football on television for six hours." "If Liz pays the household bills and washes the car, she is entitled to go out and play cards." There is evidence to suggest that when treating hostile couples, the "good faith" procedure is often more effective than the quid pro quo. Knox (1973) combined both of these procedures, applying the good faith contract first, and then introducing quid pro quo agreements when positive changes had accrued.

I concur with O'Leary and Turkewitz (1978) that *contracts for sexual behavior are usually ill-advised.* To demand sexual intercourse on the basis of an obligation is likely to arouse resentment. Many people find sexual interchanges highly unpleasant in the absence of positive emotions. "If John sweeps the garage Mary will go to bed with him," can prove positive only if Mary *wants* to have sex with John. If a spouse is asking for more frequent sex from his or her partner, the therapist's task is to identify specific changes in behavior that would occasion the other spouse to desire more frequent sex.

Numerous tactics can prove effective in marital therapy. For example, for many years, I have made use of *prescribed dinners.* "I want you to set aside one evening per week in which you go out for dinner —just the two of you. It need not be anything lavish, a simple diner or hamburger house will do. The point is that you are to view it as a regular appointment, as a definite commitment. You have to have an extremely valid reason to cancel or postpone any prescribed dinners. Over dinner, I want you to imagine that you are out on a date, or that you are in the midst of courtship. Thus, you will try to be as pleasant, and as stimulating, as possible. This is not the place for quarreling or for discussing problems. It is a time for mutual enjoyment and support." This tactic is especially good for busy professional couples whose marital discord stems primarily from the fact that they are both too busy to spend much time together.

Another useful technique is what Stuart (1976; 1980) refers to as "Caring Days." Special days are set aside for a spouse to make a strenuous effort to please his/her partner by engaging in particular behaviors that the partner desires. In some couples this tends to facilitate the development of positive and loving feelings. The majority of the techniques outlined in Appendix 2 can be incorporated into multimodal marriage therapy. Among the most frequently used methods are: behavior-rehearsal, modeling, positive reinforcement, nonreinforcement, recording and self-monitoring, feeling-identification, relaxation training, correcting misconceptions, social skills and assertiveness training, contingency contracting, time-limited intercommunication, paradoxical strategies, communication training. (See Appendix 2 for a description of these techniques.) When sexual problems are present, the following techniques are of particular value: systematic exposure, threshold training (for rapid ejaculation), sexual awareness training, and graded sexual approaches (see Chapter 10).

Questions of Compatibility

As reported elsewhere (Lazarus, 1981) I have treated couples who achieved reciprocity in place of coercion; whose feuding and hostilities gave way to discussion, arbitration, and fairplay; but who nevertheless ended up getting divorced. Some people can learn to handle their disagreements maturely and sensibly, follow egalitarian principles, and thus develop a well-functioning partnership, but not a satisfying marriage. Despite the presence of interpersonal harmony, they can feel desperately alone. I was once of the opinion that almost any two people could achieve marital happiness if they adhered to basic ground rules (such as, not labeling, blaming, judging, accusing, faultfinding, demanding, ignoring, or attacking, and instead praising, listening, discussing, thanking, helping, and forgiving). I have come to appreciate the fact that a friendly coexistence is not the same as a worthwhile marriage. This requires more than teamwork, common goals, and respectful dealings. At the very least we would add strong affection, attraction, caring, and some consensus in matters of taste and interest.

I have seen many dysfunctional marriages whose partners needed no training in social skills, communication skills, contracting, or in such commonplace activities as parenting, household management, and so on. Many people know exactly how to get along well if they so choose. I have often met with couples locked in internecine combat—employing coercive tactics, destructive double-binds, negative reinforcement, aversive stimuli, character-assassination, and other negative behaviors—who were fully aware that their ad hominem assaults, insults, and snide and vicious innuendos were undermining their relationship. Moreover, individual explorations of their interpersonal modalities revealed that they possessed the necessary skills and wherewithal to implement positive interactions. Many of these problems arose from minor skirmishes that grew out of hand. False pride entered the picture, followed by specific fears and anxieties replete with defensive reactions. If the situation had escalated to the point where BASIC I.D. analyses revealed a distinct absence of affection and caring, *divorce therapy* (Kressel & Deutsch, 1977; Lazarus, 1981) was suggested. Here, the goal is to minimize the pains of separation, and to achieve an amicable and constructive parting, especially where the protection and welfare of minor children is involved.

Paradoxically, by suggesting "divorce therapy," one quite often rekindles the couples' motivation to resuscitate the marriage. In this regard, the following procedure has both diagnostic and therapeutic value. The couple is asked: "If you were informed that somebody you love very much will be tortured and killed unless the two of you treat each other with love, kindness, understanding, consideration, and caring for an entire month, could you guarantee that no harm would befall the person you love? You will be placed under 24-hour surveillance by means of television monitors. A single nasty comment, the slightest display of antagonism, and down come the monitors, the experiment is over, and the person you love is painfully put to death. Now, tell me, what are his or her chances of survival? Under these circumstances, could you achieve one month of unremitting love and kindness?"

Where one or both partners indicate that the survival of their loved one would be in great jeopardy, the process of marriage therapy is often uphill. Those who unequivocally guarantee the safety of the beloved individual are requested to role-play the situation for a week (i.e., to imagine that they are under surveillance and that the welfare of a loved one rests on their capacity to display nothing but positive behaviors) and to report their achievements at the next session. This tactic often sets off a constructive chain reaction and permits the therapy to examine issues that are less prosaic than back-rubs, eye-contact, positive feedback, and active listening. The use of *Structural Profiles* (see Chapter 4)—in which the couple is asked to rate (on a scale from 1 to 10) the extent to which they perceive themselves as active, emotional, sensual, imaginative, intellectual, people-oriented, and health-minded—provides the impetus for constructive explorations of similarities and differences. The extent to which the marriage between a highly active, independent, and intellectual woman and a passive, dependent, and emotional man (or vice versa) represents a complementary and satisfying marital unit, or reflects a distinctly incompatible liaison, requires a qualitative analysis across the seven modalities. How is this done?

When I interview each spouse separately (usually as a prelude to conjoint therapy) I ask them to describe the interactions they would especially like to see across the BASIC I.D. "What are the things you would want to do together and the activities you would prefer to pursue separately? Apart from love, what other feelings would you want to have expressed? What sensual and sensory pleasures would you wish to give and receive? What pictures or images come to mind when I say the words 'excellent marriage?' What sorts of values, attitudes, and beliefs do you think well-matched couples are inclined to share? Basically, what do you want from your spouse and what would you like to give to your spouse?" These questions evoke many associated responses that furnish the opportunity for an excursion into some fundamental issues. Following Sager (1976), one emerges with a relatively clear indication of the extent to which each partner desires close companionship or respectful distance, and how romantic, parental, and childlike expectancies influence various interactions. These implicit expectations, when violated, often express themselves in more obvious clashes pertaining to money, child-rearing, sex, friendships, and overall lifestyle. Behavioral contracts that address only these secondary issues are unlikely to achieve their objectives. In Berne's (1972) vernacular, crossed transactions tend to spell marital trouble. The goal here is to achieve complementary transactions. Thus, problems are likely to ensue if a husband desires parenting from his wife while she wishes him to pamper her in much the same way as her own father used to treat her. In these instances, contracts can be arranged for each partner to take preset turns to enact these roles. Everyone enters marriage with implicit expectations. By making these expectations quite explicit, it is possible to examine the viability of the relationship. In this connection, the use of Modality Profiles, second-order Profiles and the other tactics described in Chapters 4 and 5 prove highly effective.

The term "marital dysfunction" is, of course, extremely broad. A couple whose main bone of contention is the pathological jealousy of one spouse over the alleged infidelity of the other, poses entirely different therapeutic challenges from a couple whose disagreements center around matters of child-rearing. Marital distress that is occasioned by sexual problems is quite different from that which reflects parental interference. And newlyweds present problems different from those who have been married more than twenty or thirty years. Again, we would ask the reader to determine whether the adoption of a multimodal framework facilitates his or her treatment. Is there added value in thinking in BASIC I.D. terms, constructing Modality Profiles, using second-order BASIC I.D. Profiles when necessary, tracking interactive effects and arriving at Sequential Firing Orders, and tuning in to the client's preferred modalities?

Steinglass (1978) has drawn an interesting fictitious scenario. First, a couple visits Murray Bowen, who, among other interventions, instructs them to talk only one at a time and only to him. Next, they consult Salvador Minuchin, who demands that they talk only to each other. Next they see a master trained by the late Don Jackson, who delivers a paradoxical injunction for them to fight regularly and to talk civilly to each other only on Sundays. Steinglass's point is that, although all three masters are bona fide members of the systems-theory perspective, their views and practices are widely divergent. My point is that there are far too many therapists—masters and novices alike—who impose their theories on their clients and inflict incorrect and unsuitable techniques on them. May we enter yet another plea for therapists to stop fitting the patient to the treatment?

Shared Intimacy versus Intimate Sharing

Many people in our culture enter marriage with romantic and idealistic notions that are distorted beyond any semblance of reality. When the ecstatic passions of infatuation are expected to form the basis of enduring affection, the divorce court looms around the corner. The everyday contact of married life soon puts an end to the extravagant expectations of romantic dreams, which have no place for the inevitable processes of adjustment and readjustment that marriage demands. Successful marriages are those whose partners, over time, have built up a common pool of habits and experiences without stifling one another's essential differences.

Many people contend that marriage is a relationship that carries the principles of friendship to its ultimate and most intimate degree. In my view, the structure of marriage overlaps with friendship but is not synonymous with it. Many an excellent premarital and extramarital friendship has come to grief soon after the parties married. The structure of marriage imposes a set of statuses, roles, and expectations that transcends the boundaries of pure friendship. Furthermore, when people marry or live together, there is a reality-based and unromantic process of *habit-building* that takes place—food and eating, grooming and dressing, sleeping and waking, work and leisure, companionship and solitude. These and innumerable other individual and common needs and wishes call for synchronization and negotiation.

Basically, marriage is intimate sharing, whereas friendship is shared intimacy. Friends typically are not expected to live under the same roof year in and year out. Their shared intimacies are intensive rather than extensive. Marriage involves the sharing of many daily events in which the "feeling tone" of one partner has a direct effect on the other. Consequently, it is easy to overload the system. Moreover, the focus of marriage usually ends up being family-centered, whereas in friendship the investment is mainly between the two people. Given the burdens that marriage imposes on the relationship, some emotional privacy seems essential. Many a couple has expressed bewilderment at how distant they have grown. "We were each other's best friends. We went from A to Z. We told one another everything and we tried to share everything. We held nothing back." Marriage is not ownership! Most people are likely to feel oppressed by too much togetherness, especially when each partner's individuality, emotional privacy, and freedom of psychological and physical movement is not built into the relationship. One of the primary goals in marriage therapy is to help each couple achieve a satisfactory balance between independence and togetherness. As mentioned elsewhere (Lazarus, 1971), when discussing these issues with clients, the following simple diagrams have proved useful.

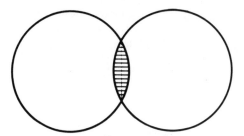

This depicts a poor marriage relationship. There is very little togetherness or common ground.

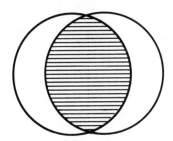

This depicts an excellent marriage. There is about 80 percent togetherness but also sufficient separateness to permit individual growth and essential privacy.

This represents the romantic ideal
where two people merge so completely that they become as one. In
practice, were this possible, it would
probably result in emotional suffoca-
tion.

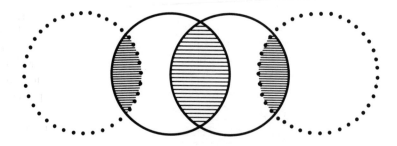

Here is a reasonably good marriage
in which each partner has an independent interest or relationship
which in no way interferes with or
threatens the marriage as it occupies
only each other's own individual territory.

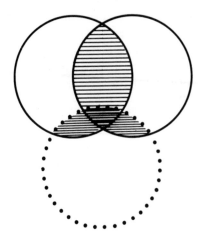

In this figure, one of the partners has an interest or relationship which not only occupies some of his or her own territory but which also intrudes into their (the marriage) territory as well as encroaching upon the other partner's individual zone.

Apart from indications of an unhealthy balance (insufficient freedom or insufficient togetherness) that may be gleaned from the Life History Questionnaire, conjoint interviews, and the Modality Profiles, the Marital Satisfaction Questionnaire (Appendix 3) affords an opportunity to examine these factors. Each item on the questionnaire is discussed with the couple. Items 1, 2, 3, 4, and 8 are especially relevant to this area of concern. When it appears that the couple tends to "live in each other's pockets," the most logical intervention is the opposite of the prescribed dinners that were mentioned for couples who do not share sufficient time together. By deliberately fostering some independent interests—a separate hobby, sport, or other activity—without creating a threatening distance between them, many couples who previously felt cloistered and confined within their marriage have achieved a satisfying modus vivendi.

A case in point concerned a female writer-poet and a male scientist, whose marriage had grown more and more turbulent over the years. Their obvious skirmishes were readily overcome, but a lingering dissatisfaction continued to undermine the relationship. Closer examination of their situation revealed that, whereas the husband did all his work away from home and regarded their house as a place in which to relax and be entertained (after doing his share of household chores), the wife demanded periods of uninterrupted privacy when she could do some creative writing. Her husband and two teenage children were unable or unwilling to honor her request—at least to the extent she deemed necessary. "All I'm asking for," she said, "is one night per week of uninterrupted work time." I made a simple recommendation. "Why not rent and furnish a one-room studio where you can go and work one night per week without interruption?" She replied, "I wouldn't have to go that far. I could work at the local library, but the point is that I feel guilty when leaving my husband and kids in the evening." This self-imposed psychological restraint was, of course, tacitly reinforced by her husband. I convinced the couple that one evening per week of independent "library work" was a sine qua non for their continued marital adjustment. Its implementation effected a significant improvement. (The therapist as a *permission-giver* is an essential role in many aspects of psychotherapy.)

In marriage, it is all too easy for one partner to encroach on the emotional territory of the other. Nondirective marriage counseling, in which the counselor merely reflects the sentiments of each partner, is probably the least likely way of enabling couples to orchestrate and negotiate a successful marriage. We concur with Guerney (1977) that we "have reached a state of sophistication that makes it feasible to offer the general public a real opportunity to acquire much useful information and many valuable life skills to aid realistic perception; rational thinking; sensible ways of dealing with emotions and with other people; ways of eliminating or reducing the harmful effects of many conflicts, frustrations, and derogations of self and others; and ways of increasing individual fulfillment and interpersonal harmony."

Chapter 10

Multimodal Sex Therapy

Sex therapy as a specialty is a phenomenon of the 1970s and seems to have been initiated by Masters and Johnson's publication of *Human Sexual Inadequacy* (1970). This was by no means the first book to stress the superiority of brief, directive counseling aimed at focal sexual problems, to insight therapies. Nevertheless, Masters and Johnson provided enough clinical and procedural details, as well as sufficient data on the effectiveness of direct sex therapy, to have gained widespread acceptance. At this juncture, clinicians are beginning to discover problems with this approach. Lief (1980), apart from referring to "the outright quacks who have invaded the field," has emphasized that: "A sex therapist is a psychotherapist. And a competent sex therapist must be able to use a variety of therapeutic approaches and from among these to choose methods of intervention that fit the special and often unique circumstances found in a given clinical situation." Leiblum and Pervin (1980) echo sentiments that we have espoused for many years: "The task of the future is to determine which techniques and approaches work with which kind of person and when."

In my opinion, there are three major shortcomings in Masters and Johnson's approach:

1. It is needlessly rigid. Masters and Johnson insist on treating couples exclusively and, then, only with a male-female treatment team. In my experience, some couples do far better when treated by one therapist, and some clients show better clinical progress when seen in individual therapy.

2. Minimal attention is devoted to the imagery modality. While Masters and Johnson cover biological and sensory factors most

187

thoroughly, and also attend to behavioral, affective, and interpersonal processes, they do not explore the clients' images and fantasies to the extent that this is often necessary.

3. The time constraint in their approach leads to inadvertent performance demands on the clients. Several clients who failed to respond to time-limited sex therapy have told me that despite the therapists' emphasis upon relaxed, nondemanding, nonperformance-oriented transactions, the knowledge that they had two weeks in which to show improvement served as an omnipresent threat and undermined the therapy. (For a detailed critique of the many shortcomings in Masters and Johnson's approach, the article by Zilbergeld and Evans [1980] is extremely incisive. Also see the stinging indictment of Masters and Johnson by Szasz, 1980.)

As emphasized throughout this book, a multimodal approach asks essentially: (1) What are the specific and interrelated problems? (2) Who or what is maintaining these problems? (3) What appears to be the best way in each individual instance of remedying these problems? These same questions are asked in all multidimensional treatment orientations, but the *multimodal* approach offers a systematic structure that ensures thoroughness and also provides specific methods for identifying idiosyncratic reactions.

Sexual problems are often part of a wider range of dysfunction. Couples who seek sex therapy often experience marital discord. A high degree of hostility and a low level of intimacy would render a couple more suitable for marriage therapy than for sex therapy. When one of the partners is clearly psychotic, it would often be counterproductive to proceed with sex therapy unless the florid problems can be first ameliorated by medication and any other necessary therapeutic intervention. In cases where individual psychopathology, though not of a distinctly psychotic variety, is evident, sex therapy tends to be a farce if these factors are not dealt with. Quite frequently, the couple or one of the partners enters sex therapy with hidden agendas that have nothing to do with the attainment of sexual harmony. One couple, for example, consulted me with the complaint that the wife was nonorgasmic and the husband usually failed to obtain an erection. It transpired that the wife was fully orgasmic with her lover and was in therapy solely to help her husband so that she could then leave him without feeling guilty. Divorce counseling was recommended, after which, if the husband still needed therapy, he could be seen individually. (As is so often the case, the couple obtained a divorce, the husband remarried and had no erectile difficulties with his second wife.)

This chapter is not intended as a summary or synthesis of sexual dysfunction. There are excellent books that provide the essential *how to's*—how to obtain a comprehensive sex history, how to apply sexual-assessment measures, how to use psychophysiological instruments, how to deal with male and female orgasmic difficulties, how to overcome male erectile dysfunction, and how to treat many special difficulties (e.g., LoPiccolo & LoPiccolo, 1978; Leiblum & Pervin, 1980). This chapter will emphasize the distinctive features that the multimodal orientation brings to the enterprise of effective sex therapy.

As mentioned in Chapter 9, certain sexual disorders do not require multimodal treatment. Where premature ejaculation is primarily a product of tension and low thresholds of arousal, relaxation coupled with direct threshold training (Semans, 1956) will often suffice. In problems of erectile dysfunction, many men have received enduring help by eliminating the spectator role, by assuming a relaxed, nondemanding outlook, and by avoiding any performance-oriented demands. Many preorgasmic women have become fully orgasmic by following a self-stimulation regimen (Lobitz & LoPiccolo, 1972). Other cases may involve a broader spectrum of treatment methods. Many years ago (Lazarus, 1965b) I reported the case of a sexually inadequate man who required cognitive restructuring, assertiveness training, masturbatory reconditioning, and a rather elaborate desensitization procedure along four separate hierarchies. The basic point about a multimodal assessment is that it readily distinguishes between focal problems and diffuse syndromes. Later on in this chapter we will be discussing several problem-identification procedures that enable the clinician to determine when to dwell on specific sexual problems and when to address associated anxieties, guilts, relationship factors, and even more subtle elements, such as feelings of personal vulnerability and the right to pleasure.

The Meaning of Sexual Intimacy

The "sexual drive" and its expression may be likened to the "hunger drive" and its ramifications. Despite some obvious differences, these basic "appetites" are stimulated by complex central and peripheral physiological processes. Both show wide individual differences in taste and appeal which, in turn, are a function of past experience and cultural conditioning. At the physiological level, there is nothing refined about the need to ingest various substances to sustain life, just as on the purely physical plane, neither love nor romance enters in to a desire to propagate the species. The hurried ingestion of an ill-cooked meal serves the same *physiological* purposes as the gourmet's epicurian preparation and elegant presentation of delicious cuisine. In matters pertaining to hunger and sex, a continuum extends from compulsive gluttony to total anorexia. And in the same way that food is often eaten for many reasons other than actual hunger or good nourishment, sex may fulfill many needs other than procreation or passion.

The analogy may be extended further. The person who refuses to eat at any place less sumptuous than a four-star restaurant, or the individual who eats nothing but meat and potatoes, exhibit a narrowness and rigidity that limits their alternatives and may undermine their health. More sensible men and women enjoy a wide range of options—they can savor the quality of a meticulously prepared dinner on some occasions and yet, at other times, will relish the food at a local pizza parlor. People who opt for balance and diversity are less likely to forego important nutritional elements (vitamins, minerals, proteins, and so on) than are those with limited or restricted dietary habits. Similarly, in matters pertaining to sex, to insist on nothing less than protracted intimacy under ideal conditions, or to adhere solely to one sexual practice or position, is bound to cause problems. Sexual frequency will be curtailed by the person who demands prolonged privacy, subdued lights, soft music, and satin sheets. Flexibility implies an ability to enjoy "four-star gourmet love-making" on some occasions, and to appreciate "local pizza parlor fare" on others. Enjoyable sex does not always have to culminate in orgasms for both partners, nor is penile-vaginal stimulation always essential. The versatile and flexible couple will settle for a "quickie" on some occasions, receive only oral or manual stimulation on others, and also be capable of indulging in the pleasures of self-stimulation.

At the biological level, sex is essentially nonaffectionate, but our psychological and sociological heritage lead us to invest sexual relations with varied meanings and values. These attitudes impede or facilitate the physiological mechanisms that subsume arousal and performance. As I have pointed out elsewhere (Lazarus, 1980) love and sex have been so inextricably linked in our culture that "making love" is a synonym for sexual intercourse. This tends to imbue the sex act with expectations or emotional preconditions. "For me, sex means love, trust, compassion, tenderness, warmth, understanding, deep concern, respect, and caring. As soon as I find someone who shows me all these qualities, I will engage in sexual intercourse." The foregoing sentiment, while somewhat exaggerated, nevertheless reflects common, fixed attitudes. "My wife wanted me to make love to her last night. How could I when only three days ago she accused me of being stingy!" "Before I let my husband make love to me I must be sure that he wants me and not just my body." These are quotes from two different couples in treatment for "desire discrepancies."

Obviously, sex can be used as a weapon, a controlling influence, an instrument of torture, a sign of love and affection, a purely physiological release, or in a myriad of other ways. To one person, sexual intimacy can mean, "I am good, I am wholesome, I am desirable, and I am lovable." To another it may signify, "I am powerful, I am in control, I am a winner and a conquerer." I have treated many couples and individuals with sexual dysfunction who had failed to respond to behavior therapy and sex therapy because their sexual images and fantasies had been inadequately explored or understood. When sexual problems stem from guilt feelings and other residua from our Puritan heritage, the correction of these misconceptions is often relatively uncomplicated. It is the more subtle doubts, meanings, and values attached to intimacy that call for detailed excursions into the imagery modality. Let us consider the case of John, 26 years old, who masturbated regularly but was unable to obtain an erection with any partner. He had seen several therapists during the previous few years. There was nothing untoward about his background—no obvious traumatic events, no undue guilts or misgivings, no apparent secondary gains. He was dating a 21-year-old woman, with whom he had had the most intimate sex play, having brought her to orgasm orally and manually on numerous occasions. He had come no closer to intercourse than having an erection on one occasion after prolonged fellation, the erection subsiding as soon as he moved into position for intromission.

John appeared to entertain certain myths about masculine prowess and performance, and I urged him to read Zilbergeld's exceptionally informative book on *Male Sexuality* (1978). In keeping with the multimodal philosophy, the most obvious therapeutic techniques were administered first—relaxation training, examination of performance anxieties, disputation of irrational beliefs, sensate focus exercises, couples training, and the exploration of possible guilt feelings. These methods all led nowhere. There was no improvement for almost two months despite a detailed exploration of his behaviors, affects, sensations, cognitions, and his relationship with his girlfriend (who made no performance demands upon him). There appeared to be no need to evaluate him medically as he regularly awoke with full erections and had no problems when masturbating (Rosen & Kopel, 1978). The imagery modality now required a thorough scrutiny.

During the initial history-taking period, John had indicated that his masturbatory fantasies were exclusively heterosexual and usually involved women he knew quite well. We proceeded to delve more deeply into his images as follows:

T: Can you recall your very first sexual memory?

C: Let me think. (pause) Well, I don't know if this is really my very first recollection, but I was around five years of age and I had an English nannie. Her name was Chrissie. Well, Chrissie was drying me after I had taken a shower and I got an erection when she was rubbing my genitals.

T: Did she say or do anything?

C: Not as I remember. In fact, I used to like Chrissie to dry me even though I was quite capable of drying myself. Sometimes when I masturbate I think of this.

T: Would you describe the scene in greater detail?

C: Oh, I merely imagine that she is rubbing my penis.

T: Do you picture yourself as a child?

C: No, well, I can't really say for sure. I'm sort of 26, but she's my nannie. It must sound crazy to you.

T: Let me stress again that nobody is in a position to call anyone's fantasies abnormal or crazy. If someone gets thrills out of fantasizing mountain goats swinging from chandeliers while a harem of Tahitian beauties fondles his genitals, or anything else imaginable, so be it. Now getting back to your fantasies. . . .

C: Well, actually, I have some weird ones. When I was about 15, I had a friend whose mother must have been about 50. She was nothing to look at, in fact she was a rather old-looking 50-year-old, a rather unattractive lady, but I used to masturbate to thoughts of sucking her breasts. And there's another thought that stands out in my mind. I was, ah, about 6 or 7, and our next door neighbor gave birth to a little girl. One day I watched her bathing the baby, after which she smeared some cream on its anus and genitals. Sometimes I imagine my friend's mother or Chrissie doing that to me, and sometimes I picture both of them doing it to me at the same time.

T: This is only during masturbation?

C: Yes.

T: Do Chrissie or your friend's mother perform any other acts?

C: Yes. (pause) Sometimes I imagine them making love to one another, and then they rub cream on me and take care of me that way.

T: Do you ever picture yourself actually having intercourse with either one of them?

C: Yes. Sometimes I am screwing Chrissie while my friend's mother rubs cream on my anus or vice versa.

T: You seem embarrassed. Is this difficult to talk about?

C: Well, it's not that. (laughs) It's given me a hard-on!

T: Well, that's understandable—these are *your fantasies.*

C: There are others mixed in there. Like one of my aunts, and an older cousin, and a woman called Jane. Now Jane was really something—she was a knockout and very, very pregnant. I was about 14 and she must have been in her thirties. We were at a swimming pool in their house, and Jane had on a black swim suit and went into the pool and as she got out of the pool, one of her breasts slipped out for a moment. Man, I'm telling you, there was something about that sleek black suit, that round belly and that smooth white breast. . . .

T: Now all these women are older than you—Chrissie, your friend's mother, your aunt, your cousin, your next door neighbor, Jane. . . .

C: No, I've never pictured myself making it with the lady next door, it was just that I saw her putting cream on her baby, that was the turn on. But, yes, they are all older, lots older.

T: Do you ever picture having sex with young girls?

C: Never.

T: Are you turned on by nude pictures or pornography?

C: I like to look at them, but I don't get erect or anything, if that's what you mean.

T: Could you or have you used nude or seminude pictures during masturbation?

C: I like to close my eyes. . . .

T: So you can attend to your fantasies?

C: That's right.

T: Well, what about your girlfriend? Do you ever masturbate to her image?

C: Well, not really. (pause) Once I imagined her watching Chrissie and me doing it.

T: Have you ever brought your mother into any of your sexual fantasies?

C: (pause) I don't know. (pause) Well, once I think I imagined myself about six months old and the lady next door was showing my mother how to bathe me and rub cream on me. Then Chrissie took over, although she didn't really start working for us until I was nearly 5.

T: A few minutes ago you said something about Chrissie and your friend's mother *taking care of you.* Your sexual fantasies all seem to involve mature women caring for babies or young children—they get bathed and dried and caressed and creamed. . . .

C: Yes, I find that very erotic, very arousing.

Further exploration of John's imagery modality strengthened the hypothesis that for him, sex was not tied into performance anxieties, or guilt feelings, or power plays, or achievement motives. Sex had a caretaker or nursemaid quality in which he was the recipient of a sort of maternal attention. Many years of masturbation to these images had reinforced their properties so that they functioned as discriminative stimuli for the elicitation of his sexual performance. He was strongly opposed to the idea of having intercourse with an older woman in actual practice, but a young, 21-year-old nubile female held little intrinsic sexual appeal for him. Would he become aroused if his girlfriend applied cream around his scrotum while he fantasized that she was Chrissie? I suggested this to John, who put it into effect, but reported no breakthrough. "One of the problems," he reported, "is that Barbara (his girlfriend) doesn't resemble Chrissie in the least." I asked whether his girlfriend resembled any of the other women. "No, not really," he concluded, whereupon I shared the following ideas with him.

Sex means different things to different people; a turn on to one person could be a distinct turn off to another. In John's case, sexual arousal was conditioned to images of certain women performing particular functions. The right "sexual chemistry" might be found with women who reminded him in some significant sense of his nursemaid, or his friend's mother, or his aunt, his cousin, or Jane. Even with such a person as a sexual partner, his initial stimulation would have to come largely from fantasies involving Chrissie, Jane, et al. Thereafter, he could shape his arousal to coincide more and more with the actual person with whom he was involved. We are all "imprinted" by early conditionings regarding sexual arousal and individual preferences. Those individuals who learn to rely on esoteric and unusual fantasies for their sexual arousal will have a difficult time displacing them with real-live sexual encounters.

John's first breakthrough occurred several months later, when dating a woman who reminded him very much of his older cousin. During a sensate-focus exercise, when she was massaging his body with a bland cream, he let his mind wander to the image of Chrissie performing cunnilingus on his friend's mother, whereupon he had successful intercourse with his girlfriend, all the while pretending that she was Jane. Thereafter, he experienced no further erectile difficulties or any other problems, and during the past two years he has remained sexually active and confident. During a follow-up interview, he reported that he required no formal shaping procedures to effect a transfer from imagery to reality. He always relied on fantasy to achieve arousal, but during intercourse he could respond to and remain aroused by the actual, ongoing sexual encounter. In Chapter 9, reference was made to the therapist as a *permission giver*. This aspect appeared to be crucial in treating John. Prior to therapy, he tended to view his masturbatory fantasies as aberrant and certainly did not think of bringing them into an actual sexual encounter. My nonjudgmental exploration of his fantasies enabled John to accept them and to utilize them at will.

In presenting the case of John at several lectures, I have paused at the point in the narrative where he failed to show any improvement after being treated by the usual behavior therapy and sex therapy procedures. I asked several audiences, "What would you do at this point?" The majority of people have recommended psychoanalysis for his apparently "deep-seated" conflicts, despite the fact that psychoanalysis is one of the least effective methods for overcoming erectile difficulties (Cooper, 1978). On one occasion a therapist who had previously attended a seminar on multimodal therapy was in the audience. "You have looked into and worked with all the modalities except for imagery," she observed. "I'd recommend conducting a thorough exploration of his sexual images." The point is that, while many sex therapists and certain behavioral clinicians are extremely competent, flexible, and innovative (Dengrove, 1967, 1971; Fensterheim & Kanter, 1980) the explicit use of the BASIC I.D. schema adds precision and direction to the overall treatment.

Sexual Adequacy: The Multimodal Perspective

At the physiological level, sexual urges may be considered a "drive," an "instinct," or a "need," but the complex cultural and social network of values, attitudes, and taboos that surround the act gives precedence in therapy to psychological and sociological factors. Sexual adequacy, like any other skill, is a product of learning. Problems may arise at all levels of personality functioning.

Behavior

Increasing the range of sexual skills and techniques will often enhance performance and enjoyment. Kissing, caressing, massaging, and various ways of stimulating one's partner are learned responses. By instructing couples to be open about their individual preferences and to be willing to give and take instructions, "errors" can be corrected and sexual enjoyment can be maximized. The use of skillful surrogates can enhance the confidence and abilities of some individuals with severe inhibitions.

Affect

Any "negative emotion" will undermine sexual performance and enjoyment. Negative emotions refer to anxiety, sadness, guilt, resentment, and so forth. Performance anxieties are perhaps the most common detractors, and certain religious teachings promote undue guilt and sexual misgivings. Traumatic events (e.g., rape, parental punishment, or coercive incest) can have entrenched affective repercussions.

Sensation

Sexual enjoyment is tied directly into the sensory modality, with particular emphasis on the wide range of tactile stimulations that one may learn to appreciate. The numerous ways of stimulating erogenous zones are part of the repertoire of any proficient lover. Sensory disturbances or displeasures (e.g., pain or discomfort) may sometimes call for a broad-spectrum treatment approach (Lazarus, 1980b), although in many instances, these are merely due to clumsiness or similar behavioral errors that are easily corrected.

Imagery

Fantasies can enhance sexual performance and enjoyment. Several popular books have appeared on the subject of men's and women's erotic fantasies. One of the main problems that enters into this area is the needless guilt some people have about enjoying their "peculiar" mental pictures. Some people experience intrusive images (e.g., pictures of parental disapproval) that disrupt their pleasures.

Cognitions

The greatest pleasures and problems in sex are associated with the attitudes that people acquire. As Ellis (1972) has strongly emphasized, "categorical imperatives"—such as *should, ought,* and *must*—together with any other strong demands, will effectively truncate if not destroy sexual performance and enjoyment. The correction of myths and irrational ideas, together with nonmoralistic insights, is often essential for the achievement of sexual fulfillment.

Interpersonal relationships

Sex can all too readily become a battleground rather than a source and expression of intimacy, affection, excitement, caring, or the heightened spiritual ecstacies that many may experience. Frequently, sexual problems may simply arise because one is having sex with the wrong partner. (I have found this to be especially true of women suffering from psychogenic dyspareunia—pain or discomfort during intercourse not due to any organic malfunction. See Lazarus, 1980b.)

Drugs

The ingestion of various drugs can facilitate or impede sexual enjoyment or performance. Small quantities of alcohol, marijuana, and certain tranquilizers may enhance arousal, perhaps mainly for their placebo effects (Dengrove, 1971), but large quantities tend to inhibit sexual performance. Sexual difficulties may stem directly from numerous organic problems—among them surgical trauma, endocrine disorders, and infections. Urological, gynecological, and other medical investigations are called for whenever organic involvement is suspected.

By traversing the BASIC I.D. the clinician comes to appreciate the extent to which problems in any one of the modalities are relatively circumscribed, or maintained by a "ripple effect" across other modalities. Often, the completed Life History Questionnaire will reveal whether specific sexual retraining or a more extensive treatment regimen is required. One man whose presenting problem was listed simply as "premature ejaculation" on the Life History Questionnaire, underlined the following items under *Modality Analysis of Current Problems:* Take drugs, odd behavior, drink too much, suicidal attempts, aggressive behavior, outbursts of temper, angry, conflicted, unhappy.

These factors may or may not be related to his sexual problem, but no responsible clinician would focus on his "premature ejaculation" and ignore any of the other behavioral, affective, cognitive, and interpersonal difficulties. There is nothing occult or elaborate about determining when to dwell on specific sexual problems and when to address other areas of concern. The initial interview and the Life History Questionnaire will often indicate whether allied problems exist and to what extent they aggravate the primary complaints.

As indicated earlier, I have found the use of imagery especially helpful when puzzling situations arise. One of my basic questions when dwelling on sexual imagery is whether the client can picture the desired goal (i.e., whether men with erectile dysfunction can form an image of themselves obtaining and maintaining an erection during sex; whether anorgasmic women can see themselves, in their mind's eye, achieving a climax). If the answer is negative, the avowed goal is usually difficult to reach. People who report that they are able to picture the desired outcome, even though they may never have experienced it, are usually easier to work with. Let me reemphasize that in many instances I consider it necessary for people to be able to imagine an event before they can achieve it. I therefore ask my clients to dissect their general goals into piecemeal segments, and then to picture themselves accomplishing each progressive step. For example, the man with erectile failure might imagine the following sequence:

1. Being relaxed though having no sign of an erection during foreplay.

2. Feeling a pleasant genital sensation as his partner stimulates his flaccid penis.

3. Eventually becoming semierect for a few moments.

4. Maintaining an erection for a slightly longer time than in #3.

5. Losing an erection while moving into a coital position, but being calm and accepting.

6. Losing an erection soon after gaining vaginal entry, but being calm and accepting.

7. Obtaining and maintaining an erection for longer and longer periods.

The transfer from imagery to actual practice is usually not automatic, but there is evidence that the deliberate use of mental imagery facilitates the process of generalization (Singer, 1974).

While I was using an image of orgasmic competence with a 29-year-old married woman who had never experienced a climax, she became upset as I urged her to imagine herself reaching orgasm. I asked, "What happens when you try to picture that scene?" She started sobbing and blurted out that she was not entitled to pleasure. As I followed this lead, we unearthed a Calvinistic ideology that emphasized the evils of pleasure and stressed that the right to happiness must be earned by performing great deeds. She had belonged to a religious sect that preached these values and was unhappy about having broken away from them at her husband's insistence. (A previous therapist who was unaware of these cognitive factors had attempted to implement self-stimulation and dyadic-pleasuring strategies!)

Sex therapy was tabled while we endeavored to achieve an elaborate cognitive restructuring. This was soon followed by couples therapy, which led into extended family therapy. (The couple and both sets of respective parents were seen together for several sessions to disentangle a network of cross-generational clashes and interference.) At the time of writing, some eight months (thirty sessions) later, a fair degree of progress has been made on several fronts (the wife is more assertive, her parents and in-laws have stopped patronizing her and interfering with her, the husband has achieved more mature transactions with his parents, the marriage relationship is closer and more egalitarian), and she can trigger orgasms with the use of a vibrator and manually during masturbation. We are now trying to effect a transfer to the heterosexual situation.

A few techniques are specific to the field of sex therapy (e.g., threshold training for premature ejaculation, the use of vibrators for anorgasmic women, the introduction of graduated dilators for vaginismus), but most of the methods employed are drawn from general psychotherapy and more especially behavior therapy. There is no specific formula for overcoming arousal problems, erectile dysfunction, orgasmic barriers, dyspareunia, or sexual deviations. Many solutions are specific to individuals and individual relationships. By proceeding multimodally (i.e., systematically covering the BASIC I.D. during assessment and problem-identification), the therapist will more readily discern critical variables that may otherwise remain unrecognized. Thereafter, as repeatedly stressed throughout this book, appropriate and effective interventions will become easier to administer.

While this chapter has dwelled heavily on the use of imagery in overcoming sexual inadequacy, it should not be thought that "imagery therapy" is tantamount to multimodal therapy for this area of dysfunction. Assessment covers the entire BASIC I.D. and, in multimodal therapy, extensive use is made of behavioral, affective, sensory, cognitive, and interpersonal strategies. As mentioned at the start of this chapter, however, the use of imagery procedures has not been given the attention it deserves, whereas all the other modalities and their specific treatments have been well documented (Hartman & Fithian, 1974; Leiblum & Pervin, 1980; LoPiccolo & LoPiccolo, 1978; Masters & Johnson, 1970; Tollison & Adams, 1979). Let me emphasize again that the use of imagery can shed light on hitherto puzzling and otherwise inaccessible problems.

Chapter 11

Multimodal Therapy in Special Situations: Working with Children, Groups, and the Severely Disturbed

How do you treat children multimodally? What is your approach in group therapy? How do you handle schizophrenia, depression, alcoholism and drug addiction?

These questions are typically raised at seminars and workshops. The reader who has perused the preceding chapters will realize that the central format in multimodal therapy remains consistent—think deliberately in terms of behavior, affect, sensation, imagery, cognition, interpersonal relationships, and biological factors; assess these seven parameters of personality systematically; examine their interactions; and tailor treatment according to the individual's requirements. This book would become unmanageably large and needlessly repetitive by devoting separate chapters to each of the foregoing questions. Brief comments will be made for illustrative purposes.

Multimodal Therapy With Children

I am not a child-therapist who has adapted and applied multimodal methods to children, but several experts in the area of child psychotherapy have reported the distinct advantages of this approach with children (e.g., Keat, 1976a, 1976b, 1979; Edwards, 1978; Green, 1978; Breunlin, 1980; O'Keefe & Castaldo, 1980). Gerler (1977, 1978a, 1978b, 1979) has applied multimodal theory and therapy to career education, school counseling, reading programs, and (Gerler & Keat, 1977) in the management of elementary classrooms. The artistry and technical repertoire of an effective child-therapist involve specific skills that are not required by a clinician who is gifted with young or elderly adults. To reach certain children, the therapist must be equipped with numerous games, songs, stories, and a flair for communicating in short words and simple phrases. I observed a masterful clinician who established instant rapport with young people by performing some impressive magic tricks; another was a talented artist who captured the imaginations of children with colorful and allegorical cartoons.

In my experience, child therapy almost always becomes family therapy, as it is the parents who control behavior-reinforcers. Multimodal parent-training (Judah, 1978) has shown the effectiveness of the BASIC I.D. framework for achieving significant changes in parents' levels of acceptance, and for decreasing authoritarian attitudes, with resultant benefits to children of elementary school age. In the multimodal orientation, Modality Profiles will point to specific therapeutic requirements—whether to concentrate on operant or other behavioral principles (Ross, 1974), when to employ programmatic classroom intervention (O'Leary & O'Leary, 1976), and when to approach the problem from a family systems perspective (Haley, 1980). When the BASIC I.D. shows an enmeshed interpersonal network of conflicting agendas and power struggles, it is often essential to work with the family and to aim for a different form of transaction among family members. Haley (ibid.) has described the necessary steps for achieving these ends. More circumscribed problems call for operant retraining (Wahler, 1976). This would include various behavior deficits (e.g., language difficulties; poor "self-help" skills, like grooming, dressing, eating; or restricted social skills), age-inappropriate behaviors (overdependent responses, bed-wetting, shyness, fears, and phobias), and other situational maladjustments. Because the child's behavior must often be studied within different environmental contexts, direct classroom observation and intervention are often necessary when school-related problems arise (O'Leary & O'Leary, 1972).

Obviously, young children are not asked to fill out a Life History Questionnaire or to draw up a Modality Profile. Nevertheless, a multimodal therapist, when working with a child, will think in BASIC I.D. terms and will make systematic inquiries about these modalities and their interactive effects. Many children are especially responsive to imagery techniques (Lazarus & Abramovitz, 1962); some respond well to specially prepared relaxation-training scripts (Keat, 1979, pp. 123–125); and it is often helpful to prescribe such books as Gardner's *The Boys and Girls Book About Divorce* (1970), or song albums, such as *Free to Be You and Me* (Hart, Pogrebin, Rogers & Thomas, 1974), which are designed to dispel myths created by our sexually biased culture. Schaefer and Millman (1977) have compiled a most useful compendium of wide-ranging articles on therapies for children. They have rewritten, in digest form, more than 130 articles on some of the most common and uncommon childhood maladies—nightmares; shy, withdrawn behaviors; school phobia and other childhood fears; reactions to trauma; enuresis; glue-sniffing; thumbsucking; aggressiveness; stealing; fire-setting; hyperactive behavior; sibling rivalry; and many other problem areas. What is unique about multimodal therapy with children is the systematic way in which the child's BASIC I.D. will be examined and dealt with when specific personal and interpersonal difficulties emerge.

Keat's book on *Multimodal Therapy With Children* (1979) shows how a gifted and imaginative clinician applies the BASIC I.D. to many problems and disorders of children. My criticism of Keat's adaptation is that it draws on somewhat spurious ideologies and techniques (e.g., he includes such interventions as megavitamin therapy, some questionable aspects of transactional analysis, kung-fu training, and adds another acronym to the BASIC I.D. that may lead critics to consider the approach *multimuddle* rather than multimodal!). Notwithstanding these criticisms, Keat is highly creative and shows that the multimodal orientation has a definite place in therapy with children.

Multimodal Group Therapy

Groups can be particularly helpful in dispelling various myths (consensual validation tends to carry more weight than the views of one person, even if that person is a highly respected authority). When interpersonal deficiencies are present, group therapy can provide a more veridical training milieu. Groups lend the opportunity for vicarious or observational learning and offer a rich variety of modeling opportunities. Role-playing, behavior-rehearsal and other enactments are enhanced by the psychodramatic nuances that groups provide (Moreno, 1958). Lonely and isolated individuals particularly tend to benefit from group therapy, especially when the group provides a springboard for the development of friendships. Furthermore, group therapy is often more expedient, more practical, and less expensive than individual therapy.

Extremely hostile, paranoid, deluded, or severely depressed individuals often have a disruptive effect on treatment groups. Likewise, people who are locked into pervasive obsessive-compulsive rituals have responded poorly in multimodal groups. These people are better treated individually or, preferably, in a marital or family context.

While some of my colleagues conduct multimodal groups with children and adolescents, my own expertise is limited to adults. The easiest groups to conduct are relatively homogeneous and have clearly defined goals. These include assertiveness training groups, couples groups, and groups for people who wish to lose weight, stop smoking, or overcome specific phobias. We have found that groups are best conducted with four to ten members (usually led by male and female co-therapists) on a weekly basis, with meetings lasting about 1½–2 hours.

Initial anxieties are usually quelled by the therapists' introductory remarks emphasizing the cooperative pooling of resources, the deliberate creation of helpful togetherness, constructive rather than destructive criticism, confidentiality, and social interaction (Lazarus, 1971). As an icebreaker, we have found it helpful to follow the orienting remarks by constructing Structural Profiles (see Chapter 4), for which each group member rates him- or herself on a 10-point scale across the BASIC I.D. The therapist emphasizes that no profile is more or less desirable than another, but that people may nevertheless readily perceive areas that call for correction (e.g., very low ratings on interpersonal and biological modalities would reflect social and medical problems). A discussion of the general implications of each member's Structural Profile usually generates lively interchanges and leads to the discovery of like-minded or temperamentally compatible persons in the group.

During the second meeting, the BASIC I.D. format is discussed in detail, and the bulk of the session is devoted to the construction of Modality Profiles by each group member (see Chapter 4). Thereafter, therapy is geared to eliminate specific excesses and deficits on each group member's profile. While multimodal groups are task-oriented, goal-directed, and are aimed at ameliorating particular problems, the group atmosphere is usually informal and often good-humored. We make a conscious attempt to create an atmosphere in which members feel safe, relaxed, respected, and accepted (Lazarus, 1974).

Group-process material is discussed from time to time, especially when some members appear to have hidden agendas that subvert the group's major goal of removing excesses and deficits within each member's BASIC I.D. The majority of the techniques outlined in Appendix 2 may be applied in group settings. Among the most frequently used group methods are behavior-rehearsal and role-playing, modeling, positive reinforcement (mainly in the form of sincere praise, when appropriate), recording and self-monitoring, the Empty Chair, anger-expression, feeling-identification, relaxation training, meditation, Ellis' A-B-C-D-E paradigm, bibliotherapy, social skills and assertiveness training, friendship training, and communication training.

Having experimented with several different formats and ways of conducting multimodal groups (Lazarus, 1975a; 1975b) I have found time-limited groups to be the most effective (i.e., group members are informed at the first meeting that the group will meet for twenty sessions and then disband). Clients who so desire may then enter individual therapy or join a different group. At one time I used to encourage certain clients to be seen individually as well as in a group, but since this tended to create some confusion and conflict, I now prefer to have group members committed exclusively to their twenty weeks of group therapy. Clients who were receiving individual as well as group therapy also tended to hold back in group meetings and saved sensitive material for their individual sessions. This practice tended to undermine group morale.

When group members become familiar with the BASIC I.D. concept, they tend to enjoy monitoring their own problems within each dimension while seeking corroboration or correction from the group leaders and other members. In my experience, most members derive benefit from tracking the firing order of particular modalities (see Chapter 5). Interchanges amongst the participants about specific remedies are usually very productive. Here is a brief excerpt:

MARGE: It's the damdest thing! (turning to the therapist) You were right about my anxieties usually starting with a cognition and then moving straight into imagery. I mean, I used to think that my attacks came out of nowhere—all I knew was that, Bang! suddenly I felt anxious. But when I started tracking it, I saw how I would almost always start in with some stupid *thinking.* If I could only shut off that stupid part of my brain that starts up this nonsense. . . .

SUE: I'm the same way. It's all in my head. That's where it all starts.

BERT: With me it's the opposite. First, I get the sensations. I notice the feelings and then I start worrying. . . .

THERAPIST: How many of you carried out the tracking? Who tried to find their firing orders? (Marge, Sue, Bert, and Connie raise their hands.) George and Tony, you two didn't get into it?

TONY: It's two weeks now since I've been doing the positive imagery. I find that it nips things in the bud.

GEORGE: I didn't realize that it was a homework assignment.

THERAPIST: You're right. It was merely a suggestion. Anyhow, maybe we can all pitch in and see if we can come up with some ideas about warding off anxiety.

CONNIE: Can we also talk about depression? I've noticed that I depress myself by thinking of Martin and what went wrong with us, and then I dredge up other things that I regret and end up feeling sorry for myself. It's a vicious circle.

CO-THERAPIST: Am I right, Connie, that you wanted to work on depression, and, George, you had mentioned guilt feelings as a major area, while everyone else talked about anxiety?

CONNIE: Well, the funny thing with me is that I get myself depressed by thinking about the past, but my anxieties usually start when I feel sick to the stomach and I begin thinking about the hepatitis and all that stuff.

GEORGE: I've been saying, "Don't take responsibility for other peoples' feelings." That really helps.

THERAPIST: Great! Now let's pull this all together. Connie, when you start up one of your reveries by dwelling on all the things you could and should have done and by giving yourself a hard time for being a fallible human being, you could try out *thought-stopping* to begin with. As soon as you notice yourself delving into these regrets, start screaming STOP! STOP! inwardly and try to picture a huge neon sign reading S T O P! Will you try that?

GEORGE: I find it even more helpful to scream STOP! inside to myself and then to imagine myself painting the letters "S," "T," and so on, on a huge billboard.

CO-THERAPIST: That's a terrific idea.

THERAPIST: I agree. Will you try that out Connie? Now Marge and Sue, you both said that you get anxious by starting up with some *cognition*. Bert, you said that in your case, the *sensations* precede the *cognitions*. I want to hear more about that in a moment, but, first, whenever the cognitive modality enters into the picture and generates anxiety, there are usually two words that are responsible—*"what if. . . ."* You anticipate some negative event. "What if this or that happens?" "What if this or that goes wrong?" The antidote is the word *"so,"* or *"so what if. . . ."* You say, "So what if this happens? I'll deal with it; I'll cope with it."

BERT: (laughing) What if it kills you?

TONY: Well, then your worries and troubles are over. Dead men aren't anxious.

CO-THERAPIST: Perhaps that's the ultimate fear. The worst thing that could happen is that we might die.

MARGE: The point is that we make ourselves anxious about silly, stupid things. We think about all the dumb little things that can happen—at least I do.

THERAPIST: Do you fully believe that if X, Y, or Z happens, you can deal with it? "So what if it occurs. I will handle it there and then."

MARGE: I'll give it a try.

THERAPIST: Marge, since you tend to start with a cognition and then you get into negative imagery, would you hit both modalities? Start with a "so what if" and then move right into some positive mental pictures.

At times, multimodal therapy takes place *in* the group, whereas at other times, it is carried out *by* the group. Therapy *in* a group implies that client and therapist are interacting much as they would in individual treatment sessions, except for the fact that other people are present. Therapy *by* a group refers to those times when the other people actively assist one another through support and by contributing knowledge from their own backgrounds. Many clients have to be taught how to extract maximum benefits from group participation. It is extremely important for group members to have the capacity to extract personally relevant information even when the spotlight of attention is not focused on them. An unmarried person listening to the tribulations of a married couple may erroneously conclude that since he or she is single, there is little to be gained or learned from their interactions. This person is led to appreciate the chance to obtain valuable clues for achieving more satisfying *interpersonal relationships,* whether the particular emphasis happens to be on husband-wife, parent-child, employer-employee, or any other specific relationship. In my view, one of the main reasons for conducting groups is that, if two heads are better than one, ten heads may be more than five times better than two!

Schizophrenic Disorders and Depressive Disorders

People who are grossly psychotic—delusional, extremely confused, markedly withdrawn and behaviorally inappropriate, homicidal, or suicidal—usually require drug therapy to become amenable to psychotherapy. In multimodal vernacular, you have to commence with the D modality. If, like certain organic psychiatrists, you deal solely with biological considerations, a network of crucial factors across the BASIC I will go untreated. Even with bipolar affective disorders, for which many authorities consider lithium carbonate the treatment of choice (Dunner & Fieve, 1978), one has to consider factors across the other modalities that might prevent the patient from taking the drug —false ideas, negative feelings and sensations, aversive images, interpersonal difficulties (e.g., family pressures, poor relationship with the therapist), or a history of poor compliance. As Fay (1976) has underscored, "It is clear that the taking of drugs is affected by the six other modalities and in turn produces results which affect the other modalities."

The first published report on multimodal therapy (Lazarus, 1973b) described the treatment of a 24-year-old woman who had been diagnosed as schizophrenic, and had been admitted to mental hospitals three times since age 18. While a psychiatrist monitored her medication (Trilafon, Vivactil, and Cogentin), thirty-one specific problems were identified and treated across her BASIC I. She was seen in individual therapy for thirteen months, was also in multimodal group therapy, and had eight family therapy sessions with her parents. Despite the poor prognosis suggested by her hospital reports, she was coping so well at the end of therapy that her psychiatrist discontinued her medication. I last heard from her two years ago. She was married, was about to graduate from college, and asked for my counsel about a career in social work.

Seriously disturbed individuals usually require more detailed and more tedious attention to each modality. Whereas many clients enjoy working in several modalities at a time, those with major mental disorders usually prefer and require step-by-step management covering one or two specific areas. While I question the validity of Whitehorn and Betz's (1960) A-B scale (which purports to differentiate among therapists who are most and least successful with schizophrenic patients) some therapists undoubtedly have a special ability to work with psychotic individuals, and others do not. A good match between therapist and client is often necessary, but—to reiterate our contention—durable results will be in direct proportion to the number of specific modalities deliberately assessed and treated.

In treating depressed patients, even those who have major biological determinants, it is important to examine and treat the sufferer's behaviors, affective responses, sensations, images, cognitions, and his or her interpersonal relationships, in addition to ensuring that the necessary pharmacological ingredients are prescribed. My follow-ups strongly indicate that stability of treatment outcome is closely tied to the thoroughness with which specific problems across a client's BASIC I.D. are systematically resolved. The value of the multimodal approach is suggested by the favorable and durable results with the many depressed clients who had previously undergone five to twenty years of unsuccessful therapy employing one or two modalities. Fay and Lazarus (1981) recount cases of chronic, so-called characterologic depression that had not responded to several unimodal or bimodal treatments, but in whom substantial benefits followed multimodal interventions.

A brief treatment outline may clarify the foregoing points. A 32-year-old woman who consulted me complained that she felt depressed. She had all the biological indications of a unipolar depression—a family history (her mother and two paternal aunts had been treated by ECT); a diurnal variation in mood (much worse early in the day); a fitfull sleep pattern; anorexia and weight-loss; constipation; listlessness; and statements of self-abnegation. There were no apparent causal or precipitating events—"These feelings gradually came on and got worse and worse." She had first consulted her family doctor, who had prescribed Valium. I recommended her to a psychiatrist who examined her and prescribed Parnate. In addition to the medication, her multimodal treatment recommendations included the following:

Behavior	Pay more attention to grooming. Increase general activity level (e.g., force yourself to engage in formerly pleasurable activities like golf and swimming).
Affect	Express anger. If people (especially husband and children) annoy you, do not suppress your feelings—tell them that you are angry.
Sensation	Expose yourself to several pleasant sensory experiences, no matter how minimal—seek pleasure in food, in a hot shower, in your favorite music, etc.
Imagery	Picture yourself coming out of the depression; see yourself in the near future having fun.
Cognition	Repeatedly challenge and dispute irrational and pessimistic self-statements.

Interpersonal   Acquire and practice a repertoire of assertive responses. Deliberately seek out company even when least in the mood for other people.

Initially, she was seen twice a week (including some family sessions with her husband and two children), and by the sixth session she was feeling very much better (probably as a result of the Parnate more than anything else). We continued to meet weekly. Although her depression was no longer a problem, it became obvious that she entertained numerous irrational ideas, that she was extremely deficient in assertiveness and other interpersonal skills, and that there were conflicts within the marriage. It took more than a year of regular, weekly therapy sessions to reach the point where she felt self-confident, self-assertive, and happy with her overall lifestyle. I also worked with her husband, who was having job-related problems, and the treatment also included at least ten sessions of conjoint marriage therapy.

Let us assume, as so often happens, that she had been treated with Parnate and some supportive psychiatry. This would hardly have enabled her to overcome the cognitive excesses and interpersonal deficits that existed premorbidly, nor would significant marital issues have been resolved. Although the biological elements would have been attended to, her unresolved problems in other modalities quite possibly would have rendered her prone to relapse. The distinctive feature of the multimodal approach is that it attempts to be systematic and comprehensive in assessment and in treatment.

Alcoholism and Substance Abuse

In an early report on a multidimensional approach to alcoholism (Lazarus, 1965a), I covered five components that foreshadowed the development of multimodal therapy.

1. Medical care was necessary to restore the client's physical well-being.

2. Aversion therapy was administered to attenuate the client's uncontrolled drinking.

3. Assessment was conducted on the specific antecedents of anxiety in the client's environment.

4. Many techniques were used to eliminate or reduce the client's

SPECIAL SITUATIONS 211

anxieties—systematic desensitization, assertiveness training, behavior-rehearsal, and hypnosis.

5. Specific steps were taken to develop a cooperative relationship with the client's spouse, especially with regard to altering the client's living situation in such a way as to mitigate some of the major determinants of his excessive drinking.

Nathan (1976), in an extensive review of the research literature on alcoholism, concluded that it is necessary to adopt a wide-ranging approach, employing a variety of concurrent methods addressed to behavioral excesses and deficits. He stated: "When they include explicit efforts to train alcoholics deficient in social, familial, and vocational skills, they would appear to hold real promise." The multimodal approach is even more thorough and systematic, as the following Modality Profile of a 32-year-old woman diagnosed as "alcoholic" depicts:

Modality	Problem	Proposed treatment
Behavior	Excessive drinking	Aversive imagery and other self-control procedures
	Avoids confronting most people	Assertiveness training
	Negative self-statements	Positive self-talk
	Tic of right shoulder	Massed practice
	Always drinks to excess when alone at home at night	Change stimulus conditions by developing social outlets
	Screams at her children	Teach operant training principles in child-management
Affect	Holds back anger (except with her children)	Assertiveness training
	Anxiety feelings	Self-hypnosis with positive imagery
	Depression	Increase range of positive reinforcement
Sensation	Butterflies in stomach	Abdominal breathing exercises

	Pressure at back of head	Relaxation of neck muscles
Imagery	Vivid pictures of her parents fighting	Desensitization
	Beatings from father	Retaliation images
	Being locked in bedroom as a child	Images of escape and/or release of anger
Cognition	Irrational self-talk about low self-worth	Disputing irrational ideas
	Numerous regrets	Elimination of categorical imperatives (remove shoulds, musts, oughts).
Interpersonal relationships	Ambivalent responses to husband and children	Possible family therapy and specific training in the use of positive reinforcement
	Secretive and suspicious	Discussion and train ing in greater self-disclosure
Drugs/biological	Using alcohol as anti-depressant and as a tranquilizer	If necessary ask M.D. about antidepressants and perhaps antabuse

The Modality Profile shows that the client's "alcoholism" or excessive drinking is part of a general series of specific and interrelated problems. As therapy proceeded, additional problems became evident; certain proposed treatment tactics were abandoned in favor of others; and a clearer understanding emerged of the client as a wife, a mother, a daughter, and especially as a unique individual. In this way, she was able to overcome her excessive drinking and to achieve significant changes in virtually all aspects of her personality (BASIC I.D.). In many cases of alcoholism, I have found it useful for clients to became members of Alcoholics Anonymous and to attend regular meetings.

In the treatment of alcoholism or any other form of substance abuse, the multimodal approach calls for a systematic inquiry across the BASIC I.D. followed by the deliberate application of procedures designed to remedy each problem. In cases of drug abuse, medically trained experts are often required to deal with organic factors associated with detoxification and withdrawal. In their topical and informative chapter on substance-use disorders, Nathan and Harris (1980) point out that no current treatment method has achieved significant success with drug addicts. It seems to us that unimodal therapies have been too vigorously promoted at the expense of multimodal interventions. For example, methadone maintenance as the sole treatment for hard-core narcotics addicts is like treating alcoholics with aversion therapy alone. To overlook any aspect of the BASIC I.D. is to leave potentially crucial problem areas untouched, which, in our estimation, renders the client vulnerable to relapse and to the development of additional maladaptive habits.

Appendix 1

Multimodal Life History Questionnaire

Purpose of This Questionnaire:

The purpose of this questionnaire is to obtain a comprehensive picture of your background. In psychotherapy, records are necessary, since they permit a more thorough dealing with one's problems. By completing these questions as fully and as accurately as you can, you will facilitate your therapeutic program. You are requested to answer these routine questions in your own time instead of using up your actual consulting time. It is understandable that you might be concerned about what happens to the information about you because much or all of this information is highly personal. Case records are strictly confidential. **NO OUTSIDER IS PERMITTED TO SEE YOUR CASE RECORD WITHOUT YOUR PERMISSION.**

If you do not desire to answer any questions, merely write "Do Not Care to Answer."

Date: _____

1. General Information:

Name: _____

Address: _____

_____

Telephone Numbers: (days) _____ (evenings) _____

Age: _____ Occupation _____ Sex _____

By whom were you referred? _____

Marital Status (circle one): Single   Engaged   Married   Separated
Divorced   Widowed

Remarried (how many times? _____)   Living with someone

Published by:
Multimodal Therapy Institute
28 Main Street
Kingston, New Jersey 08528

Do you live in: house, hotel, room, apartment _____

2. Description of Presenting Problems:
State in your own words the nature of your main problems _____

_____
_____
_____
_____
_____

On the scale below please estimate the severity of your problem(s):

Mildly   Moderately   Very   Extremely   Totally
Upsetting____Upsetting____Severe____Severe____Incapacitating____
When did your problems begin (give dates): _____

_____
_____
_____

Please describe significant events occuring at that time, or since then, which may relate to the development or maintenance of your problems: ____

_____

What solutions to your problems have been most helpful? _____

_____

Have you been in therapy before or received any prior professional assistance for your problems? If so, please give name(s), professional title(s), dates of treatments and results: _____

_____

3. Personal and Social History
(a) Date of Birth _____ Place of Birth _____
(b) Siblings: Number of Brothers _____ Brothers' Ages: _____
                 Number of Sisters _____ Sisters' Ages: ____
(c) Father: Living? _____ If alive, give father's present age

_____

                 Deceased? _____ If deceased, give his age at time
                 of death _____
                          How old were you at the time? _____
                 Cause of Death _____
                 Occupation _____ Health _____
(d) Mother: Living? _____ If alive, give mother's present

age _____
Deceased? _____ If deceased, give her age at
time of her death _____
How old were you at the time? _____
Cause of Death _____
Occupation _____ Health _____

(e) Religion: As a Child: _____ As an Adult:
(f) Education: What is the last grade completed (degree)? ____
(g) Scholastic Strengths and Weaknesses: _____

_____

(h) Underline any of the following that applied during your childhood-
/adolescence:

Happy Childhood   School Problems   Medical Problems
  Unhappy Childhood   Family Problems   Alcohol Abuse
Emotional/Behavior
Problems   Strong Religous Convictions   Others:
Legal Trouble   Drug Abuse
(i) What sort of work are you doing now?   _____
(j) What kinds of jobs have you held in the past?   _____

_____

(k) Does your present work satisfy you?   If not, please explain   ____

_____

(l) What is your annual family income? _____ How much
does it cost you to live?   _____
(m) What were your past ambitions?   _____

_____

(n) What are your current ambitions?   _____

_____

(o) What is your height? _____ ft. _____ inches   What is your
weight? _____ lbs.
(p) Have you ever been hospitalized for psychological problems? Yes
_____ No _____ If yes, when and where?   _____
(q) Do you have a family physician? Yes _____ No _____ If so, please
give his/her name(s) and telephone number(s)   _____
(r) Have you ever attempted suicide? Yes _____ No _____
(s) Does any member of your family suffer from alcoholism, epilepsy, depression or anything else that might be considered a "mental disorder?" ____
(t) Has any relative attempted or committed suicide?   _____

(u) Has any relative had serious problems with the "law"? _____

MODALITY ANALYSIS OF CURRENT PROBLEMS

The following section is designed to help you describe your current problems in greater detail and to identify problems which might otherwise go unnoticed. This will enable us to design a comprehensive treatment program and tailor it to your specific needs. The following section is organized according to the seven (7) modalities of *Behavior, Feelings, Physical Sensations, Images, Thoughts, Interpersonal Relationships and Biological Factors.*

4. Behavior:
   Underline any of the following behaviors that apply to you:

Overeat	Suicidal attempts	Can't keep a job
Take drugs	Compulsions	Insomnia
Vomiting	Smoke	Take too many risks
Odd behavior	Withdrawal	Lazy
Drink too much	Nervous tics	Eating problems
Work too hard	Concentration difficulties	Aggressive behavior
Procrastination	Sleep disturbance	Crying
Impulsive reactions	Phobic avoidance	Outbursts of temper
Loss of control		

Are there any specific behaviors, actions or habits that you would like to change? _____

What are some special talents or skills that you feel proud of? _____

What would you like to do more of? _____
What would you like to do less of? _____
What would you like to start doing? _____
What would you like to stop doing? _____
How is your free time spent? _____

Do you keep yourself compulsively busy doing an endless list of chores or meaningless activities? _____

Do you practice relaxation or meditation regularly? _____

5. Feelings
    Underline any of the following feelings that often apply to you:

Angry	Guilty	Unhappy
Annoyed	Happy	Bored
Sad	Conflicted	Restless
Depressed	Regretful	Lonely
Anxious	Hopeless	Contented
Fearful	Hopeful	Excited
Panicky	Helpless	Optimistic
Energetic	Relaxed	Tense
Envy	Jealous	Others:

List your five main fears:

1.
2.
3.
4.
5.
What feelings would you most like to experience more often? _____

What feelings would you like to experience less often? _____

What are some positive feelings you have experienced recently? ____
_____

When are you most likely to lose control of your feelings? _____
_____

Describe any situations that make you feel calm or relaxed _____
_____
_____

Please complete the following:
If I told you what I'm feeling now _____
One of the things I feel proud of is   _____
One of the things I feel guilty about is _____
I am happiest when   _____
One of the things that saddens me the most is   _____
If I weren't afraid to be myself, I might   _____
I get so angry when _____

If I get angry with you _____

What kinds of hobbies or leisure activities do you enjoy or find relaxing?
_____

Do you have trouble relaxing and enjoying weekends and vacations? (If "yes", please explain) _____
_____

6. Physical Sensations:
Underline any of the following that often apply to you:

Headaches	Stomach trouble	Skin problems
Dizziness	Tics	Dry mouth
Palpitations	Fatigue	Burning or itchy skin
Muscle Spasms	Twitches	Chest pains
Tension	Back pain	Rapid heart beat
Sexual disturbances	Tremors	Don't like being touched
Unable to relax	Fainting spells	Blackouts
Bowel disturbances	Hear things	Excessive sweating
Tingling	Watery eyes	Visual disturbances
Numbness	Flushes	Hearing problems

MENSTRUAL HISTORY:
Age of first period _____ Were you informed or did it come as a shock? _____

Are you regular? _____ Date of last period _____

_____ Duration _____ Do you have pain? _____

_____ Do your periods affect your mood? _____

What sensations are especially:
Pleasant for you? _____
_____

Unpleasant for you? _____
_____

7. Images
Underline any of the following that apply to you:

Pleasant sexual images	Unpleasant sexual images
Unpleasant childhood images	Lonely images
Helpless images	Seduction images
Aggressive images	Images of being loved

LIFE HISTORY QUESTIONNAIRE

Check which of the following applies to you:

I PICTURE MYSELF:

being hurt	hurting others
not coping	being in charge
succeeding	failing
losing control	being trapped
being followed	being laughed at
being talked about	being promiscuous

Others:

What picture comes into your mind most often?

Describe a very pleasant image, mental picture, or fantasy.

Describe a very unpleasant image, mental picture, or fantasy.

Describe your image of a completely "safe place".

How often do you have nightmares?

8. Thoughts:
Underline each of the following thoughts that apply to you:

I am worthless, a nobody, useless and/or unlovable.
I am unattractive, incompetent, stupid and/or undesirable.
I am evil, crazy, degenerate and/or deviant.
Life is empty, a waste; there is nothing to look forward to.
I make too many mistakes, can't do anything right.

Underline each of the following words that you might use to describe yourself:

intelligent, confident, worthwhile, ambitious, sensitive, loyal, trustworthy, full of regrets, worthless, a nobody, useless, evil, crazy, morally degenerate, considerate, a deviant, unattractive, unlovable, inadequate, confused, ugly, stupid, naive, honest, incompetent, horrible thoughts, conflicted, concentration difficulties, memory problems, attractive, can't make decisions, suicidal ideas, persevering, good sense of humor, hard-working.

What do you consider to be your most irrational thought or idea?

Are you bothered by thoughts that occur over and over again?

On each of the following items, please circle the number that most accurately reflects your opinions:

	STRONGLY DISAGREE	DISAGREE	NEUTRAL	AGREE	STRONGLY AGREE
I should not make mistakes.	1	2	3	4	5
I should be good at everything I do.	1	2	3	4	5
When I do not know, I should pretend that I do.	1	2	3	4	5
I should not disclose personal information.	1	2	3	4	5
I am a victim of circumstances.	1	2	3	4	5
My life is controlled by outside forces.	1	2	3	4	5
Other people are happier than I am.	1	2	3	4	5
It is very important to please other people.	1	2	3	4	5
Play it safe; don't take any risks.	1	2	3	4	5
I don't deserve to be happy.	1	2	3	4	5
If I ignore my problems, they will disappear.	1	2	3	4	5
It is my responsibility to make other people happy.	1	2	3	4	5
I should strive for perfection.	1	2	3	4	5
Basically, there are two ways of doing things—the right way and the wrong way.	1	2	3	4	5

Expectations regarding therapy:

In a few words, what do you think therapy is all about?

How long do you think your therapy should last?

How do you think a therapist should interact with his or her clients? What personal qualities do you think the ideal therapist should possess?

(Please complete the following:)
I am a person who _____
All my life _____
Ever since I was a child _____
It's hard for me to admit _____
One of the things I can't forgive is _____
A good thing about having problems is _____
The bad thing about growing up is _____
One of the ways I could help myself but don't is _____

9. Interpersonal Relationships

A. Family of Origin

(1) If you were not brought up by your parents, who raised you and between what years?

(2) Give a description of your father's (or father substitute's) personality and his attitude towards you (past and present)

(3) Give a description of your mother's (or mother substitute's) personality and her attitude toward you (past and present):

(4) In what ways were you disciplined (punished) by your parents as a child?

(5) Give an impression of your home atmosphere (i.e., the home in which you grew up). Mention state of compatibility between parents and between children.

(6) Were you able to confide in your parents?
(7) Did your parents understand you?
(8) Basically, did you feel loved and respected by your parents?
(9) If you have a step-parent, give your age when parent remarried.
(10) Has anyone (parents, relatives, friends) ever interfered in you marriage, occupation, etc.?
(11) Who are the most important people in your life?

B. Friendships

(1) Do you make friends easily?
(2) Do you keep them?
(3) Were you ever bullied or severly teased?
(4) Describe any relationship that gives you:
      (a) Joy

      (b) Grief

(5) Rate the degree to which you generally feel comfortable and relaxed in social situations: Very relaxed _____ Relatively comfortable _____ _____ Relatively uncomfortable _____ Very anxious ____ _____

(6) Generally, do you express your feelings, opinions, and wishes to others in an open, appropriate manner? Describe those individuals with whom (or those situations in which) you have trouble asserting yourself.

(7) Did you date much during High School? College?

(8) Do you have one or more friends with whom you feel comfortable sharing your most private thoughts and feelings?

C. Marriage:

(1) How long did you know your spouse before your engagement?
(2) How long have you been married?
(3) What is your spouse's age?
(4) What is your spouse's occupation?
(5) Describe your spouse's personality.

(6) In what areas are you compatible?

(7) In what areas are you incompatible?

(8) How do you get along with your in-laws (this includes brothers and sisters-in-law)?

(9) How many children do you have? _____ Please give their names, ages and sexes:

(10) Do any of your children present special problems?
(11) Any relevant information regarding abortions or miscarriages?

D. Sexual Relationships:

(1) Describe your parents' attitude toward sex. Was sex discussed in your home?

(2) When and how did you derive your first knowledge of sex?

(3) When did you first become aware of your own sexual impulses?

(4) Have you ever experienced any anxiety or guilt feelings arising out of sex or masturbation? If yes, please explain.

(5) Any relevant details regarding your first or subsequent sexual experiences?

(6) Is your present sex life satisfactory? If not, please explain.

(7) Provide information about any significant homosexual reactions or relationships.

(8) Please note any sexual concerns not discussed above.

E. Other Relationships:

(1) Are there any problems in your relationships with people at work? If so, please describe.

(2) Please complete the following:
    (a) One of the ways people hurt me is _____

    (b) I could shock you by _____

    (c) A mother should _____

    (d) A father should _____

    (e) A true friend should _____

(3) Give a brief description of yourself as you would be described by:
    (a) Your spouse (if married)

    (b) Your best friend:

    (c) Someone who dislikes you:

(4) Are you currently troubled by any past rejections or loss of a love relationship? If so, please explain.

10. Biological factors:

Do you have any current concerns about your physical health? Please specify:

Please list any medicines you are currently taking, or have taken during the past 6 months (including aspirin, birth control pills, or any medicines that were prescribed or taken over the counter) _____

Do you eat three well-balanced meals each day? If not, please explain

Do you get regular physical exercise? If so, what type and how often?

_____

Check any of the following that apply to you:

	NEVER	RARELY	FREQUENTLY	VERY OFTEN
Marijuana				
Tranquilizers				
Sedatives				
Aspirin				
Cocaine				
Painkillers				
Alcohol				
Coffee				
Cigarettes				
Narcotics				
Stimulants				
Hallucinogens (LSD, etc.)				
Diarrhea				
Constipation				
Allergies				
High blood pressure				
Heart problems				
Nausea				
Vomiting				
Insomnia				
Headaches				
Backache				
Early morning awakening				
Fitful sleep				
Overeat				
Poor appetite				
Eat "junk foods"				

Underline any of the following that apply to you or members of your family: thyroid disease, kidney disease, asthma, neurological disease, infectious diseases, diabetes, cancer, gastrointestinal disease, prostate problems, glaucoma, epilepsy, other:

Have you ever had any head injuries or loss of consciousness? Please give details. _____

_____

Please describe any surgery you have had (give dates) ——————

Please describe any accidents or injuries you have suffered (give dates)

Sequential History

Please outline your most significant memories and experiences within the following ages:

0–5 ——————————————————————————

6–10 ——————————————————————————

11–15 ——————————————————————————

16–20 ——————————————————————————

21–25 ——————————————————————————

26–30 ——————————————————————————

31–35 ——————————————————————————

36–40 ——————————————————————————

41–45 ——————————————————————————

46–50 ——————————————————————————

51–55 _____

56–60 _____

61–65 _____

Over 65 _____

Appendix 2

Glossary of Principal Techniques

Anger-expression: Unlike those who believe that "catharsis" is necessarily therapeutic, we do not regard anger-expression as an end in itself. Many clients have difficulty in recognizing their anger; others are afraid of it. Once the anger is owned, it can be eliminated through rational disputation, or channeled into appropriate assertive expression. Coaxing the client, especially in group settings, to state "I am angry!" over and over, louder and louder, is a well-known method of bringing the person in touch with his or her anger. Thereafter, *behavior-rehearsal* (q.v.) may be employed to deal with legitimate resentments. Pounding foam rubber cushions and staging pillow fights are other well-known means of eliciting anger. Toy shops usually sell inflatable objects that can be pummeled and kicked. An inhibited woman found enjoyment and relief in kicking and punching a large rubber doll shaped like a clown while picturing her estranged husband. Thereafter, she was more willing to contemplate logical steps that she could take to upgrade her divorce settlement.

Anti-future shock imagery: Apart from helping clients solve their ongoing problems, it is important to prepare them for changes that are likely to occur within the coming months and years. So many people are taken unaware by events in their lives that could readily have been anticipated. One asks, What are the prevailing conditions in the work setting and in the home? What changes are likely to occur? (For instance, young married couples are likely to become parents; middle-aged couples may soon face an "empty nest"; certain business executives are likely to be promoted and/or moved to new locations; others may be passed over, or even forced to retire.) By taking stock of the most probable changes that are likely to occur,

229

and by encouraging the client to *visualize* himself or herself coping with these changes, you facilitate the client's acceptance of the inevitable. These "emotional fire-drills" tend to reduce relapse rates.

Anxiety-management training: Clients are first taught general *relaxation training* (q.v.) and *goal-rehearsal or coping imagery* (q.v.) as basic anxiety-reducing techniques. On achieving some proficiency with these methods, they are encouraged to generate anxiety—to dwell on unpleasant sensory concomitants, negative imagery, catastrophic cognitions, and whatever else will produce feelings of anxiety. Immediately thereafter, they are asked to perform the opposite operations—to relax and to dwell on calm sensations, to picture serene images, to dispute irrational ideas, to concentrate on optimistic and relaxing thoughts, and to focus on peaceful and rewarding inputs. By learning to turn anxiety on and off in this manner, receptive clients are apt to develop self-control and self-confidence.

Associated imagery: The value of dipping into and tracking ongoing thought processes has been underscored by William James in his writings on "the stream of consciousness" and by Freud's method of free association. Clients frequently experience unpleasant sensations and emotions that they are unable to account for. While experiencing an untoward emotion, they are asked immediately to focus on any image that comes to mind, to see it as vividly as possible. Other images may begin to take its place. If so, each one is to be visualized as clearly as possible. If new images do not come to mind, the original image is to be magnified as through a zoom lens. Different parts of the same image are thus examined, and this process often evokes other images that may be tracked. As each image is attended to, the mosaic may begin to take shape, and some clients will report significant self-revelations.

Aversive imagery: There is a long history to the technique of associating unpleasant thoughts and feelings with behavior that is undesirable but self-reinforcing (e.g., alcoholism, sexual deviations, overeating). Instead of using emetic drugs and electric shocks to discourage undesirable behavior, many have found the use of extremely unpleasant mental pictures sufficient. For instance, an obese individual who is tempted by rich deserts or any food interdicted by his or her diet, can be trained to imagine that someone has vomited over the cake, ice-cream, or other food that is better avoided. A pedophile may be conditioned to imagine his hands immediately breaking out in feculent, puss-ridden in feculent, puss-ridden sores as soon as he touches a child sexually. They spread rapidly all over his body, but disappear if he drops all sexual overtures.

Behavior-rehearsal: People who are unable to conduct themselves appropriately in specific situations, or who cannot cope with particular interactions, are rehearsed much like a character actor mastering a role. Let us take the example of a man who feels entitled to a salary increment but is at a loss for words when confronting his employer. Typically, the therapist will commence by playing the part of the employer; the client is to request a raise much as he would in the actual encounter. The dialogue is usually tape-recorded (video-recordings are ideal), so that client and therapist may analyse the playback. They then reverse roles—the client plays the employer while the therapist requests a raise in salary. Again, recorded play-backs are reviewed, and the client enacts the role again and again until he and the therapist are satisfied with his performance. At this stage, he is encouraged to test his skills in the actual situation.

Bibliotherapy: If a picture can be worth a thousand words, a well-chosen book can be worth more than a dozen sessions. Many excellent self-help books can be used to facilitate progress in therapy. When I recommend a book to a client, I ask that it be read carefully, underlined at points that seem important, and even summarized in a notebook that can be kept for ready reference. The readings are discussed during the session so that the therapist can ascertain what impact the book has had, and any ambiguities can be clarified. Of course, one is not limited to self-help books. Clients who enjoy reading can benefit from a variety of literary sources.

Biofeedback: A variety of procedures exists that systematically monitor specific areas of a person's physiological functioning and transmit that information, usually in the form of a visual or auditory signal. The purpose of biofeedback is to bring about a desired change in these autonomic or physiological functions. Let's consider a client who suffers from painful tension in his jaws. Using a machine designed to give electromyographic (EMG) feedback, the therapist attaches electrodes to the client's jaw muscles so that minute contractions are registered, amplified, and connected to an auditory signal. The tonal feedback would vary with the degree of muscular tension —the more the tension, the louder the sound. The client learns to maintain a low decibel level or to eliminate the tone altogether.

There are biofeedback devices for modifying brain-wave activity, heart rate, galvanic skin response, skin temperature, and several other physiological functions.

Communication training: It is often lamented that our society provides few opportunities for people to learn how to share thoughts and feelings with one another, the result of which is anomie and alienation. Communication training is comprised of *sending skills* and *receiving skills.* When expressing ideas or conveying feelings, many people send messages that are vague, ambiguous, contradictory, and difficult to follow. To improve *sending skills,* the client learns about the importance of eye-contact, voice-projection, body posture, the use of simple, concrete terms, the avoidance of blaming and pejorative remarks, forthright rather than manipulative intent, and statements of empathy. Good *receiving skills* call for active listening, verification and acknowledgment, and rewarding the sender for communicating. Role-playing and *behavior-rehearsal* (q.v.) are especially suited for promoting the development of communication skills.

Contingency contracting: The client agrees to increase, decrease, or maintain a specific behavior, with the explicit understanding that rewards will ensue from fulfilling the terms of the contract, and negative consequences will be imposed (usually self-imposed) for breaking them. Thus, an overweight woman contracted to appear in public without her two front false teeth if she deviated from her diet; for each 5 lb weight loss, she agreed to pamper herself by having a massage and a sauna.

Correcting misconceptions: Clients often harbor mistaken attitudes about society, about particular people, or about themselves. Sexual myths are rampant despite our supposedly enlightened era. Dispensing information is an integral aspect of psychotherapy. Psychotherapy as an education in living implies that one's clients be given *facts,* not myths or superstitions, to cope with the demands of daily living. It would be helpful if most therapists were themselves armed with the necessary facts and realities. *Bibliotherapy* (q.v.) is often an important component in correcting misconceptions.

Ellis' A-B-C-D-E paradigm: In his numerous writings, Albert Ellis has emphasized that people upset themselves via their own belief systems. Clients are shown how they falsely attribute their own upsets to outside or activitaing events. They learn that when feeling upset it is essential to examine their B's (beliefs) instead of blaming the A's (activating events). They are shown that activating events (A's) do not result automatically in emotional and behavioral consequences (C's), but that it is mainly the beliefs about A (i.e., B's) that are responsible for the impact at point C. By disputing (D) the irrational beliefs at point B, the effect (E) is the diminution or elimination of negative consequences (C's).

Feeling-identification: Clients seem to require two different processes in the clarification of their feelings: defining their terms and exploring affective areas. People often use terms that convey idiosyncratic meanings—anxiety, depression, guilt, anger, and so forth. For example, a client who declared himself to be "very depressed" identified concomitants usually associated with "anxiety" when questioned about his other emotions, sensations, and cognitions. He denied experiencing any sadness, or gloom, or dejection. It became apparent that, for him, the term "depression" signified "heightened autonomic arousal." In most instances, however, feeling-identification is centered on exploring the client's affective domain in order to identify significant feelings that might be obscure, occult, or misdirected. The various methods of feeling-identification have been the mainstay of traditional psychotherapy since its inception.

Focusing: This is an introspective technique adapted from the work of Eugene Gendlin. When in a quiet, relaxed state, the client is encouraged to enter a contemplative mood and is gently coaxed into examining spontaneous thoughts and feelings until one particular feeling emerges at the focus of his or her full experiential awareness. After several minutes of intense focusing, the client is asked to try to extract something new from the sensations, images, and emotions. By shifting the emphasis from talking and thinking about problems to their felt bodily expressions, the client is often able to circumvent cognitive blocks, with the result that important material may be brought to light. Focusing exercises also tend to have a desensitizing effect in some cases.

Friendship training: This overlaps with *communication training* (q.v.) and with *social skills and assertiveness training* (q.v.), but has a number of distinctive elements. It may seem trite if not absurd to stress that friendship is predicated on sharing, caring, empathy, concern, self-disclosure, give-and-take, positive reinforcement, and complementarity, whereas power plays, one-upmanship, competitive striving, and self-aggrandizement are apt to undermine friendship and truncate the development of intimacy. Yet, when observing the behavior of many people, one wonders why these self-evident truths are so frequently ignored, and why people who neglect them are perplexed by their social isolation. In friendship training, one identifies and discusses the prosocial interactions that constitute affectionate interactions, and the client is urged to put them into practice. *Behavior-rehearsal* (q.v.) is often useful in helping clients to achieve these ends.

Goal-rehearsal or coping imagery: Most people tend to rehearse upcoming events in their minds, but goal-rehearsal implies a deliberate and thorough visualization of each step in the process. The rationale is that the deliberate picturing of oneself coping with situations will enhance transfer to the actual events. Clients are told, "If you practice something in imagination, it is bound to have an effect on the real situation." Rather than picturing oneself mastering difficult events with superb aplomb (probably an unrealistic goal), clients are encouraged to see themselves faltering but coping. Thus, a person with an aversion to hospitals wished to visit a sick friend. By picturing the hospital scene vividly, replete with all of her negative feelings toward the situation, she imagined herself dealing with it and emerging with a sense of having given support to her friend. This realistic expectation enabled her to experience the actual event with minimal discomfort.

Graded sexual approaches: Men and women with sexual anxieties are advised to engage in sensual and sexual play only as long and as far as pleasurable feelings predominate. They are not to proceed to the point where anxious feelings erupt. By keeping sensual enjoyment ascendant over anxiety, the client tends to facilitate the emergence of higher levels of sexual arousal with each amorous session. Step by step, as the anxieties recede, greater degrees of intimacy become possible, so that uninhibited and total love-making is the culminating experience.

Hypnosis: People who enter therapy believing that hypnosis will facilitate their progress often have a built-in, self-fulfilling prophecy that should be incorporated into their therapy. It is useful to learn several methods of trance-induction in order to slip effortlessly from one into another, thus maximizing the chances of success with individual clients. Most hypnotic-induction techniques involve sensory fixation (e.g., staring at a spot on the ceiling) while listening to monotonous repetitions, such as "drowsy and relaxed," "heavy and sleepy." The reader is referred to Frankel and Zamansky (1978) and to Dengrove (1976) for collections of clinically relevant reports on the applications of hypnosis.

Meditation: There are numerous meditative techniques, but the most widely used practice or process consists of sitting down, relaxing, gradually closing one's eyes, and inwardly repeating a sound (known as a "mantra") over and over. Sanskrit terms are often employed, but, for all practical purposes, simply thinking the word "in" as one inhales and "out" upon exhaling will suffice. As thoughts float in and out of awareness, the meditator continues to think the words "in," "out," again and again. Some clients report that the practice of meditation assuages marked tension, lowers high blood pressure and produces a calm and more serene outlook. Unlike those who maintain that it is best to spend twenty minutes twice a day practicing meditation, we have found that some clients benefit from much shorter spans. Some derive maximum benefit from mini-meditations, two- or three-minute sessions several times a day.

Modeling: Basically, modeling consists of learning by observation. The therapist serves as a model or provides a role model for a particular behavior the client is encouraged to imitate. For example, the therapist may invite the client to accompany him or her to a store to observe the assertive return of faulty merchandise. Some people (especially in group therapy) respond better to peer-modeling and -imitation.

Nonreinforcement: Many problems are maintained by attention (social reinforcement) from other people. By not attending to the behavior, by not rewarding or reinforcing it, a therapist or other individuals in the client's social environment may facilitate its extinction. Reward those behaviors you wish to encourage; ignore those you wish to discourage. This basic aphorism captures the essence of *positive reinforcement* (q.v.) and *nonreinforcement* as two of the most fundamental mechanisms in learning and habit-formation.

Paradoxical strategies: Innumerable paradoxical interventions have been used in psychotherapy. The two most common are *symptom prescription* (e.g., a compulsive client is told to *increase* his checking and ritualistic behaviors), and *forbidding a desired response* (e.g., a man with erectile difficulty is told to engage in foreplay but *not* to have intercourse until he receives explicit permission from the therapist). In defiance of these admonitions, the compulsive client may decrease his extreme behaviors, and the sexually dysfunctional man is likely to engage in sexual intercourse. It takes considerable clinical skill to know when to encourage or agree with something we disapprove of, when to discourage what we really desire, and when to exaggerate or distort a response to achieve a desired result.

Positive imagery: The picturing of any pleasant scene, real or imagined, past, present, or future, has many benefits. As a tension-reducer, as an anxiety-inhibitor, and as a direct enjoyment-enhancer, positive imagery can play an important role. The power of positive mental imagery for healing physical afflictions is beginning to gain attention. Positive imagery can help one cope with pain, and it can induce a feeling of optimism while overcoming boredom (Lazarus, 1978a; Singer & Switzer, 1980).

Positive reinforcement: The observation that behavior is often a function of its consequences, points to the basic reality that pleasant or rewarding (positively reinforcing) stimuli will strengthen a response. In psychotherapy, positive reinforcement is usually social and is dispensed in the form of praise, recognition, and encouragement. Tangible objects such as food and money are also used as positive reinforcers, especially in dealing with children and adolescents. The use of tokens that can subsequently be exchanged for a variety of "backup" reinforcers is also employed frequently.

Problem-solving: Most problem-solving situations call for a modicum of logic and a fairly coherent or scientific progression. It is often impossible to reach solutions without first generating plausible hypotheses that can be strengthened or weakened by gathering relevant data. Clients who do not apply these elementary but fundamental principles to their ongoing problems tend to feel bewildered and overwhelmed. Since most people seek to predict and control the course of events that pervade their lives, they are more likely to achieve these ends by adhering to the rudiments of scientific methodology than by resorting to mysticism and chance. Through *modeling* (q.v.), coaching, and example, the therapist enables his or her clients to apply scientific principles to the enterprise of problem-resolution.

Recording and self-monitoring: Self-directed change often rests on the client's willingness to engage in the systematic recording, charting, and/or quantifying of target behaviors. For example, the person on a weight-reduction program who accurately computes daily caloric intake has a better chance of achieving a desired weight than the individual who will not engage in self-monitoring. The very act of counting and keeping notes tends to give clients a greater degree of self-control.

Relaxation training: Deep muscle-relaxation tends to go beyond mere physical comfort and can produce profoundly calming feelings in many people. There are two main varieties—total relaxation and differential relaxation. Total relaxation is performed while lying down on a comfortable bed or couch, or while sitting on a large, upholstered chair that fully supports the back and head. (There are several forms of total relaxation training, but one of the most effective is the alternate tensing and letting go of each major muscle area —forehead, eyes, jaws, throat, neck, shoulders, arms, hands, chest, upper back, lower back, abdomen, hips, buttocks, thighs, calf muscles, to the soles of the feet. There are several excellent relaxation-training cassettes on the market that clients can use at home to augment their relaxation training.) Differential relaxation is the deliberate relaxation of those muscles not in use while performing various activities. Thus, while standing, it is possible to relax the shoulders and facial muscles, the arms, chest, abdomen, buttocks, and back muscles. When practicing differential relaxation, a man observed that while sitting and writing he needlessly tensed his jaws, shoulders, neck, and held his breath. Deliberately letting go of tense muscles and breathing abdominally in a slow and rythmic fashion tended to promote a sense of calmness.

Self-instruction training: It is well documented that what we think and imagine will influence the way we feel and what we do. Our perceptions, evaluations, and anticipations will determine our self-regulation processes. The many writings of Albert Ellis and the experimental studies by Meichenbaum (1977) have shown that negative self-talk (self-devaluation) lies behind many peoples' failures and anxiety-ridden reactions, whereas the deliberate use of positive, self-creative statements can facilitate successful coping. For example, in place of anticipatory anxiety over an upcoming event, the client would be taught the following sequence of self-instruction: "I will develop a plan for what I have to do instead of worrying. I will handle the situation one step at a time. If I become anxious I will pause and take in a few deep breaths. I do not have to eliminate all fear; I can keep it manageable. I will focus on what I need to do. When I control my ideas I control my fear. It will get easier each time I do it." By directly influencing clients to change what they say to themselves, an important link in the chain of negative feelings and sensations—fear, anger, pain, guilt—can be broken.

Sensate focus training: So-named by Masters and Johnson (1970), sensate focus refers to sensual rather than sexual pleasuring by a couple. It consists of tactile stimulation—massaging, touching, fondling—of any part of the body that the recipient enjoys having stimulated, except for genitals and female breasts, which are to be avoided. There is to be no "sexual" stimulation. Sensate focus training is usually prescribed to sexually dysfunctional couples to introduce togetherness, intimacy, pleasuring, and closeness without the pressures or expectations of sexual performance. The couple shapes sensate focus experiences in terms of their mutual desires.

Social skills and assertiveness training: Many people need to learn how to stand up for their personal rights, how to express thoughts, feelings, and beliefs in direct, honest, and appropriate ways without violating any other person's rights. The essence of assertive behavior can be reduced to four specific response patterns: the ability to say "no"; the ability to ask for favors or to make requests; the ability to express positive and negative feelings; the ability to initiate, continue, and terminate conversations. *Behavior-rehearsal* (q.v.), and *modeling* (q.v.) are two of the major techniques employed when training clients to develop social skills and assertive responses. It should be emphasized that in addition to appropriate anger-expressing behaviors, social skills training is concerned with forthright expressions of love, appreciation, affection, and other positive feelings.

Stimulus-control: The presence of certain stimuli tends to increase the frequency of certain behaviors. For example, an abundance of tempting foods is likely to increase eating. A person trying to lose weight can exercise "stimulus-control" by keeping snacks and deserts out of the house; a person who wishes to smoke less may light up a cigarette only under specified stimulus conditions (e.g., while sitting in a particular chair, in a given place, in the presence of a specific ashtray). Those who wish to use stimulus-control to increase given behaviors can arrange environmental cues to trigger desired responses. For example, a college student who wishes to study more can arrange his desk so that no distracting stimuli are present; he will sit at the desk only while studying and not while listening to records or talking to friends. Thus, sitting-at-the-desk sets the stimulus conditions for studying.

Systematic exposure: Refusal to take emotional risks and avoidance of fearful or unpleasant situations are two of the most common characteristics of troubled individuals. Clients are encouraged, step by step, to expose themselves to their feared situations. Depending on the client's needs and preferences, the therapist or a paraprofessional assistant may accompany him or her into the actual situations. Clients may first use *goal-rehearsal or coping imagery* (q.v.) to ease their actual excursions into unpleasant situations. Many other techniques may be employed to achieve the all-important nonavoidance or systematic exposure objectives—*modeling, positive imagery, differential relaxation,* and *self-instruction training.*

The empty chair: Typically, the client sits facing an empty chair that he or she imagines is occupied by a significant other (parent, sibling, relative, friend, employer, or even one's alter ego). The imagined person could be someone who is dead, or someone out of the future, such as a yet-to-be-met bride or bridegroom. The client commences by accusing, or attacking, or forgiving, or requesting something of the imagined occupant of the empty chair. The client then moves into the empty chair and becomes the other person, who then directs all remarks to the chair that the client had occupied, as if talking to the client. Again the client changes chairs and becomes himself or herself and continues the dialogue. Switching from one chair to the other while assuming the role of the significant other and then oneself is usually continued until some resolution is reached. The therapist may offer prompts while the client is playing either role. "Tell him about the time you were crying in the bedroom." "Ask her to tell you exactly how she would have wanted you to respond." "Do you think she was telling the truth?" "Why don't you point out that he is making at least three irrational assumptions?" This procedure provides diagnostic insights and also has a variety of therapeutic effects. It is especially useful in permitting clients to appreciate the other person's point of view.

The step-up technique: Many people are unduly anxious about upcoming events—a public speech, a job interview, a dinner party, a blind date, and so forth. The step-up technique consists of picturing the worst thing that can possibly happen and then imagining oneself coping with the situation—surviving even the most negative outcome. Once the client successfully pictures himself or herself coping with unlikely horrors that were deliberately called into fantasy, anticipatory anxiety tends to recede. When the real situation rolls around, it poses little threat. Difficult cases may require the potentiating effects of *self-instruction training* (q.v.) and other strategies.

Threshold training: This has become a common technique for the treatment of premature or rapid ejaculation. The female manually stimulates the man's penis. When he feels a sensation that is, for him, premonitory to orgasm, he says "stop" and/or removes her hand until the sensation abates. Stimulation is resumed and is interrupted by the man when the preorgasmic sensation returns. By continuing the start-stop technique, ejaculation can often be postponed for longer time intervals. The next step is to use a bland cream or other means to lubricate the penis while the procedure is repeated. After about ten training sessions over two or three weeks, many men are capable of effecting vaginal entry and withdrawing as soon as they feel a preorgasmic urge. When the sensation subsides, they reenter and resume coitus, withdrawing again preorgasmically, and repeating the procedure. Within a few weeks, many males become capable of delaying ejaculation for long periods of time.

Time-limited intercommunication: This technique is used mainly for treating marital discord. The couple is instructed to set aside at least three, separate, hour-long appointments each week for prescribed communications. They flip a coin to determine who opens the dialogue—who talks and who listens. A timer is set for five minutes. During those five minutes the talker discusses whatsoever he or she pleases. The listener may not interrupt. He or she may take notes in preparation for rebuttal, but no verbal input may occur until the five minutes elapse and the bell sounds. At that point, the talker is to stop immediately whatever he or she is saying. The timer is then set for another five minutes, with the listener now doing the talking under the same ground rules. Each partner has six five-minute intervals in which to talk and six to attend to the other person's verbalizations. At the end of the hour, the couple is to hug each other and to drop any further discussion of the issues that were raised until the next preset appointment. Those who adhere to the rules of time-limited intercommunications find it an effective means of achieving more equitable levels of understanding and communication within a mean of two or three weeks. Some couples have difficulty tolerating hour-long sessions, in which case the time-frame can be adjusted accordingly.

Time projection (forward or backward): Clients with fairly vivid imaginations can readily picture themselves going forward or backward in time. Some clients experience immense relief after reliving and working through past events. By going several months into the future and picturing themselves adding more and more rewarding events to their daily lives, some depressed individuals experience a diminution in negative affect. The enterprising and imaginative clinician will think of many ways in which "time tripping" can be employed with receptive clients.

Thought-blocking: A simple but effective way of combatting certain obsessive and intrusive thoughts is simply to scream "STOP!" subvocally over and over again. Some clients also picture huge neon signs flashing the letters "S T O P" on and off. Others while thinking "STOP!" find it effective to add the distraction of flicking their wrists with a rubber band. A man who was unable to fall asleep at night for fear that his house might burn down had been in traditional therapy with no success. By applying thought-blocking, he was able to bring his catastrophic fears under control.

Appendix 3

Marital Satisfaction Questionnaire

10	9	8	7	6	5	4	3	2	1	0

Pleased	Half yes	Not pleased
	Half no	

After each question, write down the number that most closely approximates your present feelings about your marriage or your spouse.

I AM:

(1) Pleased with the amount we talk to each other.

(2) Happy with the friends we share in common.

(3) Satisfied with our sex life.

(4) In agreement with the amount of time you or we spend at work and at home.

(5) In agreement with the way we are spending money.

(6) Pleased with the kind of parent you are. (If you have no children, are you pleased with your mutual plans for having, or not having, children?)

(7) Of the opinion that you are "on my team."

(8) Pleased with our leisure time together (e.g., sports, vacations, outings, etc.).

(9) Basically in agreement with your outlook on life (e.g., values, attitudes, religious beliefs, politics, etc.).

(10) Generally pleased with the way you relate to members of your own family (parents, siblings, etc.).

(11) Satisfied with the way you relate to members of my family (e.g., my parents, siblings, etc.).

(12) Pleased with your general habits, mannerisms, and overall appearance.

Add up your total score.

84 and more means that you have a VERY GOOD marriage.

Between 72–83 reflects SATISFACTORY to GOOD feelings and interactions.

Below 60 indicates a POOR level of marital satisfaction.

References

Adler, A. Individual psychology. In G. B. Levitas (Ed.), *The world of psychology*. New York: Braziller, 1963.

Agras, W. S., Kazdin, A. E., & Wilson, G. T. *Behavior therapy: Toward an applied clinical science*. San Francisco: W. H. Freeman, 1979.

Alberti, R. E., & Emmons, M. L. *Your perfect right* (3rd ed.). San Luis Obispo, Calif.: Impact Publishers, 1978.

Alexander, F. *The medical value of psychoanalysis*. New York: Norton, 1932.

Alexander, F. *Psychosomatic medicine*. New York: Norton, 1950.

Allport, G. W. *Personality: A psychological interpretation*. London: Constable, 1937.

Argyris, C. Conditions for competence acquisition and therapy. *Journal of Applied Behavioral Science*, 1968, *4*, 147–177.

Arlow, J. A. Psychoanalysis. In R. J. Corsini (Ed.), *Current psychotherapies* (2nd ed.). Itasca, Ill.: Peacock, 1979.

Azrin, N. H., Naster, B. J., & Jones, R. Reciprocity counseling: A rapid learning-based procedure for marital counseling. *Behaviour Research and Therapy*, 1973, *11*, 365–382.

Azrin, N. H., & Nunn. R. G. *Habit control in a day*. New York: Simon and Schuster, 1977.

Bair, S. L. & Levenberg, S. B. A multimodal behavioral approach to the treatment and management of essential hypertension. *Psychotherapy: Theory, Research and Practice*, 1979, *16*, 310–315.

Bandler, R., & Grinder, J. *The structure of magic: A book about language and therapy* (Vol. I). Palo Alto, Calif.: Science and Behavior Books, 1975.

Bandler, R., & Grinder, J. *The structure of magic: A book about communication and change* (Vol. II). Palo Alto, Calif.: Science and Behavior Books, 1976.

Bandura, A. *Principles of behavior modification*. New York: Holt, Rinehart and Winston, 1969.

Bandura, A. Behavior theory and the models of man. *American Psychologist*, 1974, *29*, 859–869.

Bandura, A. *Social learning theory*. Englewood Cliffs, N.J.: Prentice-Hall, 1977.

Bandura, A. The self-system in reciprocal determinism. *American Psychologist*, 1978, *33*, 344–358.

Barlow, D. H., Abel, G. G., Blanchard, E. B., Bristow, A. R., & Young, L. D. A heterosocial skills behavior checklist for males. *Behavior Therapy*, 1977, *8*, 229–239.

Beck, A. T. *Cognitive therapy and the emotional disorders*. New York: International Universities Press, 1976.

Benson, H. *The relaxation response*. New York: Morrow, 1975.

Bergin, A. E., & Lambert, M. J. The evaluation of therapeutic outcomes. In S. L. Garfield & A. E. Bergin (Eds.), *Handbook of psychotherapy and behavior change* (2nd ed.). New York: Wiley, 1978.

Berne, E. *Transactional analysis in psychotherapy*. New York: Grove Press, 1961.

Berne, E. *What do you say after you say hello?* New York: Grove Press, 1972.

Birk, L. Behavior therapy—intergration with dynamic psychiatry. *Behavior Therapy*, 1970, *1*, 522–526.

Bloomfield, H., Cain, M., & Jaffe, D. *TM: Discovering inner energy and overcoming stress*. New York: Delacorte Press, 1975.

Breunlin, D. C. Multimodal behavioral treatment of a child's eliminative disturbance. *Psychotherapy: Theory, Research and Practice*, 1980, *17*, 17–23.

Brewer, W. F. There is no convincing evidence for operant and classical conditioning in adult humans. In W. B. Weimer & D. S. Palermo (Eds.), *Cognition and the symbolic processes*. New York: Halsted Press, 1974.

Brody, S. Simultaneous psychotherapy of married couples. In J. Masserman (Ed.), *Current psychiatric therapies*. New York: Grune & Stratton, 1961.

Brunell, L. F. A multimodal treatment model for a mental hospital: Designing specific treatments for specific problems. *Professional Psychology*, November 1978, 570–579.

Brunell, L. F., & Young, W. T. (Eds.). *A multimodal handbook for a mental hospital: Designing specific treatments for specific problems*. New York: Springer, 1981, in press.

Carrington, P. *Freedom in meditation*. New York: Doubleday, 1977.

Carter, R. D., & Thomas, E. J. A case application of a signal system (SGM) to the assessment and modification of selected problems of marital communication. *Behavior Therapy*, 1973, *4*, 629–645.

Ciminero, A. R., Calhoun, K. S., & Adams, H. E. *Handbook of behavioral assessment*. New York: Wiley, 1977.

Colby, K. M. Discussion of papers on therapist's contribution. In H. H. Strupp & L. Luborsky (Eds.), *Research in psychotherapy* (Vol. II). Washington, D.C.: American Psychological Association, 1962.

Cone, J. D. The behavioral assessment grid (BAS): A conceptual framework and a taxonomy. *Behavior Therapy*, 1978, *9*, 882–888.

Cooper, A. J. Treatments of male potency: The present status. In J. Lopiccolo & L. Lopiccolo (Eds.), *Handbook of sex therapy*. New York: Plenum Press, 1978.

Dengrove, E. Behavior therapy of the sexual disorders. *Journal of Sex Research*, 1967, *3*, 49–61.

Dengrove, E. Behavior therapy of impotence. *Journal of Sex Research*, 1971, *7*, 177–183.

Dengrove, E. (Ed.) *Hypnosis and behavior therapy*. Springfield, Ill.: Charles C. Thomas, 1976.

Dunner, D. L., & Fieve, R. R. The lithium ion: Its impact on diagnostic practice. In H. S. Akiskal & W. L. Webb (Eds.), *Psychiatric diagnosis: Exploration of biological predictors*. New York: Spectrum Publications, 1978.

Edwards, S. S. Multimodal therapy with children: A case analysis of insect phobia. *Elementary School Guidance and Counseling*, 1978, *13*, 23–29.

Eisler, R. M., Hersen, M., Miller, P. M., & Blanchard, E. B. Situational determinants of assertive behaviors. *Journal of Consulting and Clinical Psychology*, 1975, *29*, 295–299.

Ellis, A. *Reason and emotion in psychotherapy*. New York: Lyle Stuart, 1962.

Ellis, A. *The sensuous person: Critique and corrections*. Secaucus, N.J.: Lyle Stuart, 1972.

Ellis, A. *How to live with a neurotic* (2nd ed.). New York: Crown, 1975.

Ellis, A. The basic clinical theory of rational-emotive therapy. In A. Ellis & R. Grieger (Eds.), *Handbook of rational-emotive therapy.* New York: Springer, 1977(a).

Ellis, A. *How to live with and without anger.* New York: Readers Digest Press, 1977(b).

Ellis, A. Psychotherapy and the value of a human being. In A. Ellis & R. Grieger (Eds.), *Handbook of rational-emotive therapy.* New York: Springer, 1977(c).

Ellis, A., & Grieger, R. *Handbook of rational-emotive therapy.* New York: Springer, 1977.

Erickson, M. H. Therapy of a psychosomatic headache. *Journal of Clinical and Experimental Hypnosis,* 1953, *1,* 2–6.

Eysenck, H. J. A mish-mash of theories. *International Journal of Psychiatry,* 1970, *9,* 140–146.

Fay, A. The drug modality. In A. A. Lazarus (Ed.), *Multimodal behavior therapy.* New York: Springer, 1976.

Fay, A. *Making things better by making them worse.* New York: Hawthorn, 1978.

Fay, A. *The invisible diet.* New York: Manor Books, 1980.

Fay, A., & Lazarus, A. A. Multimodal therapy and the problems of depression. In J. F. Clarkin & H. Glazer (Eds.), *Depression: Behavioral and directive treatment strategies.* New York: Garland Press, 1981.

Feather, B. W., & Rhoads, J. M. Psychodynamic behavior therapy: I Theory and rationale. *Archives of General Psychiatry,* 1972, *26,* 496–502.

Fensterheim, H., & Baer, J. *Don't say yes when you want to say no.* New York: McKay, 1975.

Fensterheim, H., & Kanter, J. S. The behavioral approach to sexual disorders. In B. Wolman & J. Money (Eds.), *Handbook of human sexuality.* Englewood Cliffs, N.J.: Prentice-Hall, 1980.

Ferrise, F. Personal Communication, 1980.

Foa, E. B., & Goldstein, A. Continuous exposure and complete response prevention in the treatment of obsessive-compulsive neurosis. *Behavior Therapy,* 1978, *9,* 821–829.

Frank, J. D. Psychotherapists need theories. *International Journal of Psychiatry,* 1970, *9,* 146–149.

Frank, J. D., Hoehn-Saric, R., Imber, S. D., Liberman, B. L., & Stone, A. R. *Effective ingredients of successful psychotherapy.* New York: Brunner/Mazel, 1978.

Frankel, F. H., & Zamansky, H. S. (Eds.) *Hypnosis at its bicentennial: Selected papers.* New York: Plenum, 1978.

Frankl, V. E. Paradoxical intention: A logotherapeutic technique. *American Journal of Psychotherapy,* 1960, *14,* 520–535.

Frankl, V. E. *The unheard cry for meaning.* New York: Simon and Schuster, 1978.

Franks, C. M., & Wilson, G. T. *Annual review of behavior therapy: Theory and practice.* New York: Brunner/Mazel, 1980.

Freedman, A. M., Kaplan, H. I., & Sadock, B. J. *Comprehensive textbook of psychiatry.* Baltimore: Williams & Wilkins, 1980.

Fromm, E. *To have or to be?* New York: Harper & Row, 1976.

Galin, D. Implications for psychiatry of left and right cerebral specialization. *Archives of General Psychiatry,* 1974, *31,* 572–583.

Gardner, R. *The boys and girls book about divorce.* New York: Bantam, 1970.

Garson, E. B. *The application of positive imagery in the maintenance of smoking reduction following broad-spectrum treatment.* Unpublished Ph.D. dissertation, Rutgers University.

Gerler, E. R. The "BASIC ID" in career education. *The Vocational Guidance Quarterly,* 1977, *25,* 238–244.

Gerler, E. R. The school counselor and multimodal education. *The School Counselor,* January 1978(a), 166–171.

Gerler, E. R. Counselor-teacher collaboration in a multimodal reading program. *Elementary School Guidance and Counseling,* 1978(b), *13,* 67–64.

Gerler, E. R. Preventing the delusion of uniqueness: Multimodal education in mainstreamed classrooms. *The Elementary School Journal,* September 1979, 35–40.

Gerler, E. R., & Keat, D. B. Multimodal education: Treating the "BASIC ID" of the elementary classroom. *The Humanist Educator,* 1977, *15,* 148–154.

Goldfried, M. R., & Davison, G. C. *Clinical behavior therapy.* New York: Holt, Rinehart & Winston, 1976.

Goldman, L. A revolution in counseling research. *Journal of Counseling Psychology,* 1976, *23,* 543–552.

Goldstein, A. P. *Psychotherapeutic attraction.* New York: Pergamon Press, 1971.

Goldstein, A. P. Relationship-enhancement methods. In F. H. Kanfer & A. P. Goldstein (Eds.), *Helping people change.* New York: Pergamon Press, 1975.

Golembiewski, R. T., & Blumberg, A. (Eds.). *Sensitivity training and the laboratory approach* (3rd ed.). Itasca, Ill.: Peacock, 1977.

Green, B. J. HELPING children of divorce: A multimodal approach. *Elementary School Guidance and Counseling,* 1978, *13,* 31–45.

Guerney, B. G. *Relationship enhancement: Skill training programs for therapy, problem prevention and enrichment.* San Francisco: Jossey-Bass, 1977.

Gurman, A. S. The effects and effectiveness of marital therapy: A review of outcome research. *Family Process,* 1973, *12,* 145–170.

Haley, J. Marriage therapy. *Archives of General Psychiatry,* 1963, *8,* 213–234.

Haley, J. *Uncommon therapy.* New York: Norton, 1973.

Haley, J. *Problem solving therapy.* San Francisco: Jossey-Bass, 1976.

Haley, J. *Leaving home: The therapy of disturbed young people.* New York: McGraw-Hill, 1980.

Halleck, S. L. *The treatment of emotional disorders.* New York: Jason Aronson, 1978.

Hammond, D. C., & Stanfield, K. *Multidimensional psychotherapy.* Champaign, Ill.: Institute for Personality and Ability Testing, 1977.

Hart, C., Pogrebin, L. C., Rogers, M., & Thomas, M. *Free to be you and me.* New York: McGraw-Hill, 1974.

Hartman, W. E., & Fithian, M. A. *Treatment of sexual dysfunction.* New York: Jason Aronson, 1974.

Hayakawa, S. I. *Language in thought and action.* New York: Harcourt, Brace & World, 1964.

Haynes, S. N., & Wilson, C. C. *Behavioral assessment.* San Francisco: Jossey-Bass, 1979.

Horney, K. *Neurosis and human growth.* New York: Norton, 1950.

Herink, R. (Ed.). *The psychotherapy handbook.* New York: New American Library, 1980.

Hersen, M., & Bellack, A. S. *Behavioral assessment: A practical handbook.* New York: Pergamon Press, 1976.

Hersen, M., & Bellack, A. S. Assessment of social skills. In A. R. Ciminero, K. S.

Calhoun, & H. E. Adams (Eds.), *Handbook for behavioral assessment*. New York: Wiley, 1977.

Jackson, D. D. Family rules—marital quid pro quo. *Archives of General Psychiatry*, 1965, *12*, 589–594.

Janov, A. *The primary revolution: Toward a real world*. New York: Simon and Schuster, 1972.

Jourard, S. M. *The transparent self* (rev. ed.). New York: Van Nostrand Reinhold, 1971.

Judah, R. D. Multimodal parent training. *Elementary School Guidance and Counseling*, 1978, *13*, 46–54.

Kanfer, F. H. The maintenance of behavior by self-generated stimuli and reinforcement. In A. Jacobs & L. Sachs (Eds.), *The psychology of private events*. New York: Academic Press, 1971.

Kanfer, F. H., & Saslow, G. Behavioral diagnosis. In C. M. Franks (Ed.), *Behavior therapy: Appraisal and status*. New York: McGraw-Hill, 1969.

Kazdin, A. E., & Wilson, G. T. *Evaluation of behavior therapy: Issues, evidence and research strategies*. Cambridge, Mass.: Ballinger, 1978.

Keat, D. B. Multimodal counseling with children: Treating the BASIC ID. *Pennsylvania Personnel and Guidance Association Journal*, 1976(a), *4*, 21–25.

Keat, D. B. Multimodal therapy with children: Two case histories. In A. A. Lazarus (Ed.), *Multimodal behavior therapy*. New York: Springer, 1976(b).

Keat, D. B. *Multimodal therapy with children*. New York: Pergamon Press, 1979.

Kimura, D. The asymmetry of the human brain. *Scientific American*, 1973, *228*, 70–78.

Knox, D. Behavior contracts in marriage counseling. *Journal of Family Counseling*, 1973, *1*, 22–28.

Koch, S. Psychology and its human clientele: Beneficiaries or victims? In R. A. Kasschau & F. S. Kessel (Eds.), *Psychology and society: In search of symbiosis*. New York: Wiley, 1980.

Korzybski, A. *Science and sanity*. Lancaster, Pa.: Science Press, 1933.

Kressel, K., & Deutsch, M. Divorce therapy: An in-depth survey of therapists' views. *Family Process*, 1977, *16*, 413–443.

Kwee, M. G. T. Gedragstherapie en neurotische depressie. In J. W. Orlemans, W. Brinkman, W. P. Haaijman, & E. J. Zwaan (Eds.). *Handboek voor gedragstherapie*. Deventer: Van Loghum, 1978.

Kwee, M. G. T. Over de ontwikkeling van een multimodale strategie van assessment en therapie. *Tijdschrift voor Psychotherapie*, 1979, *5*, 172–188.

Kwee, M. G. T., & de Waal, W. Multimodale gedragstherapie, toegepast bij een chronische agorafobie: Verslag van een intensieve behandeling. *Tijdschrift voor Psychotherapie*, 1975, *1*, 221–229.

Lange, A. J., & Jakubowski, P. *Responsible assertive behavior*. Champaign, Ill.: Research Press, 1976.

Lazarus, A. A. New methods in psychotherapy: A case study. *South African Medical Journal*, 1958, *32*, 660–664.

Lazarus, A. A. Group therapy of phobic disorders by systematic desensitization. *Journal of Abnormal and Social Psychology*, 1961, *63*, 505–510.

Lazarus, A. A. The treatment of chronic frigidity by systematic desensitization. *Journal of Nervous and Mental Disease*, 1963, *136*, 272–278.

Lazarus, A. A. Towards the understanding and effective treatment of alcoholism. *South African Medical Journal*, 1965(a), *39*, 736–741.

Lazarus, A. A. The treatment of a sexually inadequate man. In L. P. Ullmann & L. Krasner (Eds.), *Case studies in behavior modification.* New York: Holt, Rinehart & Winston, 1965(b).

Lazarus, A. A. Broad spectrum behavior therapy and the treatment of agoraphobia. *Behaviour Research and Therapy,* 1966, *4,* 95–97.

Lazarus, A. A. In support of technical eclecticism. *Psychological Reports,* 1967, *21,* 415–416.

Lazarus, A. A. Behavior therapy in groups. In G. M. Gazda (Ed.), *Basic approaches to group psychotherapy and group counseling.* Springfield, Ill.: Charles C. Thomas, 1968(a).

Lazarus, A. A. Learning theory and the treatment of depression. *Behaviour Research and Therapy,* 1968(b), *6,* 83–89.

Lazarus, A. A. *Behavior therapy and beyond.* New York: McGraw-Hill, 1971.

Lazarus, A. A. "Hypnosis" as a facilitator in behavior therapy. *International Journal of Clinical and Experimental Hypnosis,* 1973(a), *21,* 25–31.

Lazarus, A. A. Multimodal behavior therapy: Treating the BASIC ID. *Journal of Nervous and Mental Disease,* 1973(b), *156,* 404–411.

Lazarus, A. A. Understanding and modifying aggression in behavioral groups. In A. Jacobs & W. Spradlin (Eds.), *The group as agent of change.* New York: Behavioral Publications, 1974.

Lazarus, A. A. Group therapy and the "BASIC ID." In C. M. Franks & G. T. Wilson (Eds.), *Annual Review of Behavior Therapy,* 1975(a), *3,* 721–732.

Lazarus, A. A. Multimodal behavior therapy in groups. In G. M. Gazda (Ed.), *Basic approaches to group psychotherapy and group counseling* (2nd ed.), Springfield, Ill.: Charles C. Thomas, 1975(b).

Lazarus, A. A. *Multimodal behavior therapy.* New York: Springer, 1976(a).

Lazarus, A. A. Psychiatric problems precipitated by transcendental meditation. *Psychological Reports,* 1976(b), *39,* 601–602.

Lazarus, A. A. *In the mind's eye.* New York: Rawson, 1978(a).

Lazarus, A. A. Multimodal behavior therapy. Part 3. In E. Shostrom (Ed.), *Three approaches to psychotherapy II.* (Three 16 mm films or ¾" videocassettes). Orange, Calif.: Psychological Films, 1978(b).

Lazarus, A. A. Can sex be diminished by love? In A. Arkoff (Ed.), *Psychology and personal growth* (2nd ed.). Boston: Allyn and Bacon, 1980(a).

Lazarus, A. A. Psychological treatment of dyspareunia. In A. R. Leiblum & L. A. Pervin (Eds.), *Principles and practice of sex therapy.* New York: Guilford Press, 1980(b).

Lazarus, A. A. Divorce counseling or marriage therapy? A therapeutic option. *Journal of Marital and Family Therapy,* 1981, in press.

Lazarus, A. A., & Abramovitz, A. The use of "emotive imagery" in the treatment of children's phobias. *Journal of Mental Science,* 1962, *108,* 191–195.

Lazarus, A. A., & Fay, A. *I can if I want to.* New York: Morrow, 1975. (Paperback, Warner Books, 1977).

Lazarus, A. A., & Nieves, L. Assertiveness training in the multimodal therapy framework. *Comprehensive Psychotherapy,* 1980, *1,* 39–46.

Lazarus, R. S. Emotions and adaptation: Conceptual and empirical relations. In W. J. Arnold (Ed.), *Nebraska symposium on motivation.* Lincoln: University of Nebraska Press, 1968.

Lazarus, R. S., & Opton, E. M. The study of psychological stress: A summary of theoretical formulations and experimental findings. In C. D. Spielberger (Ed.), *Anxiety and behavior.* New York: Academic Press, 1966.

Lazarus, R. S., Kanner, A. D., & Folkman, S. Emotions: A cognitive-phenomenological analysis. In R. Plutchik & H. Kellerman (Eds.), *Emotion: Theory, research and experience.* New York: Academic Press, 1980.

Lazarus, R. S., Speisman, J. D., Mordkoff, A. M., & Davison, L. A. A laboratory study of psychological stress produced by a motion picture film. *Psychological Monographs,* 1962, *76* (Whole No. 553).

Leiblum, S. R., & Pervin, L. A. Introduction: The development of sex therapy from a sociocultural perspective. In S. R. Leiblum & L. A. Pervin (Eds.), *Principles and practice of sex therapy.* New York: Guilford Press, 1980.

Liberman, R. P., Wheeler, E., & Sanders, N. Behavioral therapy for marital disharmony: An educational approach. *Journal of Marriage and Family Counseling,* 1976, *2,* 383–395.

Lief, H. I. Foreword. In S. R. Leiblum & L. A. Pervin (Eds.), *Principles and practice of sex therapy.* New York: Guilford Press, 1980.

Lobitz, W. C., & LoPiccolo, J. New methods in the behavioral treatment of sexual dysfunction. *Journal of Behavior Therapy and Experimental Psychiatry,* 1972, *3,* 265–271.

LoPiccolo, J., & LoPiccolo, L. (Eds.). *Handbook of sex therapy.* New York: Plenum Press, 1978.

Lum, L. C. The syndrome of habitual chronic hyperventilation. In O. Hill (Ed.), *Modern trends in psychosomatic medicine.* Vol. III. Boston: Butterworths, 1976.

McReynolds, W. T., & Paulson, B. K. Stimulus control as the behavioral basis of weight loss procedures. In G. J. Williams, S. Martin, & J. Foreyt (Eds.), *Obesity: Behavioral approaches to dietary management.* New York: Brunner/Mazel, 1976.

Mahoney, M. J. *Cognition and behavior modification.* Cambridge, Mass.: Ballinger, 1974.

Marmor, J. Dynamic psychotherapy and behavior therapy. *Archives of General Psychiatry,* 1971, *24,* 22–28.

Marmor, J., & Woods, S. M. (Eds.). *The interface between psychodynamic and behavioral therapies.* New York: Plenum, 1980.

Mash, E. J., & Terdal, L. G. *Behavior therapy assessment.* New York: Springer, 1976.

Masters, W. H., & Johnson, V. E. *Human sexual inadequacy.* Boston: Little Brown, 1970.

Meador, B. D., & Rogers, C. R. Person-centered therapy. In R. J. Corsini (Ed.), *Current psychotherapies* (2nd ed.). Itasca, Ill.: Peacock, 1979.

Meichenbaum, D. *Cognitive-behavior modification.* New York: Plenum, 1977.

Messer, S. B., & Winokur, M. Some limits to the integration of psychoanalytic and behavior therapy. *American Psychologist,* 1980, *9,* 818–827.

Minuchin, S. *Families and family therapy.* Cambridge, Mass.: Harvard University Press, 1974.

Mischel, W. Towards a cognitive social learning reconceptualization of personality. *Psychological Review,* 1973, *80,* 252–283.

Mittleman, B. The concurrent analysis of marital couples. *Psychoanalytic Quarterly,* 1948, *17,* 182–197.

Moreno, J. L. *Psychodrama.* New York: Beacon House, 1958.

252   THE PRACTICE OF MULTIMODAL THERAPY

Murphy, G. Psychology in the year 2000. *American Psychologist,* 1969, *24,* 523–530.

Nathan, P. E. Alcoholism. In H. Leitenberg (Ed.), *Handbook of behavior modification and behavior therapy.* Englewood Cliffs, N.J.: Prentice Hall, 1976.

Nathan, P. E., & Harris, S. L. *Psychopathology and society* (2nd ed.). New York: McGraw-Hill, 1980.

Nay, W. R. *Multimethod clinical assessment.* New York: Gardner Press, 1979.

Nieves, L. *College achievement through self-help.* Princeton, N.J.: Educational Testing Service, 1978(a).

Nieves, L. *The minority college student experience: A case for the use of self-control.* Princeton, N.J.: Educational Testing Service, 1978(b).

O'Keefe, E. J., & Castaldo, C. A multimodal approach to treatment in a child care agency. *Psychological Reports,* 1980, *47,* 250.

O'Leary, K. D., & O'Leary, S. G. (Eds.). *Classroom management.* New York: Pergamon Press, 1972.

O'Leary, S. G., & O'Leary, K. D. Behavior modification in the school. In H. Leitenberg (Ed.), *Handbook of behavior modification and behavior therapy.* Englewood Cliffs, N.J.: Prentice Hall, 1976.

O'Leary, K. D., & Turkewitz, H. Marital therapy from a behavioral perspective. In T. J. Paolino & B. S. McCrady (Eds.), *Marriage and marital therapy.* New York: Brunner/Mazel, 1978.

Orne, M. T., & Wender, P. H. Anticipatory socialization for psychotherapy. *American Journal of Psychiatry,* 1968, *124,* 88–98.

Palazzoli, M. S., Cecchin, G., Prata, G., & Boscolo, L. *Paradox and counterparadox.* New York: Jason Aronson, 1978.

Paul, G. L. Strategy of outcome research in psychotherapy. *Journal of Consulting Psychology,* 1967, *31,* 109–118.

Pearl, C., & Guarnaccia, V. Multimodal therapy and mental retardation. In A. A. Lazarus (Ed.), *Multimodal behavior therapy.* New York: Springer, 1976.

Peterson, D. R. A functional approach to the study of person-person interactions. In D. Magnusson & N. S. Endler (Eds.), *Personality at the crossroads: Current issues in interactional psychology.* Hillsdale, N.J.: Lawrence Erlbaum Associates, 1977.

Peterson, D. R. Assessing interpersonal relationships by means of interaction records. *Behavioral Assessment,* 1979, *1,* 221–236.

Popler, K. Agoraphobia: Indications for the application of the multimodal behavioral conceptualization. *The Journal of Nervous and Mental Disease,* 1977, *164,* 97–101.

Postman, N. *Crazy talk, stupid talk.* New York: Delta, 1976.

Plutchik, R. *Emotion: A psychoevolutionary synthesis.* New York: Harper & Row, 1980.

Prochaska, J., & Prochaska, J. Twentieth century trends in marriage and marital therapy. In T. J. Paolino & B. S. McCrady (Eds.), *Marriage and marital therapy.* New York: Brunner/Mazel, 1978.

Rabkin, R. *Strategic psychotherapy.* New York: Basic Books, 1977.

Rachman, S. J. An anatomy of obsessions. *Behavioral Analysis and Modification,* 1978, *2,* 253–278.

Rausch, H. L. Research, practice and accountability. *American Psychologist,* 1974, *29,* 678–681.

Redd, W. H., Porterfield, A. L., & Andersen, B. L. *Behavior modification: Behavioral approaches to human problems.* New York: Random House, 1979.

Reid, W. H. *Basic intensive psychotherapy.* New York: Brunner/Mazel, 1980.

Richard, J. T. Multimodal Therapy: An Integrating Model for Behavioral Medicine. *Psychological Reports,* 1978, *42*, 635–639.

Rimm, D. C., & Masters, J. C. *Behavior therapy: Techniques and empirical findings* (2nd ed.). New York: Academic Press, 1979.

Roberts, T. K., Jackson, L. J., & Phelps, R. Lazarus' multimodal therapy model applied in an institutional setting. *Professional Psychology,* February 1980, 150–156.

Rogers, C. R. A theory of therapy, personality, and interpersonal relationships, as developed in the client-centered framework. In S. Koch (Ed.), *Psychology: A study of a science* (Vol. III). New York: McGraw-Hill, 1959.

Rogers, C. R. Client-centered therapy, Film No. 1. In E. Shostrom (Ed.), *Three approaches to psychotherapy.* (Three 16 mm. color motion pictures). Orange, Calif.: Psychological Films, 1965.

Rogers, C. R. Client-centered therapy. Part 1. In E. Shostrom (Ed.), *Three approaches to psychotherapy II.* (Three 16 mm. films or ¾" videocassettes). Orange, Calif.: Psychological Films, 1978.

Rosen, R. C., & Kopel, S. A. Role of penile tumescence measurement in the behavioral treatment of sexual deviation: Issues of validity. *Journal of Consulting and Clinical Psychology,* 1978, *46*, 1519–1521.

Rosen, R. D. *Psychobabble.* New York: Atheneum, 1977.

Ross, A. O. *Psychological disorders of children: A behavioral approach to theory, research and therapy.* New York: McGraw-Hill, 1974.

Rotter, J. B. Generalized expectancies for internal versus external control of reinforcement. *Psychological Monographs,* 1966, *80* (Whole No. 609).

Sager, C. J. *Marriage contracts and couple therapy.* New York: Brunner/Mazel, 1976.

Salter, A. *Conditioned reflex therapy.* New York: Farrar, Straus, 1949.

Satir, V. Conjoint marital therapy. In B. C. Greene (Ed.), *The psychotherapy of marital disharmony.* New York: The Free Press, 1965.

Schaefer, C. E., & Millman, H. L. *Therapies for children: A handbook of effective treatments for problem behaviors.* San Francisco: Jossey-Bass, 1977.

Schwartz, G. E. Psychobiological foundations of psychotherapy and behavior change. In S. L. Garfield & A. E. Bergin (Eds.), *Handbook of psychotherapy and behavior change* (2nd ed.). New York: Wiley, 1978.

Seligman, M. E. P. *Biological boundaries of learning.* New York: Appleton-Century-Crofts, 1972.

Semans, J. H. Premature ejaculation: A new approach. *Southern Medical Journal,* 1956, *49*, 353–361.

Shelton, J. L., & Ackerman, J. M. *Homework in counseling and psychotherapy.* Springfield, Ill.: Charles C. Thomas, 1974.

Shevrin, H., & Dickman, S. The psychological unconscious: A necessary assumption for all psychological theory? *American Psychologist,* 1980, *35*, 421–434.

Singer, J. L. *Imagery and daydream methods in psychotherapy and behavior modification.* New York: Academic Press, 1974.

Singer, J. L., & Switzer, E. *Mind play.* Englewood Cliffs, N.J.: Prentice-Hall, 1980.

Sperry, R. W., Gazzaniga, M. S., & Bogen, J. E. Interhemispheric relationships: The neocortical commissures; syndromes of hemisphere disconnection. In P. J. Vinken & G. W. Bruyn (Eds.), *Handbook of clinical neurology* (Vol. 4). Amsterdam: North-Holland, 1969.

Steinglass, P. The conceptualization of marriage from a systems theory perspective.

254   THE PRACTICE OF MULTIMODAL THERAPY

In T. J. Paolino & B. S. McCrady (Eds.), *Marriage and marital therapy.* New York: Brunner/Mazel, 1978.

Strupp, H. H., Hadley, S. W., & Gomes-Schwartz, B. *Psychotherapy for better or worse: The problem of negative effects.* New York: Jason Aronson, 1977.

Stuart, R. B. Operant-interpersonal treatment for marital discord. *Journal of Consulting and Clinical Psychology,* 1969, *33,* 675–682.

Stuart, R. B. An operant interpersonal program for couples. In D. H. L. Olson (Ed.), *Treating relationships.* Lake Mills, Iowa: Graphic Publishing Co., 1976.

Stuart, R. B. *Helping couples change.* New York: The Guilford Press, 1980.

Szasz, T. *Sex by prescription.* New York: Anchor Press, 1980.

Thoresen, C. E. (Ed.) *The behavior therapist.* Monterey, Calif.: Brooks/Cole, 1980.

Thoresen, C. E., & Mahoney, M. J. *Behavioral self-control.* New York: Holt, 1974.

Tollison, C. D., & Adams, H. E. *Sexual disorders: Treatment, theory, research.* New York: Gardner Press, 1979.

Ullmann, L. P., & Krasner, L. *A psychological approach to abnormal behavior* (2nd ed.). Englewood Cliffs, N.J.: Prentice Hall, 1975.

Wachtel, P. L. *Psychoanalysis and behavior therapy: Toward an integration.* New York: Basic Books, 1977.

Wachtel, P. L. Investigation and its discontents: Some constraints on progress in psychological research. *American Psychologist,* 1980, *35,* 399–408.

Wahler, R. G. Some structural aspects of deviant child behavior. *Journal of Applied Behavior Analysis,* 1975, *8,* 27–42.

Wahler, R. G. Deviant child behavior within the family: Developmental speculations and behavior change strategies. In H. Leitenberg (Ed.), *Handbook of behavior modification and behavior therapy.* Englewood Cliffs, N.J.: Prentice Hall, 1976.

Walen, S. R., Hauserman, N. M., & Lavin, P. J. *Clinical guide to behavior therapy.* Baltimore: Williams & Wilkins, 1977.

Watson, D. L., & Tharp, R. G. *Self-directed behavior: Self-modification for personal adjustment.* Monterey, Calif.: Brooks/Cole, 1972.

Watzlawick, P. *The language of change: Elements of therapeutic communication.* New York: Basic Books, 1978.

Watzlawick, P., Weakland, J., & Fisch, R. *Change: Principles of problem formation and problem resolution.* New York: Norton, 1974.

Weiss, R. L. The conceptualization of marriage from a behavioral perspective. In T. J. Paolino & B. S. McCrady (Eds.), *Marriage and marital therapy.* New York: Brunner/Mazel, 1978.

Weiss, R. L., Hops, H., & Patterson, G. R. A framework for conceptualizing marital conflict: A technology for altering it, some data for evaluating it. In L. A. Hamerlynck, L. C. Handy, & E. J. Mash (Eds.), *Behavior change: Methodology, concepts and practice.* Champaign, Ill.: Research Press, 1973.

Whitehorn, J. C., & Betz, B. J. Further studies of the doctor as a crucial variable in the outcome of treatment with schizophrenic patients. *American Journal of Psychiatry,* 1960, *117,* 215–223.

Wilson, G. T. The importance of being theoretical: A commentary on Bandura's "Self-efficacy: Towards a unifying theory of behavioral change." *Advances in Behaviour Research and Therapy,* 1978, *1,* 217–230.

Wilson, G. T. Behavioral treatment of obesity: Maintenance strategies and long-term efficacy. In P. O. Sjödén, S. Bates, & W. S. Dockens III (Eds.), *Trends in behavior therapy.* New York: Academic Press, 1979.

Wilson, G. T. Toward specifying the "nonspecific" factors in behavior therapy: A social learning analysis. In M. J. Mahoney (Ed.), *Psychotherapy process.* New York: Plenum, 1980.

Wilson, G. T., & O'Leary, K. D. *Principles of behavior therapy.* Englewood Cliffs, N.J.: Prentice Hall, 1980.

Wolpe, J., & Lazarus, A. A. *Behavior therapy techniques.* Oxford: Pergamon Press, 1966.

Woody, R. H. *Psychobehavioral counseling and therapy: Integrating behavioral and insight techniques.* New York: Appleton-Century-Crofts, 1971.

Woolfolk, R. L. A multimodal perspective on emotion. In A. A. Lazarus (Ed.), *Multimodal behavior therapy.* New York: Springer, 1976.

Yokley, J. M., & McCarthy, B. Multimodal behavior therapy: Use of professional and paraprofessional resources. *Psychotherapy: Theory, Research and Practice,* 1980, *17,* 10–16.

Zilbergeld, B. *Male sexuality.* New York: Bantam, 1978.

Zilbergeld, B., & Evans, M. The inadequacy of Masters and Johnson. *Psychology Today,* 1980, *14,* 29–43.

Name Index

Abel, G. G., 87
Abramovitz, A., 7, 202
Ackerman, J. M., 133
Adams, H. E., 84, 200
Adler, A., 38, 39, 62
Agras, W. S., 162
Alberti, R. E., 149
Alexander, F., 133
Allport, G. W., 175
Andersen, B. L., 35
Argyris, C., 155
Arlow, J. A., 40, 133
Azrin, N. H., 155, 177

Baer, J., 150
Bair, S. L., x
Bandler, R., 79, 94, 95
Bandura, A., 35 –36
Barlow, D. H., 87
Beck, A. T., 36
Bekhterev, V. M., 34
Bellack, A. S., 84, 155
Benson, H., 21
Bergin, A. E., 99
Berne, E., 38, 39, 181
Betz, B. J., 208
Birk, L., 39
Blanchard, E. B., 87, 155
Bloomfield, H., 146
Blumberg, A., 69
Bogen, J. E., 94
Boscolo, L., 174
Bowen, M., 181

Breunlin, D. C., 201
Brewer, W. F., 35
Bristow, A. R., 87
Brody, S., 165
Brunell, L. F., 10

Cain, M., 146
Calhoun, K. S., 84
Carrington, P., 21, 91
Carter, R. D., 87
Castaldo, C., 201
Cecchin, G., 174
Ciminero, A. R., 84
Colby, K. M., 67
Cone, J. D., 84
Cooper, A. J., 195

Davison, G. C., 131
Davison, L. A., 92
Dengrove, E., 195, 197, 235
Deutch, M., 179
de Waal, W., x
Dickman, S., 38
Dunner, D. L., 208

Edwards, S. S., 201
Eisler, R. M., 155
Ellis, A., 2, 11, 36, 62, 130, 135, 152, 154,
    161, 197, 205, 232, 237
Emmons, M. L., 149
Erickson, M. H., 68

257

Subject Index

261

About the Author

Since 1972, Arnold A. Lazarus has been a Professor II at Rutgers – The State University of New Jersey, a rank that Rutgers reserves for those full professors who have achieved scholarly eminence in their fields of inquiry. Dr. Lazarus teaches in the Graduate School of Applied and Professional Psychology and is the Executive Director of several Multimodal Therapy Institutes. He lives in Princeton, New Jersey where he conducts a part-time private practice and serves as a consultant to hospitals, clinics, and several organizations throughout the state. He has also taught clinical psychology at Stanford University, Temple University Medical School, and Yale University. He is a Fellow of the American Psychological Association, a Clinical Diplomate of the American Board of Professional Psychology, a former president of several associations and societies, and the author of about one hundred professional articles and papers. Many of his books have been translated into German, French, Spanish, Dutch, and Portuguese. His public lectures, invited addresses, and workshops here and abroad number in the hundreds.